# GEOPOLITICAL SHIFTS IN WEST ASIA

*Trends and Implications*

# GEOPOLITICAL SHIFTS IN WEST ASIA

## *Trends and Implications*

*Editor*

Prasanta Kumar Pradhan

INSTITUTE FOR DEFENCE STUDIES & ANALYSES
NEW DELHI

PENTAGON PRESS

**Geopolitical Shifts in West Asia: Trends and Implications**
***Editor: Prasanta Kumar Pradhan***

First Published in 2016



ISBN 978-81-8274-877-4



*Published by*
PENTAGON PRESS
206, Peacock Lane, Shahpur Jat,
New Delhi-110049
Phones: 011-64706243, 26491568
Telefax: 011-26490600
email: rajan@pentagonpress.in
website: www.pentagonpress.in

*Branch*
Flat No.213, Athena-2,
Clover Acropolis,
Viman Nagar,
Pune-411014
Email: pentagonpresspune@gmail.com

*In association with*
Institute for Defence Studies and Analyses
No. 1, Development Enclave,
New Delhi-110010
Phone: +91-11-26717983
Website: www.idsa.in

Printed at Aegean Offset Printers, Greater Noida, U.P.

# Contents

## PART II
## TERRORISM, SECTARIANISM AND REGIONAL SECURITY



## PART III
## EXTERNAL INTERVENTIONS IN WEST ASIA



## PART IV
## REGIONAL INSTABILITY AND ENERGY SECURITY

# Foreword

The West Asian region has been witness to severe turmoil for half a decade. Beginning with the December 2010 incident of self-immolation by Mohamed Bouazizi, a Tunisian street vendor, tensions continue to persist throughout the region till date, albeit in different degrees in different countries. The last five years have witnessed large-scale protests by the people against their rulers, the overthrow of some authoritarian regimes, and limited experiments with democracy. The events have also, to a large extent, redefined the regional balance of power in West Asia. Relationships among the countries of the region, in some instances, have witnessed a change. Such dramatic developments in West Asia have drawn the attention of the external powers, whose continued intervention has further aggravated the situation. In this backdrop of immense and ongoing regional geopolitical changes, the Institute for Defence Studies and Analyses, New Delhi organised its First Annual West Asia Conference on the theme "Geopolitical Shifts in West Asia: Trends and Implications" from 10-11 September, 2014, to deliberate on the emerging challenges and trends in the region. This volume, edited by Dr. Prasanta Kumar Pradhan, Associate Fellow at the Institute, brings together the views expressed at the conference by the scholars and experts from around the world.

West Asia has been a sensitive and conflict prone region, especially since the early 20th century with the discovery of oil. It was also an enduring space for conflict during the Cold War. More recently, the phenomenon of the "Arab Spring" added another dimension to the existing geopolitical challenges in the region. The relationship between the two crucial regional players—Saudi Arabia and Iran—has worsened, making the situation even more complex. There have been allegations of Saudi-Iran proxy wars taking place in Syria, Iraq and Yemen. The increasing Iranian activism in the region and its rising capability, along with rapprochement with the West, has alarmed the Gulf Cooperation Council (GCC) states thus inhibiting the chances of any dialogue between the two sides. Intra-GCC tensions have also surfaced in recent times.

Increased intervention by external players has been another characteristic feature of recent political developments in the region. The USA has remained the most important player in the region. Also apparent are the increasing visibility of other powers such as Russia and China, that have taken positions on several important issues pertaining to West Asia. As is apparent, external intervention has its limits and has largely been unable to solve the problems facing the region; rather, it has further aggravated the situation in many instances.

Another important feature has been the rise of the Islamists on the political horizon of the region. They gained popularity amid the popular protests and made electoral gains that enabled them to come to power in some countries. While this development had the potential to completely alter the existing political systems in the region, it could not last against the push back from the established system. The lack of political experience and acumen displayed by the Islamists also impacted on their ability, in short, their failure, to deliver.

Sectarian violence is on a rise in West Asia since the beginning of the protests in 2010. Political turmoil has led to the emergence and operation of several terrorist and extremist groups in many areas. These groups not only target the existing states but also fight among themselves to establish control and authority. Immensely disturbing is the fact that some of these elements are being backed by several wealthy and powerful countries in the region. The announcement of a "caliphate" by the Islamic State in Iraq and Syria (ISIS) and establishment of a proto-state in parts of Iraq and Syria within a relatively short span of time, exemplifies the growing capability of these terrorist groups and massive vulnerability of the states in the region. These groups' attempts to redraw the boundaries of states, inhuman acts of terrorism, and the ability to attract youths from wealthy, and often liberal, societies abroad have highlighted new and real challenges to regional security and stability.

The escalation of conflict in West Asia has created anxiety among major oil importers in Asia, particularly India, China, Japan and South Korea. These Asian economic giants are heavily dependent upon the energy supplies from the Gulf region. There has been a concern among the Asian oil importers over the possibility of disruption in production and supplies of oil and gas in the face of growing unrest in the region. While energy supplies from the Gulf to these countries have not been affected thus far, but they were impacted by the sudden rise of oil prices following the Arab Spring that spread like wildfire throughout the region. The recent drop in oil prices notwithstanding, apprehensions about wild fluctuation in energy prices over the medium to long term, as a result of instability in the region, continue to persist.

India has huge political, economic and security interests in the region. India's bilateral trade with the region is around US$ 172 billion. Not only is it heavily dependent on the region for energy supplies, there are over seven million Indian nationals living and working in the region. Their safety is a concern for India. The rise of terrorism and extremism in the region, particularly the ISIS, is also a security challenge for India. Thus, India is naturally concerned about the developments in the region which she refers to as her 'extended neighbourhood'.

I appreciate the efforts of Dr. Pradhan for bringing out this useful and timely volume, and extend my gratitude to all the contributors for their considered views. I hope that this book will be useful for scholars, academics and policy makers for understanding the trends and implications of the geopolitical shifts taking place in West Asia.

**Brig. Rumel Dahiya (Retd.)**
Deputy Director General
Institute for Defence Studies and Analyses
New Delhi

# Abbreviations

| | |
|---|---|
| ADNOC | Abu Dhabi National Oil Company |
| APEC | Asia-Pacific Economic Cooperation |
| AQI | Al Qaeda in Iraq |
| ARAMCO | Saudi Arabian Oil Company |
| ARF | ASEAN Regional Forum |
| ASEAN | Association of Southeast Asian Nations |
| BCIM | Bangladesh-China-India-Myanmar |
| BRICS | Brazil, Russia, India, China and South Africa |
| CDI | Cooperative Defence Initiative |
| CIA | Central Intelligence Agency |
| CMFHQ | Combined Maritime Forces Headquarters |
| CSCE | Conference on Security and Co-operation in Europe |
| CSCPG | Conference on Security and Cooperation for the Persian Gulf |
| DIPP | Department of Industrial Policy & Promotion |
| DJP | Democratic Party of Japan |
| EEZ | Exclusive Economic Zones |
| EIA | Energy Information Administration |
| FDI | Foreign Direct Investment |
| FSA | Free Syrian Army |
| FTA | Free Trade Agreement |
| GCC | Gulf Cooperation Council |
| GDP | Gross Domestic Product |
| GSD | Gulf Security Dialogue |

| | |
|---|---|
| IEA | International Energy Agency |
| IF | Islamic Front |
| IISS | International Institute for Strategic Studies |
| IM | Indian Mujahideen |
| IPI | Iran-Pakistan-India |
| IS | Islamic State |
| ISC | Information Sharing Center |
| ISIL | Islamic State of Iraq and the Levant |
| ISIS | Islamic State of Iraq and Syria |
| KDP | Kurdistan Democratic Party |
| KNOC | Korea National Oil Corporation |
| KOGAS | Korea Gas Corporation |
| LDP | Liberal Democratic Party |
| LIFG | Libya Islamic Fighting Group |
| LNG | Liquefied Natural Gas |
| MEPP | Middle East Peace Process |
| MoU | Memorandum of Understanding |
| NAM | Non-Aligned Movement |
| NATO | North Atlantic Treaty Organisation |
| NRI | Non-Resident Indian |
| OAPEC | Organisation of Arab Petroleum Exporting Countries |
| OECD | Organisation for Economic Cooperation and Development |
| OPEC | Organisation of the Petroleum Exporting Countries |
| OSCE | Organisation for Security and Cooperation in Europe |
| PKK | Kurdistan Workers' Party |
| PLA | People's Liberation Army |
| PLAN | People's Liberation Army Navy |
| PUK | Patriotic Union of Kurdistan |
| RCEP | Regional Comprehensive Economic Partnership |
| ReCAAP | Regional Cooperation Agreement on Combating Piracy and Armed Robbery against Ships in Asia |
| SCO | Shanghai Cooperation Organisation |

| | |
|---|---|
| SDF | Self Defence Force |
| SLOCs | Sea Lines of Communication |
| SWF | Sovereign Wealth Fund |
| TPP | Trans Pacific Partnership |
| UAR | United Arab Republic |
| UNDP | United Nations Development Programme |
| UNSC | United Nations Security Council |
| WANA | West Asia and North Africa |
| WMD | Weapons of Mass Destruction |

# About the Contributors

**Prof. Gencer Özcan** is in the faculty of the Department of International Relations, Istanbul Bilgi University, Istanbul, Turkey. He graduated from Ankara University's Faculty of Political Sciences and received his Ph D from Bosphorus University. Özcan previously worked in Marmara University (1983-1999) and Yildiz Technical University (1999-2009). His research interests are diplomatic history, Turkey's foreign policy making process, the military's role in the making of Turkey's foreign policy decisions, Turkey's policy towards the Middle East, and Turkish-Israeli bilateral relations. His recent publications include "Facing Its Waterloo in Diplomacy: Turkey's Military in Foreign Policy–making Process", *New Perspectives on Turkey*, No. 40, Spring 2009; "Do New Democracies Support Democracy? Turkey's Dilemmas", *Journal of Democracy*, 22(4), 2011; and "Turkish Israeli Relations in Crisis: Living with the Gordion Knot", *Hellenic Studies*, No. 1, 2012.

**Dr. N. Janardhan** is a political analyst based in the UAE since 2000 and author of *Boom amid Gloom: Spirit of Possibility in the 21st Century Gulf* (2011) and co-editor of *India and the Gulf: What Next?* (2013) and *A New Gulf Security Architecture: Prospects and Challenges for an Asian Role* (2014). He is also an honorary fellow at the Centre for Gulf Studies, University of Exeter, and Managing Assistant Editor of *Journal of Arabian Studies* (Routledge). With a broad-based interest in the socio-political developments in the Middle East, Dr. Janardhan's research areas include political reforms, international relations, education, media, gender, labour, migration, human rights and human trafficking in the Gulf region. After obtaining his Ph D in Gulf studies from the School of International Studies, Jawaharlal Nehru University, New Delhi, he was Programme Manager, Gulf-Asia Relations, and Editor, 'Gulf in the Media', at Gulf Research Center, Dubai. He is a regular contributor to various newspapers and websites in the Middle East, as well as international academic publications.

**Dr. Mostafa Zahrani** is the Director General of the Institute for Political and International Studies (IPIS), Tehran. He received his Ph D in International

Relations from the University of Tehran in 2002. His did his masters in International Relations from the University of Tarbiat Modarres in Tehran in 1993. Dr. Zahrani became a member of Islamic Republic Foreign Ministry in 1981. He was first posted in Vienna from 1982 to 1984. He then moved to work under the political deputy of the then Prime Minister Mousavi, from 1985 to 1990. There he became part of the negotiating team for UN resolution 598 to end the eight year long Iran-Iraq war. From 1999 to 2004 he was posted to the Iran mission in New York. Dr. Zahrani has also been Faculty member in School of International Relations in University of Tehran since 1992. His publications are mainly on Iran-US Relations, and his latest book is on the subject of critical studies of US foreign policy .

**Amb. Mohamed Fathy Abdel Hamid El Shazly** (Retd.) is a veteran Egyptian diplomat and is currently National Project Director, Executive Secretariat for the De-mining and Development of the North West Coast, Ministry of International Cooperation, Egypt. Prior to that he served as the Head, Project Monitoring Unit, EU/Egypt project on Human Rights Promotion, Democratisation, and Civil Society, Ministry of International Cooperation from June 2006 to April 2010; and Deputy Head, General Coordination Secretariat for the Implementation of the Egyptian European Partnership Agreement-Ministry of International Cooperation from November 2004 till January 2007. He has been Egyptian ambassador to Saudi Arabia and Turkey and was deputed as permanent representative to the Organisation of Islamic Conference. Ambassador El Shazly has also served as Assistant Foreign Minister for European Affairs in Egypt. He has been a member of high level delegations and committees of the Egyptian government. He has been honoured with King Abdul Aziz decoration 1st rank -Saudi Arabia in 1995 and with Polar Star Decoration, Rank Commodore in September 1983. Amb. El Shazly has written extensively on Egypt's national security, foreign policy and regional security as well.

**Amb. Ahmed Salem Saleh Al Wahishi** (Retd.) is the Executive Director of Yemeni International Affairs' Center (YIAC), Ambassador Wahishi has conducted research work on political, economic, environmental and international law issues in the Middle East as well as issues related to peace, security, disarmament and sustainable development. He served as Chief Representative of the League of Arab States to New Delhi, and was earlier appointed as Ambassador of Yemen in Indonesia, Singapore and Brunei, Darusaalam and as Head of Mission in Dubai and Tokyo. He has been teaching at the Aden University, since 1977. He has been actively participating in track-2 meeting all over the world. Amb. Wahishi earned his Ph D in Economics from Czech Republic in 1988, B.Sc. (Chemistry) from Kuwait University in 1977, a Diploma in International Law from Moscow

University in 1991, and a Fellowship in International Law from UNITAR, Geneva, 1999.

**Amb. Talmiz Ahmad** was the Indian Ambassador to Saudi Arabia (2000-03; 2010-11); Oman (2003-04), and the UAE (2007-10). He was also Additional Secretary for International Cooperation in the Ministry of Petroleum and Natural Gas in 2004-06. After retirement from foreign service, he is working with an energy services company in Dubai. He has published three books: *Reform in the Arab World: External Influences and Regional Debates* (2005); *Children of Abraham at War: the Clash of Messianic Militarisms* (2010), and *The Islamist Challenge in West Asia: Doctrinal and Political Competitions after the Arab Spring* (2013). He writes and lectures frequently on Political Islam, the politics of West Asia and energy security issues.

**Dr. Muhammad Abdul Ghaffar** prior to his appointment as Advisor to HM the King for Diplomatic Affairs and Chairman of the Board of Trustees for Derasat, served as Ambassador of the Kingdom of Bahrain to the European Union and as the non-resident Ambassador to Luxemburg. Previously, Dr. Ghaffar was a Member of Cabinet, where he held the portfolios of Minister of Information and Minister of State for Foreign Affairs. He has also held the posts of the Ambassador of Bahrain to the US, non-resident Ambassador to Canada and Argentina and as Ambassador and Permanent Representative of Bahrain to the United Nations. He obtained a Bachelor's Degree in Political Science from Poona University in India, a Master's Degree in Political Science from the New School for Social Research in New York and a Ph D, also in Political Science, from the State University of New York, Binghamton.

**Dr. Abdulwahab Al Qassab** is an Associate Researcher at the Arab Center for Research and Policy Studies, Doha. He is currently coordinating the Strategic Program, and overseeing a number of projects, including 'Armament in the Arab World', 'Energy and Oil in the Arabian Gulf', and 'Water Resources in the Arab World - Glimpses for Crisis?' Dr. Qassab previously served in the Iraqi Armed Forces, earning the rank of Major General, before entering a career in research and academia. He has acted as a consultant for Naval Affairs and overlooked research and development for the Chief of the General Staff in the Iraqi Armed Forces. As a researcher, he worked with the Center for Arab World Studies, Al Mustansiriya University, and the Center for International Studies, Baghdad University. He was a member of the Steering Committee for the Political Department and the Futurist Studies Department at Baytulhikma, Baghdad. Dr. Qassab established Al Zaman Center for Strategic Studies in Baghdad in 2003. He taught strategy to post graduate students in Al Nahrain University, Baghdad from 1997 until 2005. From 2006 until 2010, Dr. Qassab was a consultant to the Iraqi Center for Strategic Studies in Amman and the Center for Strategic Studies of the Qatar Armed Forces. His research interests include geostrategic aspects in the Arabian Gulf environment, military history, history of political and international relations in the Levant, Iraq and the Arabian Gulf, power relations in the Arabian Gulf, armament and disarmament, power and energy.

**Col. Rajeev Agarwal** was commissioned into the Regiment of Artillery in June 1990 and has had varied operational and service experience for over 24 years. He has also been a military observer with the United Nations in DRC and holds a Master's degree in Defence and Strategic Studies from Madras University. His published work include "Security in the Gulf Region: India's Concerns, Vulnerabilities, Interests and Engagement Options" in Rumel Dahiya (ed.) *Developments in the Gulf Region: Prospects and Challenges For India in the Next Two Decades* (2013). "'Arab Spring' and Democracy: Possibility or an Elusive Idea", *Indian Foreign Affairs Journal*, 8(4), October-December 2013. Monograph on *Turkey and its Quest for Leadership Role in the West Asian Region*, IDSA Monograph Series No. 32, January 2014. "US Pivot to the Asia Pacific: Impact and Implications for West Asia" (Co-authored) in S.D. Muni and Vivek Chadha (eds.) *Asian Strategic Review 2014: US Pivot and Asian Security*, (2014), and "Threat of Israel's Regional Isolation and Imperatives for the Future", IDSA Occasional Paper No. 34, June 2014.

**Prof. P. R. Kumaraswamy** is professor of Middle Eastern studies at Jawaharlal Nehru University (JNU), New Delhi. From 1992 to 1999 he was a research fellow at the Harry S. Truman Research Institute for the Advancement of Peace, Jerusalem. Since joining JNU in September 1999, he has been researching, teaching, and writing on various aspects of the West Asian Region. His works include *India's Israel Policy* (2010) and *Historical Dictionary of the Arab Israeli Conflict* (2006). Over the years, he has authored a number of monographs on the region and they include *Israel Confronts Iran: Rational, Responses and Fallouts* (2012); *Reading the Silence: India and the Arab Spring* (2012); *Indo-Iranian relations and the Arab Prism* (2008); *Beyond the Veil: Israel-Pakistan Relations* (2000); *India and Israel: Evolving Strategic Partnership* (1998); *Political Legitimacy of the Minorities: Israeli Arabs and the 1996 Knesset Elections* (1998); and *Israel's China Odyssey* (1994). He has edited a number of volumes which include: *Caught in Crossfire: Civilians in Conflicts in the Middle East* (2008); *Israel and the Islamic World* (co-edited, 2008); *Revisiting the Yom Kippur War* (2000), *The Fateful Triangle: Israel Hashemites and Palestinians* (co-edited, 2000); and *China and the Middle East* (1999). He has published research articles in various edited volumes and in refereed and non-refereed international journals and regularly contributes to Indian as well as international media outlets.

**Dr. Waiel Awwad** is South Asia based independent journalist since 1979 has travelled extensively in most of South and South East Asian countries. He has been a war correspondent, covered Sri Lanka, Kashmir, Afghanistan, West Asia and Gulf Region. He worked as Bureau Chief of MBC, London, MBC FM Radio, Kuwait, Oman and Damascus Radio and prior to that run a special program: 'Dateline South Asia' in Arabic first of its kind with Asian News International (ANI). He was the South Asia Bureau Chief of Al Arabiya TV Channel (Dubai Media City), till 2011. Many of his writings are published in English and Arabic in major newspapers and magazines. He has interviewed many world leaders and participated in international conferences, seminar and Panel discussions. Dr. Awwad covered wars in South Asia and was detained in Afghanistan before the fall of Taliban government and also was captured in an ambush during the American invasion of Iraq in 2003 while he was embedded with American Troops. He is currently the president of the Foreign Correspondents' Club of South Asia (FCC).

**Dr. Jon B. Alterman** is a Senior Vice President at the Center for Strategic and International Studies (CSIS), Washington D.C., and holds the Zbigniew Brzezinski Chair in Global Security and Geostrategy, and the Director of the Center's Middle East Program. Prior to joining CSIS in 2002, he served as a member of the Policy Planning Staff at the U.S. Department of State and as a special assistant to the assistant secretary of state for Near Eastern affairs. He is a member of the Chief of Naval Operations Executive Panel and served as an expert adviser to the Iraq Study Group (also known as the Baker-Hamilton Commission). In addition to his policy work, he teaches Middle Eastern studies at the Johns Hopkins School of Advanced International Studies and the George Washington University. From 1993 to 1997, Alterman was an award-winning teacher at Harvard University, where he received his Ph D in history. He is the author or co-author of four books on the Middle East and the editor of two more. In addition to his academic work, he is sought out as a consultant to business and government and is a frequent commentator in print, on radio, and on television. His opinion pieces have appeared in the *New York Times*, *Washington Post*, *Wall Street Journal*, *Financial Times*, and other major publications. Alterman has lectured in more than 30 countries on five continents on subjects related to the Middle East and US policy toward the region.

**Prof. Henner Furtig** is the Acting Vice President of the German Institute of Global and Area Studies, Hamburg and Professor at the History Department of the University of Hamburg. His main areas of interest are contemporary history and politics of the Middle East, especially the Gulf region and Egypt. Some select publications include, "Iran and Venezuela: Ideology-Driven Foreign Policies in

Comparison", in D. Flemes (ed.), *Regional Leadership in the Global System. Ideas, Interests and Strategies of Regional Powers. London* (2010), (with S. Gratius); "The Absence of Nonsectarian Parties in the Iraqi Political Arena" in Jamal Sanad Al Suwaidi (ed.), *The Arabian Gulf between Continuity and Change* (2009); "Iran's Sisyphean Labour – 30 Years of Spreading "Islam's Revolutionary Message", in A. Christmann and J. P. Hartung, (eds.), Islamica, *Journal of Semitic Studies*, Supplement 26, Oxford, 2009.

**Prof. Girijesh Pant** is an Economist by training. Having done his MA in Economics from Allahabad University with rank, he joined Jawaharlal Nehru University (JNU) for his doctorate. He began his career with Federation of Indian Chambers of Commerce and Industry New Delhi but moved to academics. He is the former Dean of the School of International Studies in JNU. Starting his work in Development Studies, Prof. Pant's initial writings were on Political Economy with focus on South East Asia and Third World Economies. At the Centre his work has been on West Asian economies, oil economics and international energy issues. He has been Director of Gulf Studies programme and Chairman Centre for West Asian and African Studies. He has travelled extensively and has been Senior Fulbright Visiting Scholar, University of Illinois, USA. His other assignments include, Member of UGC Standing Committee on Area Studies, UGC nominee in Managing Committee of Third World Academy in Jamia Millia Islamia and Member of Editorial Board of *Indian Foreign Affairs Journal*, New Delhi. He was also the Vice Chancellor of GGD University Bilaspur, and Doon University, Dehradun. He has been a Member of India International Centre New Delhi and Member of the International Institute of Strategic Studies, London.

**Prof. Toshitaka Takeuchi** is with the Osaka School of International Public Policy, Osaka University, Osaka, Japan. He got his BS in Environmental Engineering from Kyoto University in 1975 and BA in Political Science from University of Oregon. He completed his MA in Political Science from University of Washington in 1980 an AM (MA) in East Asian Studies from Stanford University in 1981. He has been Associate Professor at Osaka University of Foreign Studies 1991-2002 and Professor from 2002 to 2007. From 2007 he has been adviser to the Ship for World Youth and legal adviser to the delegation of Japan to the Conference of Disarmament, Ministry of foreign Affairs. He took part in CTBT, CCW negotiations 1995-1997. He has been part of US State Department's International Visitors Program, all on security related subjects military bases in the US proper and took part in conferences in 1992, the Pacific Command in Hawaii in 1999 and US bases in Okinawa in 2003. He has recently edited the following volumes: *Understanding International Relations: The world and Japan*, (2013), *Contemporary International Relations*, 2012 (in Japanese), *Game Theory* *for Policy Analysis*, (2011) (in Japanese), The Japan-US Alliance, (2011) (in Japanese), *Guidebook on International Relations*, (2008) (in Japanese).

**Prof. Jeongmin Seo** chairs the Department of Middle East and African Studies at Graduate School of International Area Studies, Hankuk University of Foreign Studies in Seoul, South Korea. Before he got the teaching position, Prof. Seo was working as a Middle East correspondent in Cairo for the *Joongang Daily* Newspaper. He holds a D. Phil. in politics from University of Oxford and two MAs from the American University in Cairo and Graduate School of Interpretation and Translation in Seoul. His main fields of research are religion and politics of the contemporary Middle East, political economy and state-society relations of the region. His recent publications include "The Religious Establishment and the Arab Spring: The Case of Egypt", *Korean Journal of the Middle East Studies*, 35 (1), June 2014; "South Korea's Interests in the Gulf: From Construction to Military Cooperation", in Ranjit Gupta and N. Janardhan (eds.) *A New Gulf Security Architecture: Prospects and Challenges for an Asian Role*, (2014); "The Three Bonds and Five Relationships of Confucianism in Islam". *Korean Journal of Islamic Studies Association*, 23 (2), June 2013; "Quantitative Culture Code in Arab-Middle East Films", *Korean Journal of Middle East Studies*, 33 (1), June 2012; "Tribalism in the Arab Political Change", *Korean Journal of Islamic Studies Association*, 22 (1), Spring 2011.

**Ms. Shebonti Ray Dadwal** is a Research Fellow with the Institute for Defence Studies and Analyses, New Delhi, specialising on energy security and climate change-related issues. She has worked as Senior Editor in *The Financial Express* and has also served as Deputy Secretary at the National Security Council Secretariat. She has presented several papers in national and international conferences and has written several peer-reviewed articles and papers on her area of work. Ms. Dadwal was awarded the FCO Chevening Fellowship on 'The Economics of Energy' in April 2009. In 2002, she published a book, *Rethinking Energy Security in India*, and is now working on the politics of energy and climate change.

**Dr. Prasanta Kumar Pradhan** is an Associate Fellow at the Institute for Defence Studies and Analyses (IDSA), New Delhi. He holds a doctorate degree from Jawaharlal Nehru University, New Delhi. Since joining IDSA, he has been researching on foreign policy, security and strategic issues in West Asia, and India's relationship with West Asia and the wider Arab world. He is also working on the implications of the Arab Spring for the region and India. He is the author of the monograph *India's Relationship with the Gulf Cooperation Council: Need to Look beyond Business*. He has also published articles in reputed journals and contributed articles to several edited volumes on West Asia. At IDSA, he is presently working on the 'Sectarian Faultlines in West Asia'.

# List of Maps, Figures and Tables

# Keynote Address by Hon'ble Minister of State for External Affairs General Vijay Kumar Singh (Retd.)

September 10, 2014

The Arab uprisings, and in particular the current crises in Iraq, Israel-Palestine, Libya and Syria have continued to challenge the traditional actors and alliances in the region. In the emerging order, there will be greater devolution of powers to the regional actors, although it is unclear how much space there will be for outside players, which will, however, continue to have leverages. Within this framework, is there scope for India to play a more strategic role? Undoubtedly, any instability in this region affects our vital interests directly.

I would like to emphasise on three points: one, to define our stakes in the Gulf and West Asia and North Africa (WANA) region; two, to elaborate on the developments and cross-cutting issues in the region; and three, to seek to outline our efforts to promote our interests within the broader regional context.

This region is an essential part of our extended neighbourhood. Civilisational links remain an area of critical importance in our proximate neighbourhood. The Gulf region remains the largest trading partner for India. Bilateral trade with the Gulf was US$ 181.4 billion (2012-13), and US$ 22 billion (2012-13) with WANA. India's top trading partners in the region were UAE (US$ 74.72 billion), Saudi Arabia (US$ 43.19 billion) and Iraq (US$ 21.35 billion). The Gulf provides over 60 percent of our oil and gas requirement. Saudi Arabia and Iraq are largest suppliers of oil to India, and Sudan/South Sudan are other important oil suppliers. The region is a major source of phosphatic and other fertilizers (Algeria, Tunisia, Morocco) and, thus, contributes to our food security.

There are about seven million Indians who live and work in the Gulf, and another 45,000 Indians live in the WANA region. India receives annual remittances of over US$ 30 billion from the region. The region is also a potential source of sizeable investments as India has the capacity to absorb large capital infusion, especially for infrastructure projects. The region is also a significant platform for operations by Indian companies.

The region is an important partner for India in counter-terrorism, intelligence sharing, homeland security, controlling money laundering, small arms trafficking, smuggling and financing of terror activities besides in anti-piracy effort.

The on-going turmoil in the Arab region is rooted in the Arab Spring, which began with popular and widespread unrest in Tunisia in December 2010, and rapidly spread to other countries in the West Asia, North Africa and the Gulf regions. In particular the after effects of the so-called Arab Spring and the spiralling internal violence in Syria and Iraq, have created a climate of political uncertainty in the countries in the region, and can have serious regional and global repercussions, which would also be felt directly by India. However, three years after the "Arab Spring", the earlier exaggerated expectations of progress towards democracy have turned out to be misplaced. The initial optimism of democratisation and regime change, has given way to serious concerns about the aftermath of the much-hyped revolutions. The "Arab Spring" has impacted the Arab World in different degrees – the first group include countries which saw a series of strong, popular and mass protests leading to regime changes such as Tunisia, Libya, Egypt and Yemen; the second tier of countries saw demonstrations that were contained by the ruling regimes through targeted but limited political and economic reforms such as Kuwait, Saudi Arabia and Oman, or by stern actions against protesters and demonstrators such as Bahrain and Jordan. The third group includes Qatar and UAE, which are yet to witness any such protests and have used this as an opportunity to enhance their regional influence.

The regional strategic balance is in flux, with Iraq perceived to have come under Iran's sway, and divisions within the Gulf Cooperation Council (GCC), evident through the withdrawal of the Ambassadors of Saudi Arabia, UAE and Bahrain from Qatar.

Religious extremism has become vastly more pronounced (Al Qaeda, Islamic State in Iraq and Syria (ISIS), and Salafists). Large number of jihadi fighters, from more than 80 countries, have joined the conflict in Syria. Given the recent ISIS activities, Syria and Iraq are likely to shift from being a 'destination' for Islamic extremism, to become the newest breeding ground for extremism. Militia infighting in Libya has seen Islamists pitted against tribal and pro-democracy rebel groups, thus threatening regional stability. The easy mobility of extremists and rising number of foreign jihadis in the region has increased fears of the possibility of the spread of radicalism in the home countries of foreign fighters.

The Shia-Sunni divide has been exacerbated by the recent events. There has been a rise in sectarian killings in Syria, Lebanon, Turkey, Iraq, Iran, Libya, and even in the GCC. These developments may have implications for Gulf unity and the stability of the WANA region. There are clear signs of a rivalry between Saudi Arabia and Iran and quest for pre-eminence in the region. Both countries have been at the forefront of the regional jostling for influence through a proxy war in Syria. Saudi Arabia has increasingly asserted itself in the region, given the earlier US resistance to intervene in Syria, the stalemated Middle East Peace Process (MEPP), and the US' potential rapprochement with Iran.

Saudi Arabia and Israel are particularly suspicious about the outcome of Iran and P5+1 nuclear negotiations. For Saudi Arabia, the reasons are theological and geopolitical. For Israel, there are issues of national/regional security: the Iran-Hezbollah-Syria axis and pressure for results on MEPP. If Iran acquires nuclear weapons, it is possible that Saudi Arabia will enhance its defence engagement with Pakistan for nuclear technology. We are hopeful that the negotiations will lead to a satisfactory permanent deal which will ease tensions in the region.

Recent conflict in Gaza resulted in large scale civilian casualties. This has put additional pressures on the region. This is compounded by lack of concrete progress on the peace talks which ended on April 29, 2014. Any outcome of the cease-fire negotiated in Cairo will ultimately have to be linked to the larger issue of comprehensive resolution of the Palestinian issue.

An apparent shift in the US role, perhaps through eroded credibility in the region is increasingly evident. Its inability to bring about a durable cease-fire after the recent conflict in Gaza, failure to stop expansion of Israeli settlements in the occupied territories, lack of a comprehensive and effective policy on Syria, disinterest in solving the ongoing violence in Libya, and its prolonged engagement in Iraq and Afghanistan without being able to restore peace and stability, coupled with domestic factors of decreasing dependence on Middle East oil, has created doubts about its commitment to the Region. But re-shifting of its focus on Syria and Iraq, means that it remains important for regional stability.

Russia has attempted to re-engage with the Middle East, and has gained in appeal as a counterweight to the West. Its positive involvement in Syrian chemical weapons deal; recently concluded defence contracts with Egypt, Iraq and reportedly with Saudi Arabia and WANA countries reinforce this perception. However, presently Russia seems preoccupied with Ukraine and its ability to influence events in the West Asian region is limited, except in Syria.

Chinese aversion to chaos may prevent it from seeking a more prominent political role. But it has embarked on an aggressive economic push in the region. Increased dependence on Middle East oil may result in greater Chinese naval presence in the region in years to come.

Qatar has moved away from its earlier policy of punching above its weight in the region, especially with the ouster of the Muslim Brotherhood (MB) led government in Egypt, and continued tensions with Saudi Arabia.

Turkey has toned down its earlier foreign policy focussed on promoting Political Islam, in its quest for a greater regional role. However, with political setbacks and growing internal challenges due to large influx of refugees and criticism from abroad for allowing jihadis to use its territory for movement into Syria, its ambition has been hit hard.

Egypt will continue to be a principal regional actor, although it has been chastened by the developments in the last three years. But it has the critical mass to get back into an institutionalised regional process as an important player.

On-going conflict in Syria has now reached a stalemate. The conflict has resulted in about 192,000 deaths, 2.9 million refugees and 6.5 million Internally Displaced Persons. Two rounds of the Geneva II talks ended inconclusively, and no further talks have materialised thereafter. The UN–Arab League Joint Special Representative, Lakhdar Brahimi, has resigned following the stalled talks between the government and the opposition. The Syrian regime held elections in early June, whose legitimacy was called into question, as elections were limited to areas controlled by the Syrian regime. Western reactions to the elections have been negative, corresponding to the belief that elections would stall any progress made between the government and opposition. Proxy war is being fought between regional powers in Syria: the West, Saudi Arabia, Qatar and Turkey on the side of the opposition and Russia, Iran and Hezbollah on the side of the Syrian regime. Involvement of jihadi groups like the ISIS and infighting between the rebel groups has led to a 'civil war within a civil war'.

A perceived refocus of ISIS from Iraq to the adjoining territories in Syria, is evident through the ISIS seizure of Tabqa air base in Raqqa province on August 24, 2014 thus ending the Syrian security forces' presence in Raqqa province. There are reports of US contemplating air strikes on ISIS targets in Syria, with or without Syrian government's consent. The US may seek the support of its NATO allies and friendly countries like Australia assistance in carrying out air strikes but genuine cooperation from the regional allies is still doubtful. The government has made partial gains in Syria through local cease-fire agreements with rebels. Now there are reports that USA and Saudi Arabia intend to provide Sunni rebel groups, especially the Free Syrian Army, with MANPADs and anti-tank missiles, and train the combatants of the moderate opposition groups.

ISIS surge in Iraq is the extension of extremism and instability into Iraq. ISIS has taken over swathes of northern Iraq since June 08, 2014 including important cities such as Mosul, Tikrit, Tal Afar, Baiji etc. Atrocities against the minority civil population in Sinjar and other places has no parallel and has caused revulsion. Sectarian blame game continues between Iraq on the one side and Saudi Arabia and Qatar on the other. Reported preparations of Hezbollah mobilising about 30,000 fighters for Iraq in another concern for regional security. India has huge stakes in Iraq. Iraq is second largest oil supplier to India. India is concerned over sectarian spill over from Iraq. There are estimated 15,000 Indians at present living in Southern Iraq and the Kurdistan region of Iraq. India has completed evacuation of 5,400 Indian nationals and there are 41 Indians still in ISIS captivity in Mosul.

The ongoing efforts of Egypt to broker sustainable ceasefire, supplemented by UN, US, Qatar and Turkey is a positive development. There is an open ended ceasefire currently in place since August 26, 2014. The terms of the proposed ceasefire are to include (i) an easing of the blockade by opening all crossings to Gaza, and (ii) allowing reconstruction of damaged infrastructure and the entry of materials needed for reconstruction. The two sides are, after a month, to begin talks on Hamas' demands to build an airport and seaport in Gaza. The ceasefire terms are along similar lines as agreed during the 2012 ceasefire between Hamas and Israel, but developments need to be watched carefully on the ground.

India provides economic/technical assistance of about US$ 30 million to Palestine. India has helped in setting up of IT centres, vocational training centre, schools, hospital/rehabilitation centre and recreation complex in Palestinian territories. India supports durable ceasefire between Israel and Palestine and has expressed deep concern over escalation in violence in Gaza, loss of civilian lives and damage to property. External Affairs Minister has stated on July 21, 2014 that there is no change in India's policy of continued strong support for Palestinian cause while maintaining good relations with Israel. This stance was also reiterated at UNSC Open debate on July 22, 2014 and India also voted in favour of Palestinian position at the United Nations Human Rights Council (UNHRC) on July 23, 2014.

Intensified militia warfare between Islamist and pro-government forces in Tripoli and Benghazi is continuing since mid-July 2014. Oil infrastructure has been severely damaged. Over 650 people have been killed and Benghazi has been declared as an "Islamic Emirate" by Al Qaeda linked Ansar Al Sharia. There have been reports of air strikes on Islamist militia by Egypt and UAE on August 23, 2014 and takeover of Tripoli airport by Misrata rebels. Situation is extremely fragile having severe implications of regional spill over. UN, US, major EU and Arab Missions in Tripoli have been closed. Indian Embassy is functional with reduced staff, although decision has been taken to relocate Embassy personnel temporarily to Djerba in Tunisia.

India imported US$ 1.7 billion worth oil from Libya in 2012-13. Investments by Indian companies like BHEL, OVL, PunjLoyd, Unitech, KEC, Shapoorji Pallonji, etc. in Libya is around US$ 4.5 billion. India has offered support in establishing democratic institutions, police training and capacity building and the Indian community in Libya was estimated to be about 6,000. India evacuated its nationals through land, sea, air routes during the turmoil. Around 3,000 Indians still remain in Libya, who are reluctant to leave.

## Policy Options for India in the Gulf & West Asia

Unprecedented changes in West Asia have compelled us to question our traditional assumptions and role. We are very willing to consider new options, in a realistic manner, and hence the need for careful strategising. India, if required, given its democratic background, principled position of non-interference in internal affairs of other countries and its non-prescriptive foreign policy, can provide political support on issues deemed of common interest in the West Asia. It can put forward alternative solutions facilitating regional take-aways for regional problems, support societal and institutional mechanisms and offer capacity building assistance - that are seen as less partial than the perceived methods of the West or even Russia and China in the region.

India is not in the business of exporting democracy. Although India is a robust practitioner of democratic pluralism and religious moderation, we don't believe in intrusive prescriptive diktats. At the same time, India needs to be realistic about its leverages as well as limitations. Vice President of India has stated that "India has limited leverages but unlimited interests" in the region. Many countries in the region have expressed a desire for India to play a more active role in the region. We should be ready for that, but with adequate preparation.

India has maintained its policy of supporting a Syrian-led, political and non-military solution to the Syrian conflict. In view of our non-prescriptive stance on the resolution of the conflict, India participated in the Geneva 2 conference held in Montreux on January 22, 2014. Our support for the elimination of Chemical Weapons (technical as well as US$ 1 million financial pledge), and US$ 2 million towards humanitarian assistance, has given us good political mileage. India has offered assistance in implementation of any agreement between government and opposition.

While strengthening high-level government to government contacts, it would be useful to have discreet contacts with key members of the opposition. This will ensure that our strategic interests in Syria and the region are not affected irrespective of the composition of the government in place.

Important fall out of the Syrian conflict has been the intensification of Shia-

Sunni fault lines across the region (proxy war between Saudi and Iran) with potential implications for India. We should stay out of sectarian alliances, while remaining prepared for any fundamentalist backlash coming from the region. The threat of the spread of extremism to the region, and the possibility that Syria (and now Iraq) could supplant Pakistan as the base for Al Qaeda and affiliates is a heavy blow to the Western backed Syrian Opposition, and of serious concern to India, the wider region and international community. There have been some reports of a few Indian jihadi fighters involved in the Syrian conflict. We need to be careful about such a development.

Defence and security cooperation on counter-terrorism, intelligence sharing, piracy, money laundering, small arms smuggling, financing terror activities etc. is emerging as increasingly important element in our ties with regional countries. Despite the so called Pakistan factor, considerable space has emerged for us to project our interests and point of view to our partners in the region. This needs to be leveraged to our advantage.

So far, despite challenges of the regional flux and sectarian divide stemming from the Syrian conflict, our bilateral relations with virtually all countries of the region have been progressing smoothly and we have managed to insulate our core interests from the negative fallout of regional developments.

We should strengthen our relations with all the regional players. Ties with GCC countries in particular, given our core energy and security interests, are valuable and need to be solidified on multiple fronts. At the same time, we will need to consolidate ties with Iran and Israel, at different levels. In parallel, we should maintain our engagement with the US which still remains important, bilaterally as well as for regional stability.

Given our large Muslim population, we will need to take a principled position on the ongoing developments in Syria and Iraq, calibrated according to our Constitution, cultural, political and secular values and based on our time-tested practices of peace and non-violence, respect for all peoples and communities. Our approach towards countries experiencing Arab Spring should not be misconstrued as being partisan or sectarian.

We can offset political unpredictability in the region through greater economic engagement with all the countries. While the regional trade volumes have increased, considerable untapped potential remains and more thorough and integrated business approach is needed. Considerable potential for use of diaspora to lobby for India's political and economic interests exists. It needs to be communicated appropriately that "old order neutrality" in a changing and unpredictable environment does not mean absence of decision making, lack of leadership or political passivity.

In conclusion I would say that, India attaches high priority to its economic, political and security relations with the countries of West Asia. These relations are poised to grow, with increasing realisation of the existing enormous potential on both sides—despite the prevailing challenges, which will need to be tackled strategically.

# Introduction

*Prasanta Kumar Pradhan*

The West Asian region continues its struggle to establish a stable political order. Since the outbreak of the Arab Spring in West Asia and North Africa in 2011, the regional geopolitical situation seems to be getting more complex day by day. The hoped-for transition from authoritarianism to democratisation has been rather painful and convulsive, and has a long way to go. Apart from Tunisia other countries affected by the Arab Spring are yet to find a viable future political roadmap for themselves. The deteriorating situation in Syria provides a geopolitical challenge for peace and stability throughout the region.

The ongoing societal and political changes have had a destabilising impact on the region, and thus, the fundamental challenge has been to envision ways to achieve ordered change in West Asia. There has been much speculation amongst scholars regarding the future trajectory of the Arab Spring; whether this tumultuous upsurge will peter out and remain an isolated event in contemporary history or will the chain of events translate into a movement leaving behind a significant mark throughout West Asia and North Africa.

Particularly disturbing not only for the region but for the immediate neighbourhoods as well is that the continuing uncertainty is creating expanding spaces for extremist and terrorist elements to entrench themselves in the region. Their increasing activities are evident on a daily basis in Iraq, Libya, Syria and Yemen, which is manifested in a growing number of attacks. The onset of sectarian politics in the region has also further contributed to the growth of radical ideologies among the people. Iran has been the most important player throwing its weight behind various Shia groups in the region. Saudi Arabia is known to be supporting the Salafists while Qatar supports the Muslim Brotherhood. The growing Shia-Sunni dimension of the conflict has severe implications for regional security in West Asia.

Iranian engagement with the P5+1 and the successful conclusion of the nuclear deal remains a concern for the Gulf Sheikhdoms. They continue to put pressure on the US and the West not to accept any deal with Iran which can potentially hamper their security and strategic interests in the region. Similarly, Israel is also concerned about the implications of Iran and P5+1 talks for regional security in West Asia.

The region has a history of external influence and even intervention in the past. Among several stakeholders, the US remains the most influential power in the region. Its attitude towards the Arab Spring and it policy of 'rebalancing towards Asia Pacific' has drawn criticism from its regional allies. The US has in the past assured its Arab Gulf allies and reiterated its commitment towards Gulf security. At the same time, Russia is emerging as a major player in the region with its support for Iran and its stance on Syria. Russian involvement in Syria has changed the regional geopolitics in West Asia.

Continuing regional instability also raises increasing concerns related to issues of energy security. The emergence of protests led to rise in international oil prices and created apprehensions regarding its uninterrupted production and supply. Since the economy of many countries in the region is primarily dependent upon the hydrocarbon sector, any disruption in production and supply of oil may have serious implications not only regionally but also much further beyond on countries dependent on oil supply from the region.

India has been following the developments in West Asia very closely. India has important political, economic and security stakes in peace and stability of West Asia. In light of the emerging political situation, the challenge facing India is to balance its political equations and economic interests with major regional and external players in the region. India is heavily dependent on energy supplies from the Gulf region. India imports around 63 percent of its total oil imports from West Asia. The region is a leading trading partner for India with a total trade of around US$ 172 billion in 2014-15. Around seven million Indians live in the region and they form an important symbiotic link between India and the region.

The importance of stability is, therefore, of paramount importance for India. Absence of a robust security architecture and deep rooted intra-regional conflicts raise concerns about the viability of regional security in West Asia. There is a realisation in some quarters that India should start getting involved in the regional security of West Asia. As India maintains warm ties with all the major countries in the region and is non-interfering in the internal affairs of these countries, it can be an important player in initiating a dialogue among regional countries on issues affecting regional security.

Realising the importance of the developments taking place in the region and huge Indian stakes in regional stability, the Institute for Defence Studies and Analyses (IDSA), New Delhi, organised its First Annual West Asia conference on September 10-11, 2014, on the topic "Geopolitical Shifts in West Asia: Trends and Implications". The conference deliberated on geopolitical, security, economic and strategic issues unfolding in the West Asian region. Scholars from India, West Asia and other countries participated in the conference and discussed in greater details the evolving trends and its implications for the regional peace and stability in West Asia. The articles in this volume reflect and analyse the continuing turbulence in the region, identify the key actors, focus on the hotspots of conflict and its implications for the region and beyond.

Gencer Özcan, in his paper "The Arab Uprisings: The More Things Changed, the More They Stayed the Same", argues that the Arab uprisings gave rise to high expectations among people in the region that the authoritarian regimes would be dismantled and be replaced with democratic ones. But except Tunisia, all other countries which experienced regime change have witnessed catastrophic results. The Sykes-Picot border agreement has been challenged by the transnational terrorist organisations who aim to abolish the borders and create multiple states of different sorts. But he also maintains that even though the borders are artificially drawn by colonial powers, these borders have 'consolidated, stood against time and appear to survive the present crises.' He concludes that due to the current turbulence though there may be some changes within the national borders of the countries of the region, the Sykes-Picot border will largely remain intact.

N. Janardhan's paper, "Arab Uprisings and Changing Geopolitical Trends in the Gulf", identifies some new trends that have emerged in the regional geopolitics in light of the Arab Spring. He notes that developments in the region since the outbreak of the Arab Spring has had its impact on the international arena as well. For him, one of the most significant fall-outs of the uprisings is the reversal of the rapprochement efforts on several fronts—such as between Iran and Gulf Cooperation Council (GCC), Iran and the West, and Syria and GCC. Meanwhile, Qatar emerged as a major player and its role changed from a 'neutral' mediator in regional conflicts to a "niche diplomacy" when it called for external intervention to help the Libyan rebels oust Muammar Gaddafi. He also believes that the Arab Spring widened the sectarian tension in the region and further intensified the Saudi-Iranian competition and hostility. Non-state actors have emerged as bigger enemies than the states during the Arab Spring. Similarly, the return of Islamists to the political mainstream is also another trend which appeared in the region.

After examining some important issues affecting the region, Mostafa Zahrani, in the paper "A New Paradigm in Understanding the Current Evolutions in the Middle East", presents an Iranian perspective of the unfolding problems. For him there are three important issues which need focussed attention. First, there seems to be an acute identity crisis prevailing among the people in the region. The boundary of the region is contested and the identity of the people is being seen as belonging to one state or another. The feeling of belonging to the region is missing from the minds of the people and the governments in the region; second, terrorism has acquired many new dimensions. The establishment of the 'caliphate' by the ISIS in Iraq and Syria is an absolutely new phenomenon. Third, Ideology is a very important issue in the region. Dismissing the sectarian dimension of the conflicts in the region he argues that the rivalry between regional and international players is the main reason for the conflicts in the region. He further states that State sovereignty has been questioned now within the region. The governments of the region have also failed in their distribution and participatory functions which is the primary reason behind the popular unrests throughout the region.

In his paper "Geopolitics in West Asia: An Egyptian Perspective", Mohamed Fathy Abdel Hamid El Shazly states that if 2011 was the year of 'Regime Fall' in the Arab Spring countries and 2012 was the year of 'Faltering Transition' and 2013 was the year of the 'Failure of Islamists in Power', then 2014 would be the year of the rise of popular demands for the return of the State. In most of the Arab countries where the uprising took place, the common noticeable phenomenon in recent times has been the move towards "Reasserting the role of the State" in contrast to the "Erosion of the State" that began from December 2010. He asserts that crisis of the Arab states happened because of the social pressures produced by the imbalance between the state and society, functional failures of the State, slow and failing transitional processes, identity conflicts, separatist trends and external pressures. He also notes that the return of the state will face numerous challenges such as social, doctrinal and regional conflicts, armed militias, separatist trends and terrorist activities as well as the differences among leaders of political and social elites.

Drawing on from the history of the region, Ahmed Salem Saleh Al Wahishi, in his paper "Geopolitical Situation in the Middle East: A View from Yemen", notes that several political trends have emerged in the region after countries of the region got independence in the middle of the 20$^{th}$ century. Dominant ideas were the pan Arab Nationalist idea at the time of Nasser in Egypt and later the radical communist forces who were supported by the Eastern bloc. After the nationalists and radicals retreated the Islamists came up to fill the vacuum. They made use of the existing political situation in the region and managed to come to power in North Africa. Thus, Wahishi is of the opinion that the present transitional situation caused in the region is not only due to the internal factors but also because of the effect of other regional and international forces. For him, there are social conditions which are responsible for creating the phenomenon like ISIS and this social condition needs to be curtailed and political reforms and economic development should be initiated by the regimes. Along with strong security measures, the participation of the citizens in the process of development and in the affairs of the state should be initiated to achieve stability and to overcome the crisis.

Talmiz Ahmad, in his paper "Sectarianism and Security Implications for West Asia", emphasises that all across West Asia, the sectarian divide has come to define political and military confrontations and thus affecting the security of the region. Thus, for more than four years sectarian conflicts have been witnessed in the countries in places such Syria, Yemen, Bahrain and Iraq. His argument is that the conflicts have provided an opportunity to jihadi elements in the region to intervene in the ongoing confrontations through the ISIS. He believes that two regional powers—Iran and Saudi Arabia—have been using sectarianism a powerful foreign policy tool for mobilisation and political competition throughout the region. He elaborates that the Saudi sense of being beleaguered after the fall of the Saddam Hussain's regime Iraq was aggravated by the events of the Arab Spring stating that the Saudi-Iranian ties have never been as sharply competitive or destructive as they are today. For him, the jihadi forces actually support the sectarian divide represented by Iran and Saudi Arabia.

While giving a GCC view of the security in the region, Muhammad Abdul Ghaffar, in the paper "The Dynamics of Regional Security in the Middle East: A GCC Perspective", points out that in the Gulf region, there are two principal players in the regional strategic scenario—the GCC (dominated by Saudi Arabia) and Iran. Reflecting on a GCC perspective he claims that Iran is using non-state actors to expand its regional influence and interests which undermines the sovereignty of nations within West Asia. On the other hand, he believes that Saudi Arabia faces challenges of a volatile situation in the region, deteriorating relations with Iran, and terrorism. He argues that the influence of the non-state actors has exponentially increased following the Arab uprisings though they have always existed in the region since the past. They have evolved into serious regional players with substantial finances, weapons and man-power and have gained control over large areas in the region. According to Ghaffar, the vacuum created by the withdrawal of the US from Iraq and the sectarian policies of Maliki have led to the emergence of the ISIS which significantly impacted the political and security landscape in the region.

Abdulwahab Al Qassab dwells on the existing situation in Iraq particularly in the context of the aftermath of the US invasion and the recent rise of ISIS. In his paper "The Present State of Affairs in Iraq: Islamic State and Prevailing Political

Disorder", Qassab asserts that the occupation of Iraq by the US forces in 2003 led to the shattering of Iraqi society, introduced unprecedented sectarian divisions, heightened intimidation of the Iraqi Government by Iran, terrorism, corruption, and finally the ISIS which has taken over the control of more than 40 percent of the country's territory. The rise of ISIS was one of the worst developments witnessed in Iraq recently. Qassab argues that the net result of the external intervention and the rise of the ISIS has been the vertical division of Iraqi society into its Shia, Sunni and Kurdish segments. Sectarian policies have been adopted by the subsequent governments in Baghdad, law and order situation deteriorated thus leading to meddling by other powers in Iraqi affairs. He, however, concludes the paper with an optimistic note reaffirming his faith in the ability of Iraqis to begin reforming themselves; which must significantly begin with the reform of the individual. The challenge, however, is to convince the Iraqis of the values of a unified Iraq, as opposed to the fragmentation of the country.

Rajeev Agarwal questions the basic premise on which the GCC was formed—that is the perceived threat from two adversaries—Iran and Iraq. In his paper "Gulf Security Architecture and the GCC: Time to Shed Past Baggage and Start Anew", Agarwal states that the formation of GCC ignored the geographical and geopolitical realities of the region. Iran is perceived to be the biggest threat to the region by the GCC. There are also security challenges emanating from balance of power dynamics in the region as well as those facing the GCC. The Gulf region has been witness to multiple, interlocking rivalries and competitions in the past including terrorism, WMD threat, problems of the rentier economy, the fear of a Shia axis, intra-GCC conflict etc. He argues that the GCC has not been able to solve the problem it faces. For him, GCC's excessive emphasis on the Iran threat and the overpowering presence of Saudi Arabia in the organisation are some of the issues which shows the failure of the GCC. He proposes a different security architecture for the region which would include Iran, Iraq, Yemen and Egypt. That should also involve participation of regional countries such as Syria, Jordan, Lebanon, Turkey and Palestine, in some form.

According to P. R. Kumaraswamy the region has a love-hate relationship with the external players. In his paper "A Love-Hate Relationship: External Interventions and Middle East", he argues that the region cannot recognise and resolve most of its core problems without external influence, interference and intervention, and at the same time, it holds the outside powers, especially the US, responsible for most of its crises. In his analyses, the external powers in the region have become an 'integral part of the political landscape' primarily because most of the problems and challenges they face are either too big for them to handle on their own or were intensified or created by them. In his opinion, though the influence of the US has declined somewhat in recent past, it still remains the only power with 'political will and military capability' to influence the region. He questions the capability of the countries of the region to tackle the challenges they face without external support. With the emergence of the ISIS he foresees even greater role for the US in the region to confront the ISIS.

Waiel Awwad is of the opinion that the current situation and turmoil in West Asia is driven by the Western policy of exploiting the natural resources of the Arab world. In his paper, "External Intervention in West Asia: Regional and Global Implications", he draws on from the developments during last century and points out that after the fall of the Ottoman Empire, the Arab world was divided into smaller countries by Britain and France (Sykes-Picot Treaty) to retain it under their influence and dominance. European powers intervened in the Arab world and encouraged coups against regimes opposing to their policies. Heavy militarisation of the region was one of the top priorities of the West and US, and they supplied weapons to support the puppet regimes. He states that the ISIS is a creation of the policies of the US in the region. ISIS emerged because of the vacuum which was created in Iraq after the withdrawal of the US. He also holds the Gulf monarchies responsible for the formation of ISIS.

Jon B. Alterman asserts that 'Middle Eastern energy has driven—and continues to drive—the economic growth of Asia and this trend of Asia-Middle East energy trade would continue in the future as well.' In his paper, "US and 'The Other Side of the World'", Alterman claims that the US has created the conditions for such trade to grow by securing the important choke points in the Indian Ocean such as the Strait of Hormuz and the Straits of Malacca. The energy from the Middle East to Asia is transported through the sea route. But when it comes to the safety of transportation the Asian powers, he argues, are disproportionately reliant on the US for security, regardless of their positive relationship with the US or not. Thus, the Asian powers are benefited because of the large US maritime presence in the Indian Ocean.

Henner Furtig, in his paper "How to deal with West Asia? Commonalities and Differences in the European and German Approaches", argues that even within the first two decades after the end of the Cold War, Germany did not pursue a consistent foreign policy towards West Asia. Germany has pursued a non-interventionist and defensive approach developed as a consequence of and a lesson from its defeat in World War II. It did not participate in the Iraq War in 2003 and it also remained neutral during military intervention in Libya in 2011. By doing this, Germany sided with Russia and China and not with its supposedly closest allies in Europe even though many Arab countries expected Germany to join the NATO intervention in Libya. Thus, Furtig argues, that it was an opportunity lost for Germany. Similarly, Germany also has taken different positions than most other European countries' position on Egypt and Syria. There are concerns that the consequences of the conflicts in the region is not clearly understood by many in the Germany policy circles which thereby leaves the policy initiatives to other powers such as the US, UK or France.

Analysing the geopolitics of energy in the region Girijesh Pant, in his paper titled "Changing Text of Energy Geopolitics and West Asia", states that energy has been a critical factor in defining the geopolitics of West Asia. A new interface between two is unfolding following the American invasion of Iraq and unleashing of forces from within after the Arab Uprisings. He argues that the terms of regional global oil engagements will be defined by the power dynamics of the region itself. This is a reversal from the context wherein global energy geopolitics was shaping the regional power dynamics. For him, the geopolitics of regional oil will be shaped by two distinct trends: one, the survival imperatives of the individual countries; and second, the intra-regional power rivalry, mainly between Saudi Arabia and Iran. Also, other formations of extremist profile like the ISIS, Al Qaeda or the Muslim Brotherhood are in the play that can use their oil power to consolidate their politics.

Toshitaka Takeuchi gives a Japanese perspective of the impact of regional instability on the energy security. In his paper "Safeguarding the SLOCs from West Asia as an Energy Security Policy: A Japanese Perspective", Takeuchi expresses concern that the regional instability in West Asia would negatively affect the energy security of the Asian countries because of the possibility of disruption in production and supply. He emphasises the point that besides the demand and supply sides of energy, its transportation becomes important in case of instability. This is especially crucial for Asian countries such as India, Japan, China and South Korea because almost all of their imported oil is transported through the Persian Gulf, the Indian Ocean and the Malacca Strait. The demand for the Middle Eastern oil is expected to increase significantly because of rapid economic growth in Asia. Thus, the Asian countries can make joint endeavours for anti-piracy operations in the Gulf of Aden and for the safety of the SLOCs. He suggests that the Asian countries can and should cooperate for their own sake for the safety of the SLOCs. Some kind of Asia-wide energy security forum can be contemplated by the Asian countries.

Similarly, Jeongmin Seo has expressed concern over the impact of regional instability on the South Korean energy security. In the paper "The Impact of Regional Instability on Energy Security: A Perspective from South Korea", Seo points out that South Korea is the fifth top energy importer worldwide with 64 percent of its oil coming from OPEC member countries. Over the last 30 years,

South Korea accounted for a rapid increase in energy use. There was a concern over the eruption of the protests in West Asia as any disruption in production and supply of energy will have disastrous impact on the economy and security of South Korea. But, he states that, South Korea's response to the current political transformation in West Asia has not been assertive, but defensive or passive because South Korea, unlike the US, Russia, and Europe, has not had any political leverage in the West Asian affairs. Therefore, the strategies and policies of South Korea on energy security have been focused on the two 'reactionary' measures such as in expanding the use of nuclear power and renewable energies building a strategic partnership with relatively stable Gulf countries like UAE and Saudi Arabia to secure its energy supply.

Shebonti Ray Dadwal, in her paper "West Asian Turmoil and the Future of the Regional Gas Sector: Implications for India", states that although regional gas producers have faced some disruption in production and export, overall, the political turmoil has had minimal impact on the international gas market. This is because of the lower status of West Asian gas supplies in the international gas market (barring Qatar) as compared to the region's oil supplies, reduced demand for gas due to the economic recession in Europe, and the increase in supply from other regions, particularly the US in the aftermath of the shale gas revolution. She states that Iran has the potential to emerge as an important player in the gas market as the sanctions are waived. India's LNG imports from the region has not been significantly affected because of the regional instability in West Asia. Demand for gas in India is increasing and it is estimated that the share of gas in India's energy basket is going to increase from nine percent at present to 20 percent by 2025. This would lead to a rise in India's import of gas in the coming years.

Finally, the paper by the editor of the volume, Prasanta Kumar Pradhan, "India's Relationship with West Asia: Facing the Challenges of Arab Spring", points out the major challenges India has faced since the unrest began in the region. The sudden rise of oil prices impacted Indian economy as India imports around two thirds of its total energy imports from the region. India has been concerned over the safety of its citizens in the region and it had to undertake massive evacuation operations to rescue its citizens from conflict zones such as Egypt, Libya and Yemen. The spread of terrorism, particularly the rise of the ISIS, has been another concern for India. India believes that ISIS is not only a threat for the West Asian region but also for the whole world. To deal with the continuing uncertainty in the region India has been actively engaging with the countries of the region. To a large extent, India has been successful in engaging with the West Asian countries to counter the challenges emanating from the unrest in the region.

It is clearly evident from the papers that there are divergence of views among scholars over the political and security situation in West Asia. Involvement of regional powers, extra-regional powers, role of non-state actors, sectarian politics, rise and spread of terrorism and extremism are some of the critical factors that have pushed the region towards further instability. The situation still continues to unfold and it is aggravating day by day with increasing violence, killings and humanitarian crises. In the absence of an agreed mechanism among the countries of the region to resolve the crises, it seems like the turbulence will continue in the foreseeable future and it will take a long time for peace and stability to establish in the region.

# PART I

## Geopolitical Trends in West Asia

# 1

# The Arab Uprisings: The More Things Changed, the More They Stayed the Same

*Gencer Özcan*

The Arab uprisings took many by surprise, brought about unforeseen changes across the region and sent shock waves all over the world. After they engulfed the whole region in early 2011, the uprisings gave rise to expectations that the authoritarian Arab states would be dismantled and be replaced with democratic ones.[1] With the exception of Tunisia, the expectations disappeared in other countries that experienced popular protests. Rather, the uprisings triggered chain reactions culminating to catastrophic results in the most populous Arab countries such as Egypt, Syria and Iraq. While the political turmoil instigated by the uprisings went out of control in Syria, it spilled over to Iraq fuelling sectarian strife throughout the country. The uprisings brought about significant changes, yet the way they turned out, it appears to have preserved, even consolidated the regimes they challenged. After some of the dust settled, it became conspicuous that at least the regimes in major Arab countries succeeded in withstanding the stir. In addition to the Gulf monarchies, Algeria, Morocco, Jordan and Lebanon managed to remain outside the maelstrom. In the wake of the *coup d'état* of July 3, 2013, the military in Egypt restored its political status. Though still staggering, the Bashar Al Assad regime in Syria has hitherto stood up to the challenges and accomplished to get back the control of critical areas that the armed opposition occupied.

The uprisings also excited anticipations that the regional order dubbed as 'Sykes-Picot Agreement' is doomed to collapse. True that the order seems to have been challenged by several transnational movements and religiously motivated organisations such as Al Qaeda in Iraq, presently named as Islamic State (IS), and to a much lesser extent, the Muslim Brotherhood, as well as another nationalist organisation like Kurdistan Workers' Party (PKK), all of them aiming to found states of their own stretching beyond the present borders. The IS clamoured that it will reverse the effects of the Sykes-Picot Agreement. A jihadist from the IS warned in the video titled *The End of Sykes-Picot* saying, "this is not the first border we will break, we will break other borders." IS' leader, Abu Bakr Al Baghdadi, in a speech at the Great Mosque of Al Nuri upon his forces' capture of the city of Mosul, vowed that "this blessed advance will not stop until we hit the last nail in the coffin of the Sykes-Picot conspiracy." In an even more spectacular way, the IS militants bulldozed the term that marked the northern border between the two countries.[2] Heralding that the geopolitical architecture founded by the Sykes-Picot Agreement disappeared, Franco-German geographer Christophe Neff claimed that the IS restructured the geopolitical structure of the Middle East in summer 2014, particularly in Syria and Iraq. The former French Prime Minister Dominique de Villepin has presented a similar geopolitical analysis in an editorial for *Le Monde* where he stated that the order based on the Sykes-Picot treaties no longer exists.[3]

Like those that foretold the doomsday of the Sykes-Picot, analysts who claimed that the regime change in Egypt would inevitably lead to the abolition of the Camp David order proved to be wrong. In this context, it is of use to remember that the regional order in the Middle East was set in the tumultuous year of 1979, the year marked several breakthroughs in the modern history of the Middle East. It began with the Iranian Revolution which transformed the balance of power in the Gulf. Being one of the pillars of Western security architecture in the Gulf, the Islamic Revolution catapulted Iran to a position of revisionist state in the Middle East. Since then, Iran has increased its weight, forged an alliance with Syria, and gradually became the pivotal power on the northern lands of the Middle East. However, it should be noted that revolutionary calls made by the Islamist government in Tehran did not resonate, if not fell on deaf ears, in other parts of the Middle East. Those who anticipated that the Iranian revolution would cause a domino effect ousting the pro-Western regimes in neighbouring countries did not come true either.

The year continued with the signing of the Camp David Agreements that ended hostilities between the two arch enemies, Israel and Egypt, which left the former free of the latter's pressure. The Egyptian decision to make a separate deal with Israel in 1979 was a final blow to the Pan Arab aspirations. Therefore, while the Islamic Revolution failed to reinvigorate Pan Islamic projects, the Egyptian-Israeli Peace Treaty catalysed the consolidation of nation state system in the Middle East. The balance of power, which relied on these two axes, defined the strategic landscape of the region. The spread of uprisings to Egypt and Syria therefore led analysts to foretell that the days of the regional order founded in 1979 are numbered. However, in the wake of the military takeover of July 3, 2013 in Egypt, let alone nullification of the Camp David Agreements, Egypt's relations with Israel became even stronger. On the part of Iran, the uprisings engulfing Syria caused grave concerns. The regime change in Damascus would mean the loss of most important strategic asset that Tehran has been having since 1979. In the light of these observations, the present paper will highlight two interrelated points. While the first point pertains to the regime resilience in the Middle East, the second is related with the resilience of the regional order. Therefore, the paper will argue that while chain reactions rekindled by the uprisings eventually solidified the national security regimes in major Arab states, the regional order forged in 1979 got further strengthened. Before delving into the details of the argumentation, it may be of use to briefly revisit the Sykes-Picot Agreements and the concept of artificial state.

## The Sykes-Picot Agreements

The Sykes-Picot Agreements handed over control of Syria, Lebanon and Turkish Cilicia to the French; and Palestine, Jordan and areas around the Persian Gulf and Baghdad to the British. Jerusalem was to be governed by an international administration. While neither France nor Britain actually 'owned' these territories, they were to effectively control them at a governmental and administrative level. Both Britain and France had large interests in those territories. The British claimed and gained the lion's share in the partition. London's strategists by the early 20th century had recognised the importance of having access to oil fields, a region lying between Britain and the British India. Paris, by contrast, had growing business relations with the large harbour cities of the Mediterranean—Beirut, Sidon and Tyrus. The Sykes-Picot Agreements intended to divide the Levant on a sectarian basis: Lebanon was envisioned as a haven for Christians (especially Maronites) and Druze; Palestine was to have a sizable Jewish community; the Bekaa Valley, on the border between the two countries, effectively left to Shia Muslims; Syria with the region's largest sectarian demographic group, Sunni Muslims. However, as it will be the case, it was impossible to partition such a vast territory populated by a complex demography as the Ottoman Middle East. Therefore, the newly created borders rarely corresponded to the prevailing sectarian, tribal, or ethnic distinctions on the ground.[4] Furthermore, the agreements marked a turning point in relations between Arabs and European Great Powers since they nullified the promises made to the Arabs for national Arab homeland in the area of Greater Syria, in exchange for their siding with

British forces against the Ottoman Empire.[5] Although it was thoroughly revised, the Sykes-Picot Agreement remained to be the hallmark of the post war colonial partitioning of the Ottoman Empire. Whenever there was a questioning reference to the regional order, the notorious document was quoted.

The agreements' principal terms were reaffirmed by the inter-Allied San Remo Conference from April 19-26, 1920 and the ratification of the resulting League of Nations mandates by the Council of the League on July 24, 1922. However, the mapping of the Middle East by the post-World War I arrangements is also noteworthy for being the first of its kind. The colonial demarcation made between 1919 and 1922 was a sheer novelty for ex-subjects of the Ottoman Empire. In this context, it needs to be underlined that nations' state borders were alien to the Middle East. As was the case between the Ottomans and Safavids/Qajars of Persia, one of the World's oldest borders, which had remained in place since the Treaty of Qasr-e-Shirin of 1638,[6] the border would be demarcated only by the first quarter of the 20th century.

## The Artificiality of States

In the wake of the initial phase of the uprisings, the concept of artificial state once again attained prominence in the international lexicon.[7] The uprisings gave rise to claims that since the states of the Middle East are artificial entities, which are constructed by the Great Powers of the 20th century, they are congenially incapable of survival. Arab states were qualified as fabrications constructed within "artificial" borders demarcated by lines drawn by rulers. For these theories, the artificiality of state formation is considered to be part and parcel of the political and social problems that these countries fail to address. Belittled as artificial polities with proclivities for disunity, the Middle Eastern states were qualified as entities which were doomed to collapse.[8]

It is interesting that arguments based on artificiality have been adopted and pronounced by a peculiar group of people—Pan Arabists, Pan Islamists of various kinds, neo-Ottomanist Turks and Israeli irredentists. Moshe Sharon, who is Emeritus Professor of Hebrew University and served as advisor to Prime Minister Menachem Begin, provides a good example of artificiality argument. He starts his argument by holding the British and French responsible for artificial creations as Syria, Lebanon, Iraq and Jordan and Saudi Arabia.

> None of these countries [Syria, Lebanon, Iraq, Jordan, Saudi Arabia], which have by now also created for themselves an artificial history, existed as even an administrative entity under the Ottomans or prior to the emergence of the Ottoman Empire. For example, what today is Syria was divided under the Turks, and virtually throughout the Islamic rule, into at least four administrative

> regions. However, in 1919, following the French takeover it was cobbled together as a "state" which became independent in 1946. This state incorporates such contradictions as the Aleppo region in the north, the Isma'ili-Ansari territory in the north-west, Homs and Damascus in the centre, and the Druze Mountain in the south, to mention only part of the ethnic, religious and cultural conglomerate making up modern Syria. While at it, the French created "Lebanon"; a mishmash of Moslem Sunnis, and Shi'tes, Christian Maronites and Druze, all thrown into a pot of some 10,000 sq km to cook together in impossible arrangements of power sharing. Jordan is even more ridiculous, Transjordan, torn away from the mandate of Palestine by the British, was created as a "kingdom" for an Arab sheikh from the Hejaz (first Emir and later King Abdullah).[9]

The artificiality argument is flawed in several respects. The first defect is that it overlooks historical realities by seeing each Arab state under the same rubric. However, from the very inception, new states were different from one another and followed different paths of development. In the latter part of the 19th century, various forms of nationalisms espousing decentralisation, cultural autonomy within the framework of Ottoman state were already burgeoning in the Arab provinces. Since the beginning of the formation of nation state system in the Ottoman Middle East, the principle of territoriality was upheld. When the war ended, the establishment of the first Arab state, Eliezer Tauber notes, "it seemed relevant to think that the dominant nationalist idea among the inhabitants of the Fertile Crescent would be the Pan Arab idea of establishing one single Arab state in the territories of the former Arab provinces of the Ottoman Empire. The Pan Arab idea did not reach an exclusive senior position despite Husayn's Arab revolt." Tauber claims that, "the particularistic movements which had emerged before the war, and which became stronger during it, continued to exist after it."[10] It was therefore, Tauber adds, "when the time came to put ideas into practice, the territorial tendencies prevailed, and the struggle for independence was for local independence: Syrian, Lebanese, or Iraqi." Before making a list of the Arab provinces for which he requested respective rights for self-rule, the memorandum Faysal submitted to the Paris Peace Conference illustrates the state of mind prevailing among the Arab nationalist circles. Tauber further argues that, "the various provinces of Arab Asia—Syria, Iraq, Jezirah, Hejaz, Nejd, and Yemen—are very different economically and socially, and it is impossible to constrain them into one frame of government."[11] Muhammad Muslih also highlights how the post war political climate in Damascus turned out to be conducive for fragmentation rather than integration. His illustration of competing local nationalisms reveals dynamics which laid the foundations of nation states.[12] Faysal is known to have made similar statements after the Paris Peace Conference emphasising that Syria and Hijaz and Iraq must each be granted separate independence.

The evidence that the 20th century Middle East history presents does not substantiate the arguments of artificiality either. It is true that the Middle Eastern territories of the Ottoman Empire were partitioned under the scheme of Mandate System inspired by the Sykes-Picot arrangements of 1916. However, this definition oversimplifies the complexities of the early stages of the statehood of these countries. The Ottoman experience of ruling the Middle East for 400 years, served as a model for the British and French, new patrons of the regions. Historical accounts provide ample evidence that they studied and maintained many Ottoman administrative practices. For instance, when they revised the Sykes-Picot arrangements in San Remo Conference, they by and large adopted Ottoman provincial divisions.[13] Although arbitrary modifications were imposed when deemed necessary for strategic considerations, the borders they envisaged had strong historical and social references which the new patrons inherited from the former ruler.

## The Resilience of the Regional Order

The historical overview of the 20th century clearly underpins that whenever faced with a challenge, so called *artificial* order could have recuperated itself and came out of the crises even stronger. It was witnessed time and again that when the regional order had indicated signs of fragmentation, the centripetal forces gained momentum. The concern articulated by Usher Susser, an Israeli expert on Jordan, over the recent turmoil, represents a centripetal reflex, "Israel presently faces a regional array of challenges that the founding fathers could never have imagined. These are very different from the dangers that the Israelis had actually expected in the first decades of independence. The founding fathers were constantly agonised over the balance of power with the Arabs, which they expected to change with time in the Arabs' favour. They could not have foreseen Arab weakness and decline or that the Arabs, instead of going from strength to strength, would become a conglomerate of failing states paving the way for the proliferation of a host of dangerous non-state actors."[14] All these do not necessarily mean that the order will be with us eternally, but that it will well remain with us unless the very nature of the challenge is changed. In this regard, another caveat needs to be underscored. There may be a sort of *Yugoslavisation* of some countries, as we already witnessed in Palestine, but as far as the colonial borders demarcated in 1920s are concerned, they will likely remain as they are.

The historical evidence is also consistent with this observation. The particularistic tendencies were conspicuous as early as 1920s and pan ideologies were assailed by nationalists, be in Damascus or Baghdad or Jerusalem. It does not necessarily mean that there were no political activists and movements that upheld Arab unity, but in practice, they were particularistic. The formation of mandates catalysed the process of nation state formation. After the mandate system was dismantled, the unionist projects never succeeded in overcoming these particularistic tendencies. The unity declared between Egypt and Syria in February 1958 and the formation of the United Arab Republic (UAR) can also be seen as another attempt to change the artificial borders. The UAR was welcomed throughout the Arab world with much enthusiasm as the nucleus of Pan Arab state. However, alarmed by the UAR, Israel and Turkey were known to intensify their contacts to hold it at bay. Israeli Prime Minister, David Ben-Gurion, considered it "as a nutcracker, closing in on Israel from above and below."[15] Furthermore, in the wake of the July 14 Revolution in Baghdad, Israel and Turkey would step up their efforts to counterbalance the unionist initiatives. However, due to the Syrian nationalist priorities, the unionist project was cancelled in September 1961. Its dissolution marks the beginning of the decline in Nasser's Pan Arabism. The prime of Pan Arabism would not be returned; even the Baathist coups changed power in Damascus and Baghdad in early 1963. In the wake of coups in two major Arab capitals, the Pan Arabic project seemed to seize another rare moment to get revitalised. However, the trilateral talks between Cairo, Damascus and Baghdad to create a union failed to renew Pan Arabist aspirations.

It was interesting that Hashemite Kingdom of Jordan, the weak construct of the mandate system, could survive many challenges at times when even its staunchest allies lost their hope that the kingdom would fail to keep its integrity. Before shedding some light on its history, one can remember that it was again Jordan that attempted to change the mandate borders in the 1948 War by occupying the West Bank. When Jordan's existence was jeopardised by Pan Arab claims, the regional dynamics preserved its territorial integrity. For instance, in 1950s, Ben-Gurion was known to have "little faith in the Kingdom's long-term survivability and, at times, he had even toyed with the idea of splitting Jordan between Israel and Iraq."[16] Later in the 1960s Jordan was seen as an easy prey to Pan Arab ideologies. Asher Susser notes that, "in the late 1950s and early 1960s the sense of common interest between Israel and Jordan was consolidated against the background of increasing scepticism about the Kingdom's future in the capitals of Jordan's traditional Western allies, the US and the UK. In the foreign ministries and intelligence services of both powers it became increasingly common to think that Jordan had no real choice but to come to terms with the inevitable victory of the Nasserite tide sweeping through the region."[17] However, it would have been Jordan, which was to survive the worst acid tests during the decades to come.

The borders between Turkey and Iraq, envisaged by the post war arrangements, were already challenged by Turkey in Mosul from 1923 to 1925, yet it was ratified by the parties at the end of 1925. The consecutive Israeli invasions of Sinai in 1956 and 1967 can be seen as other events in which the borders, that colonial powers imposed, were challenged. However, after nearly 15 years of occupation, the borders between Egypt and Israel, the latter agreed to restore them. In this regard, the Egyptian-Israeli Peace Treaty of March 1979 marks a turning point in the process of crystallisation and legitimisation of nation state system in the Middle East. The Israeli occupation of the West Bank in 1967 can also be seen as a sort of restoration of the Mandate borders, which had been run over by the Jordanian army 19 years ago. Yet the Israeli occupation of the Golan Heights still represents the most protracted challenge to the colonial borders. Although they had been decided well in advance, Iran's violation of the Qasr-e-Shirin borders in the Iran-Iraq War of 1980-1988 was another example. Iraq's invasion of Kuwait in 1990 set another example of such challenge, which was repelled a year later by a US-led coalition. As of today, the only success in revising the colonial borders belongs to the successor state of the Ottoman Empire—Turkey. Turkey took advantage of the configuration of forces in the Middle East and Europe, and secured the return of the Alexandretta in 1939.

## Conclusion

After five years of upheaval in the region, where we stand now is far from where the uprisings began. Great hopes attached to the uprisings, that they will mark the beginning of a new era in the history of Arab societies, were dashed. With some notable exceptions, the uprisings simply failed to deliver what they promised in many Arab countries. Military, police and intelligence agencies of the *mukhabarat* states became more consolidated. While the cries for *change* enchanted by crowds lost their charm, calls for *stability* and *order* are often heard.

In all Arab states the events followed their own trajectory and remained within the national borders. The events highlighted once again that the principle of territoriality is still upheld in the ex-Ottoman territories. It is also remarkable that the power vacuum left by the civil war and fratricide in the Levant and Mesopotamia instigated its own problems urging other states to act accordingly and take precautions. In this regard, two points are noteworthy. First, the nation state system reacts against pan ideologies and recuperates itself. The system is able to function to the effect that it could have been the US and Iran together to further expansion of the IS. The way the uprisings turned out to be and the course they have so far taken reveal that the two axes of the regional order, the Israeli-Egyptian and the Iranian-Syrian, will be with us in the foreseeable future.

Second, the claims that the uprisings will eventually take down the postcolonial borders have hitherto proven wrong. In spite of the calls that the borders will be broken, there is no change of official borders. Although there may be some revision within the national borders, the colonial borders dubbed as the Sykes-Picot borders would eventually remain intact.

## NOTES

1. James Gelvin, *The Arab Uprisings: What Everyone Needs to Know*, Oxford University Press, Oxford, 2012, pp.1-32.
2. Michael Crowley, "Middle East in Pieces", *Time*, 183 (25), June 30, 2014, p. 21.
3. "ISIS Announces Islamic Caliphate in Area Straddling Iraq and Syria", *The Guardian*, June 30, 2014, at www.theguardian.com/profile/matthewweaver.
4. Ihsan Serif Kaymaz, "Establishment of the British Protectorate in Northern Mesopotamia During the End of World War I/The Great War", *Elektronik Sosyal Bilimler Dergisi*, 12 (47), Autumn 2013, pp. 275-296.
5. Usha Natarjan, "Creating and Recreating Iraq: Legacies of the Mandate System in Contemporary Understandings of Third World Sovereignty", *Leiden Journal of International Law*, 24, 2011, pp. 799-822.
6. Rudi Matthee, "The Safavid-Ottoman Frontier: Iraq-i-Arab as Seen by the Safavids", in Kemal H. Karpat and Robert W. Zens, (eds.), *Ottoman Borderlands: Issues, Personalities and Political Changes*, The University of Wisconsin Press, Madison, 2003, pp.157-171.
7. For a discussion on the concept of "artificial state" see Juliet J. Fall, "Artificial States? On the Enduring Geographical Myth of Natural Borders", *Political Geography*, 29 (3), March 2010, pp. 140-147.
8. For such a perspective see Moshe Sharon, "The Artificial Map of the Middle East", at www.shalom-magazine.com/Print.php?id=500307.
9. Ibid.
10. Eliezer Tauber, *The Formation of Modern Syria and Iraq*, Frank Cass, Ilford, 1995, p. 327.
11. Ibid.
12. Muhammad Muslih, "The Rise of Local Nationalism in the Arab East", in. Rashid Halidi *et al.*, (eds.) *The Origins of Arab Nationalism*, Columbia University Press, New York, 1991, p. 174.
13. Karen Culcasi, "Disordered Ordering: Mapping the Divisions of the Ottoman Empire", *Cartographica*, 49 (1), 2014, pp. 2-17.
14. Asher Susser, "Israel's Place in a Changing Regional Order (1948–2013)", *Israel Studies*, 19 (2), p. 218.
15. Ibid., p. 220.
16. Ibid., p. 223.
17. Asher Susser, *Jordan; Case Study of a Pivotal State*, Washington Institute for Near East Policy, Washington D.C., 2000, pp.14-20.

# 2

# Arab Uprising and Changing Geopolitical Trends in the Gulf

*N. Janardhan*

Few would dispute that there is a global foreign policy crisis. The Chinese and Russian anti-West foreign policies are more confrontationist than constructive; Turkey's 'zero problem' foreign policy is witnessing an awful lots of problems; India's 'play it safe' approach is indeed safe, but non-purposeful from a global perspective; the United States' 'poke your thumb at others' noses' while its own is bleeding, is a lesson at what foreign policy ought not be; in following the United States on most issues, much of Europe has no independent foreign policy; and less said the better about the foreign policies of the West Asian countries, which are either with or against the United States and the rest of the West.

The question that arises while pondering over these realities is: what drives foreign policy? At least four Ps come to mind—principle, profit, power projection and prestige. From the West Asian perspective, how the principal security guarantor—the United States—has fared on each of these factors explains its failures during the last decade, making us wonder about future alternatives.[1] Adding another dimension to these crises is the Arab uprisings, which have been compared to the 1979 Islamic Revolution in Iran, the collapse of the Soviet Union in 1991, and the 9/11 attacks in 2001, which impacted the political-security equations in West Asia and led to geopolitical changes and ideological rivalries to fill the power vacuum in the region.[2] In 2014, the four-year-old uprising coincided with the 25$^{th}$ anniversary of the collapse of the Berlin Wall—an event that led Francis Fukuyama to predict the end of history and the beginning of universal Western liberal values.

It is ironical that Arab uprising, which began as an attempt to seek political freedom to mend economic depravity, has achieved neither. Instead, it appears that Mohammed Bouazizi did not just set himself afire in Tunisia four years ago; the flames from his self-immolation have set the entire region ablaze, triggering an international power struggle between and among nations and non-state actors, thereby sending the global balance of power into a spin. There are strong indications that a transformation of the international order—a unipolar world at present—is either in progress or would follow as a result.

## Trends

The Arab uprisings have reinforced the regional approach versus the international approach. It is understood that most of the regional crises were triggered by the adoption of Western solutions, including the use of force. This has hastened the approach of regional perspectives for resolving regional issues, which in the context of the Gulf Cooperation Council (GCC) countries, especially Saudi Arabia and Qatar, could be traced to about a decade ago.

In the present scenario, contrary to international affairs affecting the region's politics, the events following the Arab uprisings mostly impacted international affairs.[3] One of the most significant fall-outs of the uprisings is the reversal of the rapprochement efforts on several fronts. The bid to overcome the GCC-Iran friction was being championed by Qatar, and was reluctantly being considered even by Saudi Arabia until just before the outbreak of the Arab uprising. There were a number of visits by GCC and Iranian leaders to each other's countries. Mahmoud Ahmadinejad became the first Iranian president to visit the UAE since the 1979, and Iranian delegates attended the GCC summit in Doha and presented a 10-point confidence-building measures plan. Turkey was attempting to mediate between Iran and the West. Syria was on course to mending fences with the GCC countries and the West, which was evident by King Abdullah of Saudi Arabia walking hand in hand with Bashar Al Assad in Lebanon, and also British and American leaders visiting Damascus, which signalled readiness to bring back Syria and Bashar from the cold. Suddenly, most of these efforts hit roadblocks in 2011 and the very actors involved in the rapprochement were and are at loggerheads once again.

While the decade-old experiment of the GCC countries to evolve regional solutions to regional problems is a brave and wise effort, it now appears that there are serious contradictions in their approaches and the key players may have bitten off more than they can chew. The most glaring is the lack of coordination in the GCC's foreign policy management—Saudi-Qatar competition over projection of foreign policy influence has intensified as there was no unanimity on sending troops to Bahrain to quell the unrest in March 2011 and there is variance in the Saudi-UAE-Qatari approaches in dealing with Muslim Brotherhood.[4]

A key change in regional foreign policy tactics pertains to Qatar. Many analysts question 'small' Qatar's 'big' adventures, but the fact is that it is playing a big role, irrespective of its motives, *modus operandi* or impact on the ground. After playing the role of a 'neutral' mediator in regional conflicts and beyond during the last decade, Doha's "niche diplomacy" switched gears in March 2011 by calling for external intervention to help the Libyan rebels oust Muammar Gaddafi and followed it up with financing and arming Syrian rebels too. Unconfirmed reports suggest that other GCC countries, including the UAE, have also joined this game of one-upmanship by taking matters of conflict resolution into their own hands. Does it reflect loss of confidence in the United States' ability as security guarantor?[5]

The GCC stand on the Syrian crisis, in particular, became one of the factors that widened the Sunni-Shiite divisions in the region, intensifying Saudi-Iranian competition. The hostility between the two countries and the sects they represent became more pronounced than it was three years ago, thereby worsening regional sectarian division and insecurity. Nothing demonstrates this better than the gains of the Islamic State of Iraq and Syria (ISIS). Owing to internal contradictions, the GCC as an institution is facing one its toughest challenges since it came into being in 1981. But it must be noted that while Iran was a catalyst in the GCC's genesis, it has had little or no role in the GCC's current crisis.

Non-state actors have become bigger enemies than states—Osama bin laden may be dead, but signs of more radicalised outfits like the ISIS are evident across the region. Their impact and the future of the 'war on terror' is a space that needs to be watched. It assumes greater importance because of the implications of foreign intervention, which are yet to manifest fully.

West Asia has left the post-colonial era. Before the uprisings, repressive governments diverted popular discontent to American or Israeli foreign policy, leading to a sense of "infantilisation and disempowerment". Today, external actors such as the United States and Europe seem peripheral to the politics of the region.[6] The decline of influence of great powers like the United States and Russia in West Asia is leading to some sort of rapprochement between them. This has created a cooperative relationship on Syrian chemical weapons and Iran. It is argued that the Geneva II talks offered an opportunity to form an inclusive international contact group that includes the key regional actors, Saudi Arabia and, despite the associated challenges, even Iran.[7]

The rise in political tension and deteriorating security scene has also meant more indulgence in arms race. Studies released between 2010 and 2012 indicate that the GCC countries spent some US$ 40 billion on armaments. In 2012, Saudi Arabia bought US$ 34 billion worth in weapons, including 84 new F-15 fighter jets and 132 Black Hawk helicopters. And, in March 2014, Qatar announced a massive US$ 23 billion arms purchase, including massive orders of attack helicopters from Boeing and Airbus.[8] But the important question here is that have these arms been purchased for domestic security or have some of these arms become instruments of the GCC's power struggle for influence and dominance abroad?

## Winners and Losers

While analysing the geopolitical implications of the Arab uprisings and drawing up a balance sheet of winners and losers, Prince Turki Al Faisal said in January 2013 that "in the bloody, hostile miasma of the Middle East" there are only losers.[9] Some suggest that Iran is the biggest beneficiary of regional instability due to the downfall of pro-US Arab regimes in the region. Others, including Iranians, however, suggested—at least till President Hassan Rouhani won the election—that the 'Arab Spring' had given rise to an 'Iranian autumn'.[10] The Arab Spring also to some extent brought challenges for Iran. First, Iran was too embroiled in its internal political bickering to be robustly involved and become optimally effective on the regional scene during the period prior to Rouhani's election. Moreover, sanctions were certainly hurting its economic development. Second, until the beginning of 2014, regime change appeared to be the only solution to stabilise Syria in the medium to long term, which appeared to be a setback scenario for Iran. Tehran's influence in the "Shiite Crescent", which was perceived to become a "Shiite encirclement" for the GCC countries, seemed to be hitting roadblocks. It was felt that "the weakening of the Iran-Syria corridor also meant weakening of Iran's power in Israel's backyard."

But, on the other hand, Arab Spring has also been a blessing for Iran in many respects. Iran appears to have gained more ground than it may have lost. Though temporary, after 32 years without diplomatic relations, Egypt and Iran had a spate of leadership exchanges beyond the customary appearances of heads of states at multilateral forums, which sent ripples in several Arab countries, particularly the GCC countries. Similarly, after a break, Iran and Turkey are slowly, but surely, beginning to see eye to eye on some regional issues again.

Iran is also sure to continue to exert greater influence in post-US Iraq and post-NATO Afghanistan. In fact, Baghdad's steadfast support for Tehran's policies in the region was evident when (the then) Iraqi Prime Minister Nouri Al Maliki said in 2013 that a rebel victory in Syria would spark a sectarian war in Iraq and a civil war in Lebanon, divisions in Jordan and create a new haven for Al Qaeda which will destabilise the region. It is another matter that Iran was a big factor in forcing Maliki out of the job, thereby reiterating its influence in Baghdad, apart from becoming a facilitator, rather than an obstructionist, in the region's conflict resolution bid. Iran has played this role realising that Iraq's sectarian and territorial divisions are more pronounced now and the empowering of the Sunni and Kurd factions may actually compromise its sphere of influence in the Shiite-majority Arab country.

The reopening of negotiations between P5+1 and Tehran tells its own story about Iran's strength. There has been a shift in the position of both sides on the vexed nuclear issue. Any deal hereafter would obviously be good for Iran, while compromising the longstanding concerns of the GCC countries and resulting in their worst fears coming true. Since the GCC countries have no 'Plan B' to address their grouse, Iran's gains stand out. Further, the threat of military action against Iran, which frequently reared its ugly head during the last few years, even if it was not as serious as it was made out to be, is irrelevant now. This sentiment was driven home by US President Barack Obama in 2013 when he said that diplomacy will yield a more lasting solution to the dispute with Tehran, which would serve the interests of Iran, the United States and Israel.

Iran's biggest gain, perhaps, is the fact that differences within the GCC on how to deal with Iran has come out in the open and even formalised to some extent. Oman has facilitated Iran-West negotiations; Qatar has always had economic interests in South Pars in mind, thereby wearing soft gloves while dealing with Iran. Saudi Arabia, UAE and Bahrain are still inflexible because of obvious ideological, territorial and sectarian reasons, respectively; and Kuwait is both the new fence sitter and mender with the GCC.

## Stars Align for Iran-West-GCC Ties?

President Rouhani's election, coinciding with the other Arab uprising events in the region, has altered the Iran-West-GCC ties dynamics. Iran's differences with the West and the GCC countries are fundamentally different even though they are now linked by the common thread of the nuclear programme. To explain it loosely, the difference lies in what each side considers to be "threat" and "fear". The West has viewed Iran as a military and nuclear threat, primarily to Israel and partly to the Western world as well. This factor has rarely worried the GCC countries. Iran has been more of an ideological threat to the GCC countries which has manifested itself in the sectarian divide. Their fear has been that Iran's nuclear programme would expand its regional domination, widen the Sunni-Shiite gulf and even expose the region to environmental disasters. Since there is a perceptible difference between the threat and fear factors, the West and GCC countries should approach problems with Iran differently. While the West should concentrate on the nuclear threat perception in their negotiations, the GCC countries should open a completely different front to deal with their territorial, ideological-sectarian, political and environmental disaster fears and concerns.

Yet, though the concerns of the West and the GCC countries are different, the short- and long-term GCC-Iran rapproachment is largely linked to Iran-West rapproachment. The likelihood of meaningful progress in Iran-West talks is high because this could be US President Barack Obama's *only* foreign policy success over two terms. Since ISIS is perceived to be the biggest of all the threats that the region faces, by nearly all the parties concerned, the Syrian government's gains and the re-election of Bashar Al Assad has vindicated Iran's position on Syria. Irrespective of how the anti-ISIS campaign pans out in Syria, Iran will ensure that its interests do not take a beating.[11]

In this backdrop and in the event of progress in the Iran-West talks, it is possible that the GCC countries, especially Saudi Arabia, may initiate a change in stance on both Syria and Iran. This is already evident in the diminishing instances of antagonistic and offensive rhetoric by both sides, which has been partly tempered by the clear lack of consensus within the GCC fraternity on how to deal with Iran. And, for Iran, a deal with the United States is very important. Achieving it, getting economic sanctions lifted and returning to the international mainstream would be the end goal of its rapproachment mission. Making the 'necessary' promises and compromises to satisfy the West is now more possible than ever before. And, making the necessary promises and compromises to meet the expectations of the GCC countries will be a task that Iran will think tomorrow rather than worry today.

## Looking Ahead

Former Saudi Foreign Minister Saud Al Faisal laid out a Saudi vision for Gulf security at 2004 Manama Dialogue—a "unified GCC, a prosperous Yemen, a stable Iraq and a friendly Iran." However, the situation today is far from this vision. The fact that the GCC is not a united bloc any longer may actually help GCC-Iran rapproachment in the future. Yes, from the GCC's longstanding viewpoint, especially that of Saudi Arabia, the possibility of Iran becoming a 'nuclear' regional hegemon is hard to digest. However, if the GCC countries are serious about long-term regional stability, the possibility of them leaving behind ghosts from the past and looking forward to a future of regional cooperation cannot be completely ruled out. The GCC countries, including Saudi Arabia, certainly realise that prolonged sectarian strife would destroy the development gains of the last decade. They, no doubt, used the Arab uprising developments as an opportunity to curtail Iran's influence in West Asia. With contrary results, it is not impossible to conceive that they may be ready to pursue 'selective' rapporachment with Iran, like they had embarked on before the outbreak of the Arab uprising. Simultaneously, Turkey is also an important player. While it is true that some of the GCC countries have not appreciated Turkish policy towards Egypt, Ankara has the potential to help establish a balance of power between a divided GCC and Iran.

## Arab Cold War?

While the above is a positive outlook, some analysts are putting forth a pessimistic view. Egypt, Saudi Arabia, the UAE and Jordan (perhaps Morocco too) appear to be forming a new regional group. At the same time, Qatar, Iran, and Turkey may be attempting another alliance, perhaps joined by Oman. Oman may be desirous of forming a regional grouping that would include Iran and Iraq, apart from Turkey and Qatar. Keeping this in mind, one analyst posed the questions such as its impact on Iran, Syria, Shanghai Cooperation Organisation (SCO), and big powers such as US, Russia and China. He believes that the SCO is likely to support the Qatar-Iran-Turkish axis over a number of key issues, including the future of Syria. He points out that once sanctions start getting lifted against Iran, Tehran would be able to join the SCO as a full member and not just be an observer.[12] It is also claimed that the United States was pushing for the Turkey-Qatar plan as opposed to the Egypt-Saudi plan in resolving the Gaza crisis.[13] Another view suggests that there is a "New Arab Cold War" that is playing out.

> As the United States steps away from the Middle East, its allies have tried to fill the void—with disastrous results. A bitter proxy war is being waged in the Middle East. It stretches from Iraq to Lebanon and reaches into North Africa, taking lives in the Sinai Peninsula, Egypt's Western Desert, and now Libya. Although the nihilism of the Islamic State and the threat of other extremist groups have garnered virtually all the attention of the media and the governments, this violence is the result of a nasty fight between regional powers over who will lead the Middle East. It is a blood-soaked mess that will be left to the United States to clean up.
>
> The popular conception of the Middle East is one of a region divided along sectarian lines pitting Sunni against Shiite, but another simultaneous struggle is underway among predominantly Sunni powers. The recent Egyptian and Emirati airstrikes on Libyan Islamist militias is just one manifestation of this

> fight for leadership among Turkey, Qatar, Saudi Arabia, and the United Arab Emirates (UAE). All these countries have waded into conflicts in Iraq, Syria, Egypt, Bahrain, and now Libya in order to establish themselves as regional leaders.
>
> Yet these regional contenders for power have rarely achieved their goals. Instead, they have fuelled violence, political conflict, and polarisation, deepening the endemic problems in the countries they have sought to influence. And if the United States doesn't step in, the chaos will only get worse.[14]

## Gulf-Asia ties

How would the above-mentioned developments and scenarios impact the US—a "superbroke, superfrugal superpower"? Contrary to the view above, the Arab uprisings have hastened the decline of US influence in a region that was already witnessing a US fatigue of the region and a regional fatigue of the United States. The fatigue on both sides has been greatly influenced by the Obama administration's efforts to correct the military adventures of the Bush administration, which affected the US domestic economy, thereby necessitating defence budget cuts and the 'pivot' to Asia. The pronouncement in May 2014 that "US military action cannot be the only or even primary component of our leadership in every instance... Just because we have the best hammer does not mean that every problem is a nail," is an important admission in Obama's continued attempt to refashion American foreign policy.[15] This comes in the backdrop of many scholars and most US policymakers calling on Washington to get rid of ISIS. But the point is, as Mahmoud Haddad points out:

> If one's span of memory extends back few decades, it could be remembered that the supposed recipe for a fine US policy was getting rid of the Ayattolahs in Iran, followed by calls to get rid of Al Qaeda, followed by calls to get rid of the "axis of evil", followed yet again, by the insistence to get rid of Saddam Hussein, followed by calls to exterminate Taliban, Gaddafi & Co., and now ISIS to reach some undefined utopian policy goal. The US's successive policies in the region have been piecemeal, negative and destructive since the 1970s. Some kind of a positive, constructive and broad-minded alternative should be put forward by experts to end the cycle of destroying one group to move to the choice of destroying another continuously. The Middle East maybe a great market in the times of war, but could become a greater market in times of peace.[16]

But the alternatives are far from encouraging. Lack of alternatives and the US desire to make its presence felt amid diminishing relevance in the region has made Washington discourage regional solutions by regional players, which could be one reason why the unconfirmed joint air attack by the UAE and Egypt may have taken place without the knowledge and consent of the United States. The only reason the GCC countries are still holding on to the United States is due to its security cover in a region that equates 'national' security with 'regime' security. In the event that there is likely to be a credible alternative, even in the distant future, American influence is bound to diminish enormously. This is where Gulf-Asia ties become relevant. Over the last decade, the Gulf security debate has revolved around two points of view: one, less international involvement in the region's affairs; and two, more internationalisation of the region. Since the dominant view favours the second option, there have been calls for exploring the idea of incorporating several international actors who could act as security guarantors of any future regional security arrangement. Some of the GCC leaders have issued several statements in support of this argument and idea. For Saudi Arabia, guarantees for Gulf security cannot be provided unilaterally "even by the only superpower in the world" and that the region requires guarantees "provided by the collective will of the international community."[17] Qatar feels that, "the major conflicts in the world have become too big for one single power to handle them on its own."[18] According to a Saudi analyst, "it is clear that the Saudis fully intend to pursue their national security interests much more assertively, even if that leads to a strategic break with the United States."[19] As a result, there have been signs of willingness on the part of the GCC countries to have different alliances with different countries on different issues, rather than put all their eggs in one basket. This "omni-balancing" means the GCC's ties with the United States are no longer exclusive.

In this backdrop, some trends that are crystallising after the Arab uprisings could actually be traced back to the early part of this century. Firstly, the GCC countries were conditioned by a mood referred to by some as "spirit of possibility", wherein they felt it is possible to develop and implement visions of transformative and far-reaching change. This new spirit was characterised, first, by high oil prices and other economic reasons, which filled their coffers with plenty of liquidity. The second factor was the "failure of others" in dealing with regional issues. This reinforced the wisdom in exploring local solutions to local problems—as seen in Qatari and Saudi diplomatic initiatives taking over from Egyptian and Jordanian diplomacy. The third factor is what is described as the "real strategic shift" in the region's foreign policy. Owing to the failure of the United States in the region and the shift in the economic power centre from the West to the East, the GCC countries began building ties with a host of alternatives, particularly in Asia.[20]

For the doubters of the Gulf's 'Look East' policy, according to Tim Niblock, "the extent to which there are real options is not the issue. It is the perception which is important, as it is this which creates openness to envisaging new possibilities." It is in this context that some like-minded scholars have been pushing the idea of upgrading the GCC-Asia buyer-seller relationship to a strategic one and exploring possibilities for a new collective security architecture, which would involve Asian countries (including China and India, among others) and Western powers, without excluding the United States. Asian powers have to start getting used to not ridding piggyback on US naval presence in the region's waters and find their own means of securing their sea lanes by bolstering their navies. Assuming that the US engagement in the region would progressively diminish in the decades ahead, this opens interesting possibilities by diversifying the number of security players catering to the region's security and stability.[21]

## Conclusion

From a GCC-Iran-West perspective, the Iran-West deal on the nuclear issue which may facilitate a workable rapproachment between the GCC countries and Iran, would contribute to greater stability in the region. From a wider perspective, the pursuit by various actors of principle, profit, power projection and prestige via their foreign policies is transforming West Asian politics, which bears the potential to alter the geopolitical situation—currently based on a unipolar world. Any alternative multi-polar power centre that may materialise in future must not be viewed as a competitor with the US and other Western forces; rather it should be approached in the spirit of cooperation, in a "post-US world", which is not necessarily an "anti-US world".

## NOTES

1. N. Janardhan, "America's policy crisis," *Khaleej Times* (UAE), April 23, 2012.
2. Kayhan Barzegar, "A turning point in the Middle East geopolitics," *Global Affairs* (Russia), June 24, 2012, at http://eng.globalaffairs.ru/number/A-Turning-Point-in-the-Middle-East-Geopolitics—15583.
3. Mohammad Sayed Rassas, "How the Arab Spring altered the region and the world," *Al Monitor*, October 4, 2012, at http://www.al-monitor.com/pulse/politics/2012/10/geopolitical-changes-caused-by-the-arab-spring.html.
4. Saudi Arabia, the UAE and Bahrain recalled their ambassadors from Qatar in March 2014, saying it failed to uphold its end of a security agreement to stop meddling in other nations' politics and backing groups threatening regional stability. This was seen as a rebuke of Qatar's support for Islamist groups, especially the Muslim Brotherhood in Egypt, which was seen as a domestic threat by both Saudi Arabia and the UAE, and its activist foreign policy, including its backing of the *Al Jazeera* satellite network, which has unnerved governments across the region. Also read, Salman Aldossary, 'Will the Gulf lose Qatar?' *Asharq Al Awsat*, August 25, 2014, at http://english.aawsat.com/2014/08/article55335842.
5. No longer able to rely on US support, richer Arab states are more likely to take military action on their own behalf—'Libya could be just the beginning for a newly proactive Gulf', *The Guardian*, August 26, 2014. The UAE had sent 12 fighter-bombers to participate in the 2011 international air campaign that helped oust Muammar Gaddafi—"If Egypt and

UAE hit Libya with Airstrikes, here's how they might have done it", *International Business Times*, August 25, 2014, at http://www.ibtimes.com/if-egypt-united-arab-emirates-hit-libya-airstrikes-heres-how-they-might-have-done-it-1668568.

6. Mark Leonard, "Seven reasons why the Arab uprisings are eclipsing western values," *Reuters*, January 21, 2014, at http://blogs.reuters.com/mark-leonard/2014/01/21/seven-reasons-why-the-arab-uprisings-are-eclipsing-western-values/.
7. Daniel Levy and Julien Barnes-Dacey, "Syria: the imperative of de-escalation", *Open Democracy*, May 25, 2013, at https://www.opendemocracy.net/daniel-levy-julien-barnes-dacey/syria-imperative-of-de-escalation.
8. Simone Cantarini, "Dangerous arms race among Gulf States," *Asia News*, July 2, 2013, at http://www.asianews.it/news-en/Dangerous-arms-race-among-Gulf-States-27082.html; and "Qatar buys helicopters, missiles in $23 billion arms deals," *Reuters*, March 27, 2014, at http://www.reuters.com/article/2014/03/27/qatar-defence-idUSL5N0MO3VV20140327.
9. Turki bin Faisal Al Saud, "How to win the Middle East," *Project Syndicate*, January 1, 2013, at http://www.project-syndicate.org/commentary/middle-east-winners-and-losers-in-2012-by-turki-b—al-saud.
10. Reza Ekhtiari Amiri, Mohammed Agus Yusoff, and Fakhreddin Soltani, "Arab Spring: Geopolitical implications for Iran", *International Journal of Asian Social Science*, 2 (9), 2012, pp. 1533-1544.
11. President Obama calls the ISIS a "cancer." Hassan Nasrallah, leader of Lebanon's Hezbollah, describes it as a "monster." Sheikh Abdul Aziz Al-Sheikh, Grand Mufti of Saudi Arabia, ranks Al Qaeda and ISIS as "Enemy No. 1" of Islam. And President Hassan Rouhani of Iran warns Muslim states to beware of "these savage terrorists," for "tomorrow you will be targeted," too, by ISIS—'Mideast rivals come together against ISIS,' *Bloomberg Businessweek*, August 25, 2014. Starting late August 2014, the United States and Shiite militia fighters aligned with Iran battled ISIS in northern Iraq. This was the first time that the United States and militias backed by Iran worked with a common purpose against ISIS, even though the US administration said that there was no direct coordination with the militias. This marks a dramatic shift for US-Iran ties—"US and Iran unlikely allies in Iraq battle", *New York Times*, August 31, 2014, at http://www.nytimes.com/2014/09/01/world/middleeast/iraq.html?_r=0; Also, "Isil brings Saudi Arabia and Iran closer," *Gulf News*, August 25, 2014, at http://gulfnews.com/news/gulf/saudi-arabia/isil-brings-saudi-arabia-and-iran-closer-1.1376455.
12. Theodore Karasik, "Shifting sands and shifting security alliances in the Gulf," *Al Arabiya*, April 6, 2014, at http://english.alarabiya.net/en/views/news/middle-east/2014/04/06/Shifting-sands-and-shifting-security-alliances-in-the-Gulf.html.
13. "There is talk as it was when the ambassadors were pulled from Qatar that there will be a closing of the border between Saudi Arabia and Qatar as well as the potential for a sea blockade of Qatar in order to get Doha to reverse its actions. Of course if this moves through this will push Qatar closer to Turkey and to Iran, which is the emerging new bloc. We have seen that already in the negotiations regarding Gaza. The GCC states are very angry with the United States because Secretary of State John Kerry was pushing for the Turkey-Qatar plan as opposed to the Egypt-Saudi Arabia plan", Theodore Karasik, "Region in crisis", *SUSRIS*, August 22, 2014, at http://susris.com/2014/08/22/focus-ksa-special-theodore-karasik-interview-region-in-crisis/. Also "Some see Qatar's hand in collapse of Gaza talks", *Al Arabiya*, August 21, 2014, at http://english.alarabiya.net/en/perspective/analysis/2014/08/21/Some-see-Qatar-s-hand-in-collapse-of-Gaza-talks.html.
14. Steven A. Cook, Jacob Stokes, and Alexander Brock, "The new Arab cold war," *Foreign*

*Policy* (Washington), August 28, 2014, at http://foreignpolicy.com/2014/08/28/the-new-arab-cold-war/.

15. Part of US President Barack Obama's speech on at a US military academy in May 2014.
16. Mahmoud Haddad of the University of Balamand, Koura-Lebanon, expressed these views in an online forum called Gulf 2000 in August 2014.
17. Saudi Foreign Minister Saud Al Faisal's statement at the Gulf Dialogue meeting in Bahrain in December 2004.
18. Qatar's Emir Sheikh Hamad bin Khalifa Al Thani said this at the General Debate of the United National General Assembly in September 2007.
19. Nawaf Obaid, "Saudi Arabia gets tough on foreign policy," *Washington Post*, October 25, 2013.
20. Read "Introduction" by Tim Niblock in N. Janardhan, *Boom amid Gloom: Spirit of Possibility in 21st Century Gulf*, Ithaca, UK, 2011.
21. These and related issues are elaborated in Ranjit Gupta, Abubacker Bagader, Talmiz Ahmad, and N. Janardhan (eds.), *A New Gulf Security Architecture: Prospects and Challenges for an Asian Role*, Gerlach, Germany, 2014.

# 3

# A New Paradigm in Understanding the Current Evolutions in the Middle East

*Mostafa Zahrani*

This paper presents a critique of the present security structure in the Middle East and attempts to analyse the impact of the present security structure on the ideological trends in the region. Examining the possible solutions for the present situation in the Middle East, the paper provides an understanding of the main hindrances in the way of settlement of conflicts, and also provides an explanation for understanding the importance of ideology in the unfolding situation in the region.

A vast range of security issues across Middle East has always raised fundamental and lasting threats for, firstly, the Middle Eastern states, and then, to some extent, for the transcontinental ones. The trans-regional powers have always attempted to intervene in this region in order to meet their security interests. Each of the foreign actors has used its own method of precedence towards the region.

The situation in Middle East at present is quite complex. Methodologically speaking, there are three important issues which need focussed attention while studying the situation in the region. First of all, there seems to be an identity crisis prevailing among the people in the region. The boundary of the region is contested and the identity of the people is being seen as belonging to one state or another. The feeling of belonging to the region is missing from the minds of the people and the governments in the region.

Secondly, terrorism is another important issue which is haunting the region. Iran has a very good experience of dealing with terrorism. Possibly this is one reason why many scholars argue that Iran is not a part of the problem rather a part of the solution. This comes from its experience of dealing with terrorism over the years. Possibly, suicide killing was for the first time experienced by Iran carried out by some terrorist groups which were provided sanctuaries in Western countries. Thus, Iran has a long history of fighting against the terrorists. Terrorism was used as a metaphor by former US President George W. Bush in the aftermath of 9/11. He called 'terrorism with global reach' that has really materialised now. It means terrorism is spread everywhere around different parts of the globe. No country, in today's world can claim itself to be immune from terrorism. The US being an external player can only play a marginal role in the region but Iran can play a key role in the region in solving the problems. To resolve the issues in Iraq, the presence of the US is not required.

Today terrorism has acquired many new dimensions. Earlier, people talked about terrorism from below, terrorism from top and lastly international terrorism. But the spread of terrorism in Iraq and Syria and the establishment of the 'caliphate' is an absolutely new phenomenon which has emerged in the region. This is neither terrorism from below, from top nor international terrorism. It is even further than international terrorism which is 'terrorism of global reach.' The competency and capability of this new form of terrorism is massive. The Islamic State of Iraq and Syria (ISIS) is not really a group, rather in a sense, they are a strategic group who can shift and can change the status quo of the region. They have the potential to change borders and, to a greater extent, even regimes as well. They intend to change the structure of the present international system.

Thirdly, ideology of the terrorist groups is a very important question in the region. As far as ideology is concerned there are two important points to be discussed here; one is particularism and the other is universalism. Universalism means that all of the groups come from a specific school of thought. Particularism means a tiny sect of a larger group, for instance, Wahhabism as an offshoot of Sunni Islam. Particularism is seen in Taliban in Afghanistan and in the form of jihadism and tribalism as well. In Iraq, jihadism plus the remnants of the elements belonging to Saddam Hussain's regime and that of the Baathist ideology represent a dangerous combination. It is a combination of nationalistic ideology and the jihadist ideology. So the Europeans should be skeptical because when it comes to Europe, universalism will bring some particularism and this might even spread to the US as well. Thus, fundamentally speaking, this is not an ideological conflict.

However, when the Arab Spring took place in the region, no one thought of the phenomenon having an ideological undercurrent. Even though many thought of Muslim Brotherhood to have been behind the uprising, this was not entirely true. This is because this wave of protests that engulfed the region was driven by the Arab youth population that did not follow traditional thinking, adhered to Arab nationalism or Nasserism.

It is wrong to conclude that the difference between Shias and Sunnis is the catalyst of conflicts in the region. This conclusion is drawn when things are politicised. Iraq and Syria can be cited as examples of this misconception. What has happened in Syria is the rise of rivalry between regional and international players.

The second point is whether one is talking about sovereignty or State sovereignty. It is not unknown that state sovereignty in the Middle East has strongly eroded from both within and outside. It is not only a question of the military intervention of the US or globalisation but of state sovereignty which is really under question now within the region. The marriage between State and non-State actors is an important issue. The lines between state and non-state actors as decision makers are now blurred. Therefore, it is difficult to state as to whether the state can solve the issues itself or not. Surely, this protracted conflict cannot be solved by any single state alone.

The legitimacy of the State is also an important question in the region. Because of natural resources and underdevelopment of the political systems in the region, territory has become a source of legitimisation. With the proliferation of the new elements, the question of source of legitimacy becomes a problem. So, the relation between nation and the State is really another question. Usually there are four types of relations—nation-State, state-nation, multinational state or part-national state. The issue is that, fundamentally, nation building is a very important factor in the region. The process of nation building is a very long process. It is difficult to state where Middle East stands when it comes to the process of nation building.

Historically speaking, the failure and the collapse of Ottoman Empire was an important factor in shaping the course of the region. It was supposed to introduce a modern State to the Middle East, but instead of modern State a colonial State was introduced in the region and that was really one of the root causes of the problem.

Further, globalisation is a very important factor. Globalisation is a very positive process but at the same time it has some negative sides as well. The Middle East is very much left behind when it comes to globalisation. Democratically speaking, as Samuel Huntington said, this region is an exception to democracy and some others call the whole region an exception when it comes to the level of sociology. Why is this an exception for the region? When Arab Spring came, some people optimistically called it the globalisation of democracy. But now we can see that it is globalisation of crisis and not globalisation of democracy. Arab Spring did not lead to establishment of democratic system of governance in the region, rather the crisis spread from one country to another, in the process, engulfing the whole region.

Another problem facing the region is the concept of 'Rentier State'. Many states in the region are dependent upon the rent received from oil and gas. Rentier states do not have institution of taxation. In the absence of the institution of taxation, responsible and accountable governments do not exist. Without a responsible government, democratic form of governance is not possible thus making the society highly unproductive. This is heavily prevalent throughout the region. The societies are not really productive. Also the patrimonial way of thinking, political culture, and the traditional way of understanding politics in the region further hinders any kind of political openness. The conservative and authoritarian reading of Islam by some of the states in the region has furthered misunderstanding about religion and politics. This is the fundamental problem in the region, at present.

Likewise, in a rentier structure, it becomes difficult for the state to implement the minimum plans that the state promises to its people. The governments have also failed in their distribution functions and participatory functions. This is the primary reason behind the popular unrests throughout the region. Of course Arab countries have not been able to solve the fundamental issues in their foreign policy. The problems that emanated during Arab Spring stem from Islamic fundamentalism and a lack of established civil institutions.

We must look at the developments in the region in a strategic manner. As similar trends are seen throughout the region one must look at the larger picture while trying to analyse the situation. Further, no single state or group of states can claim to resolve the problems facing the region. Therefore, it is the responsibility of everybody. One should also differentiate between two things—causes and the reason of the developments taking place in the region. It is very important to think about this, from a philosophical point of view as well. When we talk about reason we are talking about an idea that is Islam. There is also a need to differentiate between the determining factor and effective factor which determines the situation in the region and in which one has an effective role.

Lastly, if globalisation is really a positive trend, the people of the region should also benefit from that. One must look at the security of the region, human beings and security of the state critically. Careful consideration should be given to thoroughly understand terrorism today, especially, in the context of globalisation. It is true that terrorism has been financed, possibly, by some states and organisations. The inevitable result of globalisation is that porous borders have given rise to narco-terrorism as a new way of financing the ISIS. Thus, the terrorists of today are exploiting the unlawful benefits of globalisation.

# 4

# Geopolitics in West Asia: An Egyptian Perspective

*Mohamed Fathy Abdel Hamid El Shazly*

In most of the Arab countries where the "Arab Spring" took place, the common noticeable phenomenon in recent times has been the move towards "Reasserting the role of the State" in contrast to the "Erosion of the State" under the impact of the revolutionary tide that swept the region beginning from December 2010. This could be easily demonstrated through the unprecedented electoral victory of President Abdel Fattah El Sisi in Egypt and the political support strongly felt for President Abdelaziz Bouteflica in Algeria, as well as the popular support for the war on terrorism in Libya and Yemen.

## The Repercussions of 'Revolutions' on Arab States

The Arab Spring protests prompted a wider debate about its repercussions on state institutions and functions in the face of unprecedented threats to its survival and ability to discharge its conventional functions. Hence, the Crisis of the State in Arab Spring countries could be attributed to the following transformations:[1] First and the most crucial reason is the social pressures produced by the imbalance between State and the Society. Salient examples could be easily found in Libya under Muammar Gaddafi and Ali Abdullah Saleh's reign in Yemen. Gaddafi tried to use the historical competitive relationships between different regions for the survival of his regime; and the similar approach of tribal alliances and rivalries was used by Saleh in Yemen leading to the crisis in their states.

Secondly, the functional failures of the State in most of these countries are also responsible for the crises. Most of those states showed inability to adequately confront security threats especially when their "monopoly of power" started to fade away with the rise of the terrorist phenomenon, and the blows directed to their repressive police forces during the revolutions.

Thirdly, the slow and failing transitional processes because of internal conflicts and the lack of national consensus on vital issues such as the distribution of power and resources led to the crisis of the state.

Fourthly, identity conflicts acquired special importance after Islamist factions came to power, especially in Egypt. This trend was aggravated with the keen attempts by the ruling Islamist parties to penetrate the State and educational institutions, curtail non Islamist opposition, and dramatically change the identity of the concerned nations, which in return caused repulsion, protest and resistance.

Fifthly, the separatist trends were created during the popular protests in some places. The open atmosphere felt in the wake of revolutions encouraged certain interest groups in some countries to publicly talk about federalism, echoing a long silent competition that has been going on in some affected countries between "Nation" and "State". This was read by some as amounting to full separation such as the independence of South Sudan and the special status of semi-independent Iraqi Kurdistan.

Finally, the external pressure and intervention has also played a role in the regional crises in the region. There have been calls by foreign officials and representatives of Western NGOs for a quick transformation into democracy. There has been direct military intervention such as the one led by North Atlantic Treaty Organisation (NATO) against Gaddafi regime Libya, the multilateral intervention in Syria and proxy war in Yemen.

## Indications and Motives of the Popular Willingness for the Return of the State

If it could be agreed that 2011 was the year of "Regime Fall" in the Arab Spring countries, 2012 was the year of "Faltering Transition" and 2013 was the year of the "Failure of Islamists in Power", then 2014 would be the year of the rise of popular demands for the "return of the State." The followings are some of the main trends which have emerged during last few years since the outbreak of the Arab Spring.

*Electoral Decisiveness*: This could be demonstrated by the victory of President El Sisi in Egypt who carried 96.9 percent of the votes casted. The victory of Sisi with such a huge margin was also considered a vote for the return of the State to face pressures created by the struggling economy and the rise of terrorism. Similar situation emerged in Algeria where Bouteflica, in spite of visibly poor health conditions, won the elections after obtaining a huge 81 percent of the total votes.

*The War Against Terror*: The return of the State is structurally connected to the feeling of fatigue and fear produced at the grass root level by the new escalating wave of destructive terrorist acts committed by the Muslim Brotherhood in Egypt. There is also an enthusiastic support to the military operations the Yemeni Army launched against Al Qaeda in Shaboa, Ebien and Maareb.

*Confronting the Chaos Created by Militias*: In Libya an alliance of militias operates against the Libyan Army under the command of General Khalifa Hafter. To illustrate the deteriorating situation in Libya, it suffices to refer to the declaration made by the Libyan Government[2] in late August 2014 that Egyptian camion drivers willing to enter Libya will have to sign documents stating that they would do that at their own risk. Later on[3] the Libyan Government declared that it cannot guarantee the safety of drivers entering its territories from the Egyptian side beyond Tubrok. Similar to this popular approving attitude was the reaction of most Yemenis regarding the decision by President Hadi to dismiss the military commanders known for their links with the "Yemeni Regroup for Reform" affiliated with the Muslim Brotherhood. The Yemeni reform group reportedly succeeded in penetrating the Yemeni military institution during the post-Saleh period through the status and services of Major General Aly Mohsen Al Ahmar.

*Confronting Trends for Separation*: In Yemen, President Hadi enjoys popular support because of his determined efforts against the Houthis. Yemeni armed forces have confronted the Houthis who have also attempted to occupy the Amran Governorate and expand from Saada at the North towards the region where the Yemeni Tribes are concentrated at Ketaf, Hegga, Damag and Arhab and encircle Sanaa.

## Challenges Facing the Return of the State

The popular pressure towards the return of the State in the Arab Spring countries could not alone put an end to the erosion of the State in those countries. For this to sustain and consolidate, the State should endeavour to meet the minimum social aspirations: safety and security, containment of political tensions, revitalisation of economic growth, promoting social justice and combating corruption.

However, social, doctrinal and regional conflicts, armed militias, separatist trends and terrorist activities as well as the differences among leaders of political and social elites may jeopardise the process of the return of the State. Therefore, it should not be concluded that the general trend towards the return of the State in Arab Spring countries may falter and be delayed in some countries especially those lacking solid institutions capable of leading the masses and re-establishing political and security stability. In some countries, the emerging leaders do not have networks of supporters due to the absence of alliances with primary social groups and of supportive political movements. This condition negatively affects the ability of those leaders to fill in the political vacuum and may compel them, to instead, distribute economic and social benefits to attract supporters and expand their popular bases. The returning State will have to confront and neutralise the attempts by regional and international powers to exploit the current state of affairs to advance their interests in the concerned countries. Therefore, several scenarios could be expected in those countries:

a) Total collapse under the pressures of acute civil conflicts, separatist trends and armed militias.
b) Structural weakness leading to the survival of the State while the balance of weaknesses would prevent any of the competing factions from taking the central stage.
c) Functional failures, meaning that the state would survive and achieve some extent of consolidation but would not be able to adequately perform, which may lead to the eruption of successive waves of unrest.

Thus, the States should endeavour to achieve political immunity through economic restructuring and meeting the societal demands.

## Egypt and Sectarian Affiliations

If religion were a human invention, Egypt should be the inventor.[4] At Luxor, seat of so many Pharaonic temples and tombs one gets to see scenes engraved on the walls since several thousand years, depicting the dead standing in court in the afterlife prior to being sentenced either to Paradise or to Hell. The book of the dead, thought to exist many centuries before Moses, explains this scene very clearly. Religion has always been central in Egypt's national identity. A field study conducted about ten years ago by the American University in Cairo has found that Egyptians were the people who use the most religious terms and connotations in their day to day spoken vocabulary. Egyptian Coptic Church, the oldest in Christianity has made great contributions to Christian theology. After adopting Islam[5] in the sixth century, which is now the religion of the majority of Egyptians, Egypt took on its charge to defend the true ideals of Islam and to guarantee the free passage to the two holy cities of Mecca and Medina. The Fatimids ruled over Egypt between the years 969 and 1171. They established Cairo which became

Egypt's capital city as well as the capital of the Fatimid empire. They also built Al Azhar, a mosque that was transformed into a university. The Fatimids didn't impose their doctrine on Egyptians but Al Azhar taught the Shiite Jurisprudence together with that of all Sunni four doctrines Hanafi, Shafei, Hanbali & Maliki. In the article written about him in the Encyclopedia Britannica, Ibn Khaldoun wonders, "whether or not Egyptians would think of the Day of Judgment." For him, Egyptians looked too liberal.

In contemporary Egypt, doctrinal divisions were almost non-existent. Only in centuries old religious marriage ceremonial pronouncement, dating back to the days of the Ottoman Empire which annexed the country in the year 1517, and which had Hanafi as its "official doctrine", the person reading the sermon would say that the marriage is being contracted in conformity with the doctrine of Al Imam Abou Hanifat Al Nomaan. Apart from that, very few would follow to the letter of any specific doctrine. Very few would declare their affiliation to a specific doctrine. As early as the 50s of last century, Al Azhar under the committed and knowledgeable guidance of Grand Imam Sheikh Mahmoud Shaltout made its own a cause timidly tackled before: the rapprochement between Sunni and Shiite Muslims. Grand Imam Shaltout issued a famous Fatwa allowing Sunnis to pray behind a Shia Imam from the Jaafari sect. However,[6] during the one year Muslim Brotherhood reign in Egypt from June 2012 to June 2013, the spirit of religious tolerance was subjected to great challenges. Leaders of the Islamic ruling coalition called for imposing on the Egyptian Christians Al Jizia, a special tax levied on non-Muslims after Egypt was brought to the World of Islam in the 6th century, for their protection by the state and ensuring their religious freedom. A number of churches were burnt down and declarations by state and ruling party officials hostile to Egyptian Christians were echoed now and then. The most appalling incident happened on June 22, 2013, only a few days before the Muslim Brotherhood regime collapsed under the pressure of the second Egyptian Revolution, when an Egyptian Shia was tortured to death in the Sixth of October City.[7] The revolution of the June 30, 2013, supported by the military, removed the Muslim Brotherhood led government in Egypt. After the success of the revolution, a roadmap for democratic transformation has been adopted. Following that, two important steps have already been taken: the adoption of a new constitution and the election of the President of the Republic. It seems a tolerant Egypt is slowly coming back to normalcy now.

## The Future of Yemen[8]

Since the February 11, 2011 Revolution which removed from power President Ali Abdullah Saleh after 32 years in power, Yemen has been passing through a very delicate period. His removal from power was the most important sign that the revolution achieved something. The revolution was not able to completely bring down the entrenched regime, and the regime was not able either to subdue the revolution. The confrontations between the two sides came to an end only upon agreeing on a political settlement proposed by Gulf Cooperation Council (GCC) calling for the formation of a national unity government and the launching of a comprehensive national dialogue conference to define the features of the modern Yemeni State. However, at present it seems like, there are three rebellious groups who pose serious threats for the Yemeni State, its future and the whole political life of Yemen: the Houthis, the Southern Movement and the Al Qaeda.

### *The Houthis*

The Houthis represent the most important threat facing the Yemeni State today. In a few years' time, the Houthis formed a real and effective social force in some Yemeni provinces. Their threat escalated with time, and the opportunity was seized by some regional powers and was used as a tool to achieve their agendas in Yemen, namely Iran, Qatar and the Kingdom of Saudi Arabia. According to *Al Ahram* daily,[9] Abdul Malik Al Houthi, head of the Houthi rebellion, threatened to take what he described as "total measures" to launch the third stage of escalation. Houthis have been setting siege around the capital Sanaa for the past several months.[10] This has prompted neighbouring Saudi Arabia, UAE and other countries to launch military strikes against the Houthi positions collaborating with the Yemeni forces and the clashes between them continue to aggravate the situation.

### *Al Qaeda in Yemen*

The apparent weakness of the Yemeni State added to the rough topography, to attract terrorist groups to take safe haven in remote Yemeni areas which lack any real State presence. Political divisions and rivalries have not enabled the Yemeni State to effectively eliminate terrorist groups. It is also claimed that Al Qaeda has succeeded in penetrating State institutions in Yemen.

### *Internal political conflicts*

For several years the relationship between the Popular Public Conference (PPC) and the Yemeni Regroup for Reform (YRR) the main Islamist opposition party has been described as a strategic alliance. The YRR was part of the ruling coalition between 1993 and 1997. When YRR left the government it turned to harsh opposition leading the "Common Encounter Parties." The period from 2008 till 2010 saw unprecedented escalation in the confrontation between the two sides until the PPC was removed from power during the 2011 revolution. The

YRR was consequently able to control most of the government positions and expand its tribal, political, military and financial influence at the expense of the PPC. In retaliation, PPC tried and succeeded in neutralising the performance of the YRR in power which had a very negative impact on the state institutions and functions.

## Regional Competitions and its Impact on the Yemeni State

Saudi Arabia and Yemen share a long geographical boundary between them. The two countries have always had common historical and cultural links as well. Saudi Arabia has had a close watch on developments in Yemen especially since the September 26 Revolution of 1962 which brought down the Imamate regime and installed a republican regime instead. This prompted a civil war between Republicans supported by Egypt and Royalists supported by Saudi Arabia. The civil war continued until late 1967 when Egypt had to redeploy its expeditionary force at Yemen to fight the June 1967 war with Israel. After the February 2011 Revolution, Saudi Arabia proposed to implement the GCC initiative. The Kingdom has also supported the Yemeni government in its war against the Houthis who are being supported by Iran. On August 30, 2014, the permanent representative of Saudi Arabia to the United Nations declared at New York that the Houthis were trying to take Yemen to the dark ages using terror and military force.[11]

Qatar is also another important player in the region. Both Saudi Arabia and Qatar took the same position of supporting the Syrian and Libyan revolutionaries against the regimes. Both also took similar stand over maintaining stability in Bahrain in the face of protests by the people. However, they took different sides in Yemen, with Qatar supporting some groups in conflict with the central Yemeni government and Saudi Arabia wholly supporting the Yemeni government led by President Hadi.

Iran is trying to do in Yemen, what it has been trying to do elsewhere in the region. Iran is pursuing its own agenda for regional dominance. It intends to promote the interests of factions loyal to it, foil any strategy against it and maximise its international and regional influence. If the competition between Saudi Arabia and Qatar has had its negative impact on the situation in Saada, the competition between the Kingdom and Iran, which is much more acute with ideological and religious tributaries, has had much more negative impact on the whole Yemeni state. The best scenario for the future of Yemen would be to have implemented the results of the "inclusive national dialogue" and disband the armed militias for the benefit of safeguarding the Army and Police Forces, which is, obviously not the case!

During the first transitional period between November 23, 2011 and February 21, 2012, after the removal of Saleh from power, the Vice President Hadi was given the temporary responsibility to act as the President until he was officially elected for the position on February 21, 2012. This was followed with the second transitional period which was supposed to only last for 2 years but was extended until the holding of presidential and parliamentarian elections. During this period the restructuring of the army and police force was embarked upon. The National Dialogue Conference was launched on March 18, 2013 and lasted until January 25, 2014, producing a comprehensive document on the future of Yemen.

According to the President of the National Center for Strategic Studies of Yemen, the failure to abide by the outcome of the National Dialogue would endanger the future of Yemen as a united polity. He ascertains that the current government has been doing its best to confront plenty of obstacles such as the persistence of small wars and attempts to involve the Army therein, the postponement of the restructuring of the Army, the challenges posed by Al Qaeda and the Houthis, the failure to contain the former President Saleh and the abstention from bringing him and his cronies to court and the financial deficit which threatens the ability of the State to perform as it is estimated to be about US$ 5 billion of a total budget of US$ 12 billion.

## Future Scenarios of the Developments in the Arab Levant

Many Shia minorities in the Arab World immediately rejoiced the success of the Iranian Islamic Revolution in 1979. The Shia minorities were generally living under miserable conditions suffering from negligence of the authorities and repulsion from the majority Sunni population. The areas in which they lived were underdeveloped, with inadequate infrastructures and lacking basic amenities. After the Iranian revolution, they became more emboldened in calling for their equal rights as citizens. For decades since the independence, Iraqi Sunnis dominated the state and to a great extent marginalised the Shia population known to represent the biggest percentage of the Iraqi people. For that reason, former Iraqi Prime Minister Nouri Al Maliki's policies reflected a spirit of vengeance against the Sunnis. The immediate impact of the emergence of the Shia after the Iranian Revolution was putting emphasis on doctrinal affiliations among Arabs which was not of much presence earlier. The hatred and fear of the Gulf Arabs towards the revolutionary Iran was further amplified by the assertiveness of the new regime in Tehran. This soon started to shape the official attitudes of Arab States towards Iran. The situation further aggravated due to the occupation by Iran of three Emirati islands of Abu Musa, Greater Tunb and Lesser Tunb in the Gulf.

In recent times, the Gulf Arabs have started to doubt the credibility of American commitment towards their security as the USA is now seen shifting its strategic interests to farther East towards the Far East and China. The USA is expected to be transformed into a net oil exporter after having perfected the technology needed to extract Shale oil for a reasonable economic cost. This may entail a reduced strategic importance of the Gulf in the eyes of a policy maker in Washington. Further, the dialogue between P5+1 and Iran and the future of the US engagement with Iran may entail a further relative reduction of the value of Gulf-USA relations.

The civil war in Syria is arriving at a stalemate with neither party having the upper hand. This status may hold on for years in the future as a military balance has been established between the forces of the Assad regime and the opposition,[12] mostly made of jihadi and salafi organisations. Some estimates expect the regime to be able to survive for further five years. It was able to regain the initiative and re-establish its control on previously lost areas such as Al Zabadany and Al Kalamon and in imposing its control on the coastal regions and important cities such as Homs, Edleb and Derea. ISIS controls Dir Azzour and the Raqqa and it has been clandestinely exporting the oil produced in these regions to generate funds needed to finance its activities. The Kurds, have seized the opportunity to establish a quasi-independent entity after the withdrawal of the Syrian Army from their areas. Some of them have already been talking about a federal state in north-eastern Syria. Hence Syria is also threat of disintegrating in to a number of loose territories if this situation continues for long.

Apart from Iraq and Syria, Jordan, too, is feeling the threat of ISIS. Some recent reports have indicated that ISIS has established a branch in Jordan to declare an Islamic Emirate there. Supportive demonstrations to ISIS took place in Jordanian cities, which prompted the Jordanian army to deploy its forces at the borders with Iraq. However, it is believed that the stability in Jordan and the efficiency of the Jordanian security apparatus and Army as well as the financial, logistical and strong military relations Jordan enjoys with both USA and Saudi Arabia would make it extremely difficult for ISIS to overrun the country. This should not exclude the eventuality of random terrorist operations by ISIS in Jordan in the future.

Lebanon has been undergoing consecutive sectarian crises since the assassination of former Prime Minister Rafik Hariri in 2005. The situation further escalated to an alarming level after the sweeping control by Hezbollah of Beirut in 2008. This brought the sectarian tensions to unprecedented levels in the country. The Syrian crisis in 2011 and the Iraqi crisis in 2014 added to the rivalries already existing between Sunnis and Shias especially after the open support given by Hezbollah to the Syrian regime against the Syrian opposition. This resulted in a dangerous sectarian polarisation in the country. ISIS targeted the southern Beirut suburb more than once, which is an indication that Lebanon is in the pipeline of interests and plans of the organisation given the fact that the suburb is one of the main bases of Hezbollah. The Lebanese government should remain vigilant regarding the activities of the terrorist organisations. Any negligence or inability on the part of Lebanon to fight the terrorists will have dangerous consequences for the security of the country.

The Arab Levant will probably witness extreme tensions among followers of different doctrines. At present the situation looks grim not only because of regional and international interferences, but also because of the religious and sectarian sedition as well as because of the growth in the capabilities of terrorist groups.

## Terrorism Disguised under Islamic Banners

A thorough study about ISIS[13] has been conducted by Haytham Manna which is worth mentioning here. After the Afghan war ended,[14] the comrades of jihad separated. Some of them continued the fight in Chechnya and others in Bosnia and Algeria. Those who went home were always regarded with suspicion. The relocation of a substantial number of Afghan Arabs in Iraq was the result of the chaos created by the mismanagement of its administration by Paul Bremer, who was the first presidential envoy of USA in Iraq after the invasion. Thus, Abu Musab Al Zarqawi soon became the leading figure of the resistance against the US. The US administration tolerated and even blessed to cover up for its fatal mistakes in Iraq. There are relevant questions relating to the transformation of that state of affairs leading to the formation of the ISIS: what was the role the security and intelligence agencies of both Saudi Arabia and Qatar in the creation of ISIS, what is the role of Turkish government in facilitating the crossing of thousands of fighters from Turkey to Syria and Iraq.[15] The research paper later reviews the history of ISIS through reviewing the history of its leaders starting by Zarqawi, then Abu Omar Al Baghdadi until its current leader Abu Bakr Al Baghdadi, born in Samarra in Iraq in 1971 and a graduate of the Islamic university at Baghdad. He worked as Imam in one of Baghdad mosques. He established the Sunni and Al Jamaa Army before moving to other similar organisations until he was elected Khalifa of the Islamic State of Iraq on May 16, 2010. He ordered several criteria to be followed as policies of the organisation: benefitting of the military experience of former Iraqi officers, raising huge financial resources to fund the ambitious program of the organisation, underlining the importance of mass media to convey a message that should instill fright in the hearts of opponents, negotiating with local population to secure their support, showing toughness regarding any other jihadi organisation that may dare deal with the organisation on equal footing, and cleansing of any non-Sunni group from the operations areas of the organisation.

The former officers of the Iraqi Army now form the core of ISIS. They have several common beliefs: the importance of re-building the Iraqi state and Army away from the American influence and Iraqi government, the hatred of Iran, the willingness to revenge of Iraqis who submitted themselves to Shiite and Kurdish dominated governments and the disregard for democracy and rejecting the idea of "the rule of the non-Sunni majority". Out of that last belief the organisation thought of adding Syria to its area of operations as a land where the Sunni are the majority.

Manna includes a letter addressed by one of ISIS Syrian leaders to Ayman Al Zawahiri. That letter expresses the principles of ISIS showing an extremist Salafi attitude, refusing to submit to Al Qaeda in the lands ruled by the "Islamic State". It admits that the ISIS would leave to Al Qaeda the leadership of the Islamic jihad on the international level. The letter elaborates that the ISIS left to Al Qaeda the theatres in Tunisia, Egypt and Libya, but Al Qaeda refused to withdraw from Syria. ISIS claimed that the Kuwaiti constitution is heretic, and accused several Arab leaders of heresy including President Mahmoud Abbas of Palestine, former Egyptian President Mohammed Morsi and his party, and President Sisi. The letter also made the same accusation of heresy regarding the Armies of Egypt, Pakistan, Afghanistan, Tunisia, Libya and Yemen.

## ISIS and US

There is some confusion as to what extent the American management of the Syrian crisis has contributed to the creation of ISIS. According to certain quarters,[16] the Obama administration policies in Syria led to the creation of ISIS. Ira Straus, the executive director of Democracy International and US coordinator of the committee on Eastern Europe and Russia in NATO writing in *National Review* clearly expressed by stating that, "air strikes against IS are too little and too late. Militarily, the refusal to put boots on the ground means that we lack the guidance needed for fully effective air strikes. Politically, Obama has relied on Iraq's democratic parliamentary process to make essential changes, and the most it has been capable of delivering is another leader from within Maliki's Shia party, hardly a good beginning for winning back Sunni trust."[17]

There are some confusion created due to earlier declarations by American officials concerning ISIS, in which US position regarding the ISIS was not clear. President Obama's press conference in Tallinn, Estonia of September 3, 2014, "pledged to punish ISIS" for its beheading of two American journalists. He said, "our objective is clear, and that is: degrade and destroy ISIS so that it no longer a threat not just to Iraq but also to the region and to the United States."[18] The same day, Vice President Joe Biden said, "US will follow ISIS to the gates of hell."[19] The US Secretary of Defence, dismissing confusion still persistent after Obama's press conference, declared that: "The US isn't trying to contain ISIS. It's trying to destroy it." He reiterated that the mission is to degrade and destroy.

## NOTES

1. Mohamed Abdallah Younis, "Re-establishing the State—A trend towards re-establishing sovereignty in some States of the Arab Revolutions", *Event Trends*, 1, Future Centre for Research and Advanced Studies, Abu Dhabi, August 2014, pp. 32-36.
2. *Al Ahram*, Cairo, August 31, 2014 (all references to *Al Ahram* daily could be retrieved at www.ahram.org.eg).
3. *Al Ahram*, Cairo, September 1, 2014.
4. Fathy El Shazly, "Diplomacy & International Security", a one day Lecture & workshop, Bulgarian Diplomatic Institute, April 25, 2007.
5. Fathy El Shazly, "Dialogue between religions & cultures from the perspective of a Moslem Diplomat", Bahrain Centre for Studies & Research, *Journal of Strategic Studies*, Spring 2009, pp. 14-15.
6. To follow the developments in Egypt after the January 25, 2011 Revolution until recently in early 2014, kindly refer to Cherif Bassiouni, Emeritus Professor of Law, De Paul University of Law, Chicago, USA. "Egypt Update Background Papers", at www.mcherifbassioni.com.
7. *Al Ahram*, Cairo, June 23, 2013.
8. Fares El Sakkaf, "The future of the Yemeni State", *Events Trends*, 1, August 2014. (The article was published originally in Arabic).
9. *Al Ahram*, Cairo, August 30, 2014.
10. Ibid.
11. *Al Ahram*, Cairo, Aug 31, 2014.
12. Mohamed Megahed Al Zayyat, "Probable division: Future scenarios in the Arab Levant, *Event Trends*, August 2014, pp. 40-43.
13. Haytham Manna, "ISIS Khalifate: From emigration of illusion to blood lakes", July 21, 2014, published in Arabic by the Scandinavian Institute for Human Rights, at http://sihr.net/wp-content/uploads/2014/07/DAEESH-first-part1.pdf.
14. I have always maintained that the term "Jihad" in its contemporary meaning and connotation was simply a term the CIA reinvented in order to manipulate the Gulf financial support and Egypt's soft power and human resources for the launching of a real war of attrition against the USSR in Afghanistan. During that war, USA turned a blind eye against many dictum and principles in the conduct of its foreign relations including for instance the fight against illegal trade in narcotics.
15. *Al Ahram* Newspaper published on September 1, 2014 that a Turkish daily published the day before that the ISIS fighters undergo training in a camp in Ghaziantep city in south eastern Turkey and that this piece was originally broadcasted by the German ARD network claiming that the Turkish intelligence service plans and coordinates ISIS operations in Turkey and provides the logistical support. *Al Ahram* also published the same day that the head of a German domestic intelligence service that more than 400 persons left Germany to fight

alongside ISIS adding that we should expect those fighters to return one day to their homes with whatever experience and opinions they may have obtained.

16. John Dougherty, "ISIS: Made in U.S.A.—How the Obama Administration Equipped a Terrorist Organization", *Absolute Rights*, September 1, 2014, at http://absoluterights.com/isis-made-in-u-s-a-how-the-obama-administration-equipped-a-terrorist-organization/.
17. Ira Straus, "How Obama Caused ISIS", *National Review*, August 27, 2014, at http://www.nationalreview.com/article/386354/how-obama-caused-isis-ira-straus.
18. "Obama says beheading videos won't intimidate US", *The Washington Times*, September 3, 2014, at http://www.washingtontimes.com/news/2014/sep/3/us-says-sotloff-beheading-video-is-authentic/?page=all.
19. Maya Rhodan, "Biden Says U.S. Will Follow ISIS 'to the Gates of Hell'", *Time*, September 4, 2014, at http://time.com/3264582/joe-biden-isis-iraq-syria/.

# 5

# Geopolitical Situation in the Middle East: A View from Yemen

*Ahmed Salem Saleh Al Wahishi*

Several political analysts have expressed concern on the growing hotbeds of conflict in the West Asia and North African (WANA) region emphasising that there is a need to enhance the regional and international efforts to face these challenges of the present time. There are also serious concerns among analysts over the region's ability to agree on the ways and means needed to overcome the shortcomings that lead to deterioration of the situation and further aggravation of conflicts. There is an urgent need to elaborate policies to achieve stability, development and ensure the wider participation of the citizens in the development and decision making process. The states should bear the wider responsibility of bringing out policies to ensure that the citizens enjoy their rights, and to build the future of the region based on the principle of democracy, freedom and sustainable growth.

Several political trends were dominating in the region when countries got their independence in the middle of the 20th century. Firstly, the Pan Arab Nationalist idea was dominating, particularly at the time of Nasser in Egypt. Secondly, from the end of the 1960s until the end of the Cold War era, the radical forces were popular in the region supported by the Eastern bloc at that time. At the time when Nasser was in power in Egypt, Arab Nationalism was the main trend in politics in general and it was popular among the masses. But there was a shift in this trend after the 1967 war and, from the end of the 1960s until the end of the Cold War, the most popular trend politically in the WANA region was the emergence of the left forces. Many nationalists used to be leftists because of their relations with Soviet Union and Europe. But after the collapse of the Soviet Union and end of Cold War the forces of instability retreated. There was a vacuum, and the Islamist forces who were there for more than seven to eight decades in the region mobilising the people, came and filled this vacuum. But some of them went to the extent of gaining popularity by getting involved in dangerous terrorist acts which is continuing even today. With the winds of change that came to the region at the beginning of the second decade of this century, political Islamist reached the power in several North African countries and were struggling to do so in a number of Middle Eastern countries making use of the present situation in these two regions.

The political turbulence caused in the Middle East was not only due to the internal factors but also because of the effect of other regional and international forces. The huge petroleum and natural gas resources are a big attraction for the external powers for getting involved in the political and security affairs of the region. This, naturally, raises the question as to whether the rich natural resources and the strategic location of the Middle East is a curse or a blessing for the region?

The emergence of new terrorist organisations like the Islamic State of Iraq and Syria (ISIS) is a big challenge for the countries of the region. The ISIS now acquires large parts of Iraq and Syria, and extends close to the borders of Lebanon. Among others, the ISIS has been able to acquire several important oil refineries, oil fields, and water resources such as dams and rivers in the region they have occupied. The ISIS has been selling oil in the black market at a cheaper price to sustain its operations. Using the money, they are also buying weapons, to behave like a State in a very wide territory. It has been widening its terror network into other parts of the region beyond Iraq and Syria and has launched attacks on other countries such as Saudi Arabia, Kuwait, Libya, Egypt and so on. Fighting against the ISIS requires a strong cooperation among the regional and external powers in the region. According to a French minister, the fight to defeat ISIS will last for several years. The US President Barack Obama stated that this new phenomena of ISIS will not only endanger the Middle East but could also beyond the region.[1] The whole world was shocked in response to the act of the Islamic State. Killing of the American citizens added up to a deeper and longer US involvement more than what the White House initially outlined. President Obama said he is pursuing a more "systematic" approach to compact ISIS.

There are a number of conflicts and civil wars taking place in the region simultaneously. That is why it is not possible for any single country to root out the ISIS. It would require cooperation and building a coalition among the stake holders. All those who have stakes involved in the security and stability of the region need to come together to fight against the ISIS. South Asian countries should also join the fight against the ISIS and terrorism in Middle East as Ayman Al Zawahiri has recently declared that Al Qaeda was planning to open cells and extend its attacks in South Asia.[2]

Since the beginning of the Arab Spring, the Islamists have tasted power in North Africa and have been making consistent efforts to capture power in the Middle East. It is a wind of change which is linked to the transitional period in the region. This change happened partially because of the regional forces' involvement to engineer change. There is also involvement of the international forces as well affecting the politics and security in the Middle East. At present it looks like these developments and this crisis will last for years to come.

Though the conflicts and civil wars are going on in the WANA region, the impact of the crisis and the challenge go beyond the region. Even King Abdullah of Saudi Arabia in a statement warned that the West and the US should see that this threat will reach them as well.[3] There are social conditions which are also responsible for emergence of such phenomenon as the ISIS. Such social conditions need to be controlled. It is necessary that social conditions such as the existing inequality and despair that helped the ISIS grow need to be altered. Political reforms and economic development should be initiated to defeat the negative effects of the social conditions that promote terrorism and extremism. Also, the political and economic situations that have been existing in the region since the last two decades need to be addressed to defeat the ISIS. Adopting only strong security measures will not be sufficient to deal with this phenomenon. The international community should also share the responsibility of playing a role in restoring peace and stability in the region. The international community, particularly the West, should not revert to the spirit of Cold War and make Europe as their key focus. Dealing with the phenomenon of terrorism and instability of such high magnitude requires an international coalition to combat terrorism. To deal with such a challenge, the participation of the US and Europe is important. The world is also looking to US and other forces in the world to play their role in dealing with ISIS in Iraq and the region. The growing hotbeds of conflict in the WANA region is challenging and is really a big concern for the people and the governments of the region as well as the world over. This requires that the forces in the region as well as at the international level should bring their efforts together to face these challenges. It cannot be achieved by the people of the region alone.

To overcome these shortcomings which led to the crisis, the countries of the region need to elaborate their policies to achieve stability. Here, besides adopting strong security measures, the participation of the citizens in the process of development and in the affairs of the state should be initiated to achieve stability and to overcome the crisis. For this, the relationship between the state and the citizens should be based on global norms well known to us such as democracy, freedom and development.

Some analysts believe that the regional geopolitical shift might lead to new democracies with growing role of the new forces that brought these changes such as youth, women and the civil society organisations with liberal tendencies. Yet, this transitional situation in the WANA region still depends on number of possibilities that the new forces can manage to achieve. Role of education and social media among others would be crucial for religious tolerance and maintaining religious and cultural diversity of the region which is the source of Judaism, Christianity and Islam among other beliefs.

Another challenge is the growing military build-up including the Weapons of Mass Destruction (WMD) in the region. This will endanger geopolitical situation and threaten peace and security of the region and beyond. The role of Israel is very much crucial in this regard. The Israeli ruling circles should realise that there is a growing consensus among Arabs and Israelis as well as internationally about their role in the Palestinian conflict. If the siege of Gaza and the suffering of the Palestinian people will continue this will create further hopelessness regarding the prospect of the solution of the Palestinian-Israeli conflict and make peace ever more elusive.

The contemporary challenges on the level of peace, security, stability, environment protection and development process due to the political shift in the WANA region can be faced with the support of the international community including US, EU, BRICS among others. To change these geopolitical situations from conflicts to cooperation within the region, experienced leaders should be elected democratically by the people. The role of national, powerful and disciplined institutions such as the national armies to help in framing a roadmap of the transitional period is very important. Cooperation with South Asian region, particularly India, the largest democracy in the world, can provide much needed political support to deal with such instability.

## Transition in Yemen

Since the end of 2010, Yemen among several Arab Countries witnessed a popular movement demanding regime change. Yemen has been listed as one of the failed states in the world. The peaceful mass movement in Yemen started in the south of the country in 2007. But with the spread of Arab Spring it hit Yemen in the beginning of 2011 and protests and demonstrations were held all over the country. The protesters demanded the removal of the regime of President Ali Abdullah

Saleh ruling for more than 33 years. The Gulf Cooperation Council (GCC) proposed a political initiative[4] as a way out for the change, with a scheduled mechanism, for the former President Saleh to handover the power to Vice President Abdo Rabo Mansor Hadi to form a new coalition government equally divided between the former ruling party (the congress and its allies), and the opposition. This initiative was supported by the United Nations Security Council (UNSC) resolutions 2014 and 2051.

In the transitional period the coalition government, according to GCC initiative, should reorganise the army and security wherein countries such as US, UK, Saudi Arabia and Jordan will provide assistance and experience at the military and security level. Moreover, based on the two UNSC resolutions the UN mandated special envoy, Gamal Ben Omar, to facilitate the implementation of the transitional period tasks, including the National Dialogue which was held from March 2013 till January 2014. Furthermore, based on the National Dialogue outcome, the UNSC adopted resolution 2140[5] which emphasised the importance of the National Dialogue outcome including the drafting of a new constitution of a federal democratic civil state, to carry a referendum on this constitution and organise accordingly the election of the president, the parliament and the regional assemblies of the six federal regions in the country. The UNSC resolution also decided to establish a committee to follow the developments of the transitional period to take necessary measures towards those who will be an obstacle to the National Dialogue outcome as well as to report on the human rights violation during the peaceful opposition demonstration and the achievement of the transitional Justice Law.

Yemeni people aspire for a new constitution for their country. Yemenis must realise that free societies result from social pluralism, and that the notions of the constitution are justice-seeking instruments. Also, constitutional systems are systems of checks and balances. The civil society in Yemen emphasises the point that the organisation of state requires, more than any other organisation, to be kept on course by a structure of rewards and punishments as well as rights and duties. The constitution should also form the structure and discipline of the Yemeni state decision-making processes, yet the constitution should not replace the bodies such as the parliament and the executive.

The drafting committee also discussed a choice between parliamentary and presidential system in the new Yemeni constitution. In a presidential system, president appoints and discharge cabinet members. National Dialogue proposed semi-presidential system for Yemen as presidential systems are rigid and parliamentary systems are soft. So the National Dialogue chose a middle path of semi-presidential one as a flexible system. The drafting committee realises the importance of electoral systems.

Yemen is going through a transitional period. But, unfortunately, at the moment the situation is very critical and it seems some of the warlords are not happy with the regime change of Saleh and, therefore, they are escalating tensions in Yemen. They may also be attempting to start and aggravate a civil war in the country to bring in further instability in Yemen. The transitional period of Yemen needs the support of the international community as well as the UN. The tensions in Yemen, has been further escalated, particularly as the Houthi armed militias made their advancement in to other regions including the capital Saana since August 2014. They have captured parts of the capital Saana and thereby forced President Hadi to move to Aden and subsequently to Saudi Arabia. The situation in Yemen is moving towards a civil war as the Houthi rebels have been able to acquire heavy weapons of the government army. Untill now, there is no sign of understanding between the parties concerned to frame a roadmap for the future. At present, with no concrete solution in sight, it seems like the internal strife and instability in Yemen will continue in the foreseeable future.

## NOTES

1. "Statement by the President on ISIL", The White House, September 10, 2014, at https://www.whitehouse.gov/the-press-office/2014/09/10/statement-president-isil-1.
2. "Al-Qaeda declares new front to wage war on India, calls for jihad in the subcontinent", *The Indian Express*, September 4, 2014, at http://indianexpress.com/article/india/india-others/al-qaeda-leader-ayman-al-zawahiri-announces-formation-of-india-al-qaeda/.
3. "Saudi king: Islamic State will reach 'Europe in a month and America in another month'", *The Washington Times*, August 30, 2014, at http://www.washingtontimes.com/news/2014/aug/30/saudi-king-islamic-state-will-reach-europe-in-a-mo/.
4. See the full text of the GCC initiative at http://peacemaker.un.org/sites/peacemaker.un.org/files/YE_111205_Agreement%20on%20the%20implementation%20mechanism %20 for%20the%20transition.pdf.
5. "Security Council Adopts Resolution 2140 (2014), Welcoming Yemen's Peaceful Transition towards New Constitution, General Elections", United Nations, SC/11296, February 26, 2014, at http://www.un.org/press/en/2014/sc11296.doc.htm.

# PART II

## Terrorism, Sectarianism and Regional Security

# 6

# Sectarianism and Security Implications for West Asia

*Talmiz Ahmad*

Sectarianism has been defined as "the promotion and deliberate deployment of sect-based allegiance in the pursuit of political ends."[1] In the Islamic context, sectarianism refers to the doctrinal and political cleavages between the two principal sects of Islam—the Sunni and the Shia—which emerged in Islam just after the death of Prophet Mohammed in 632 AD. The divide originated in a dispute over succession, with one group promoting the right of Hazrat Ali, the Prophet's cousin and son-in-law, to be his successor as caliph on the basis of kinship, while the other group promoted the caliphate of the Prophet's oldest companion and supporter, Abu Bakr Siddique, on the basis of his seniority and excellent personal qualities. In the event, the latter were triumphant. After Abu Bakr, three caliphs succeeded one another after the Prophet's death, with Hazrat Ali being the fourth caliph, the four being referred to collectively as 'the Rightly Guided Caliphs.' However, the division that started as a succession dispute, got aggravated with civil war and the defeat of Hazrat Ali during his caliphate at the hands of the Umayyads, who traced their lineage to the third caliph Othman. This divide was finally consolidated in the defeat and death of Hazrat Ali's son, Imam Hussain, at Karbala in 680 AD, an epochal event in Shia iconography from which commenced their faith in the imamate restricted to the descendants of Ali. The group allied with Hazrat Ali called itself *Shiat Ali* (partisans of Ali), being referred to in short as Shia. The other group called themselves *Ahl Al Sunna*, i.e., the followers of the Sunna (traditions) of Prophet Mohammed.[2]

The Shia have remained a minority in Islam and have rarely enjoyed political authority. For a short period a Shia dynasty, the Fatimids, ruled in North Africa between the 10th and 12th centuries, while in the year 1501, the Persian ruler Shah Ismail I declared his affiliation to the Shia sect and over time all of Iran became Shia and has remained a Shia-dominated country, with its rulers affiliated with this sect. All the other Muslim dynasties and empires in West Asia have been Sunni, culminating with the Ottoman Empire that ruled until the beginning of the 20th century.

Today, in a global Muslim community of 1.4 billion, the world Shia population is 13 percent, i.e., 180 million, 60 percent of which is Arab and Iranian. The Shia population in the Gulf and West Asia is 55 percent of the total native population; if Iran is excluded, the Arab Shia constitute one-third of the total native population. Among the Gulf Arab countries, the Iraqi Shia population is about 60 percent of the total population of 35 million. Bahrain is the other Arab Gulf country that has a majority Shia population in that two-thirds of the native population of half million is Shia. In Kuwait, 30 percent of the native population of 1.2 million is Shia, while in Saudi Arabia, out of the total native population of 20 million, 13 percent is Shia. However, Shia are overwhelmingly represented in certain specific provinces such as in the Eastern Province where out of the 3.9 million native population, 2.6 million are Shia; in Najran, out of a total native population of half million, 75 percent are Ismaili Shia; and, in Jizan province out of 1.5 million, 20 percent are Ismaili Shia. Syria is the other Arab country where the Shia of the Alawi sub-sect constitute just 12 percent of the total population of 23 million.[3] However, the Assad family, which has ruled Syria since 1971 belongs to the Alawi sect; members of this community dominate the military and security services, with 80 percent of the armed forces officers being Alawi.

## Sectarian Politics

While Islam has not experienced large scale inter-sectarian war, in the current turbulent political environment in West Asia, we are witnessing considerable mobilisation on sectarian basis, leading the Finnish scholar Mari Luomi to suggest that the sectarian divide could emerge as an "era-defining" feature of the West Asian political scenario after Saddam Hussain.[4] Looking at the ongoing sectarian mobilisation and conflict, certain commentators have asserted that these modern-day contentions are merely the contemporary manifestations of age-old animosities; most observers however tend to reject this perspective. As Murtaza Hassan has pointed out:

> Such beliefs represent not only a misreading of history but a complete and utter fabrication of it. While there are distinct theological differences between Sunnis and Shias, the claim that these two groups have been in a perpetual state of war and animosity throughout their existence is an absurd falsehood.[5]

However, while the present-day sectarian strife may not be a replay of ancient feuds, among Arab leaders in West Asia there have been several who have seen in recent developments a Shia resurgence which, in their view, constitutes a threat to Sunni interests. In 2004, King Abdullah of Jordan spoke of a "Shia Crescent" that had emerged in West Asia, embracing Iran, Iraq, Syria and Lebanon, concerns that were echoed by President Hosni Mubarak and former Saudi Foreign Minister Prince Saud Al Faisal. This expression captured the imagination of several commentators who saw its validity in the emergence of Hezbollah as major role-players in Lebanon; the rule of the minority Alawites in Syria; the nascent Shia empowerment and governmental leadership in Iraq; and, the emergence of a new Zaydi fighting force in Yemen, the Houthis, amidst accusations that this group enjoyed sectarian-based support from Iran, with the Islamic republic being at the heart of this powerful reversal of sectarian balance of power across West Asia.

However, the concept of a "Shia Crescent", though seductive, has several limitations, primarily because it suggests a cohesive and undifferentiated bloc while the reality is quite different. First, there is no centralised Shia religious authority that enjoys the support of the entire community. For several decades, doctrinal influence has been divided between Najaf in Iraq and Qom in Iran, with a number of other schools that enjoy considerable local influence. Even Khomeini's concept of *velayet-e-faqih*, which gives Shia clergy full political authority in the country, has been disputed by prominent clergymen in Iran and has not been accepted in Najaf.[6]

Second, political mobilisation of the Shia community has also not been monolithic; there has been a divide between the transnational activist networks of Shia Islam into the *Daawa* and the *Message: the* first emerged in Najaf, while the latter took root in Karbala, being inspired by the influential cleric Mohammed Al Shirazi. The *Daawa* has been influential among the Hezbollah in Lebanon, and in Kuwait and Bahrain, while the Message movement has been more prominent in Saudi Arabia and in sections of the Bahraini Shia. Again, the principal Shia political activism in the Gulf and West Asia has had limited connections with Iran, and has focused not so much on Shia empowerment as on promoting pluralism in the nation and seeking reform in the polity that would accommodate the Shia as equal partners, rather than seeking to overthrow the political leaderships.[7]

Third, the situation relating to the Shia in Iraq has always been very complex and discourages a broad-brush approach that gives central significance to sectarian identity. Saddam Hussain's rule, for instance, was not projected as a case of "Sunni" power; his regime was ultimately founded on narrow familial and tribal loyalties, and in eliminating threats to his regime, Saddam did not discriminate on sectarian basis. Support for the Iran-Iraq war of the 1980s was mobilised by him primarily on national and Pan Arab bases, appeals that were sufficiently persuasive as to encourage thousands of Shia soldiers to fight their co-sectarian brethren across the border and fiercely defend their country when attacked. Even now, in the post-Saddam era, Shia groups do not project a unified monolithic force; they have deep divisions amongst themselves, and governments can be formed only through temporary alliances among Shia groups with the support of Sunni parties.[8]

Four, even Iran, the bastion of Shia Islam, has rarely projected its revolution in sectarian terms. Iranian rhetoric has consistently spoken of the resurgence of *Islam* rather than of the Shia. In fact, in the 1950s, Iranian clerics, who would later become prominent in the Islamic revolution, established close ties with the Sunni Muslim Brotherhood members and saw the Brotherhood ideologue, Sayyid Qutb, as a hero of Islam.[9]

Finally, the principal issue that has concerned West Asia politics, i.e., the Palestine issue, has not evoked support on sectarian basis. Iran has been robustly supportive of the Palestinian cause and has enjoyed considerable popularity in the Palestinian community. In 2006-07, Hezbollah and its leader Hassan Nasrallah were regarded as heroes across the Arab world for their "victory" over Israel. Iran has also established strong links with Hamas, a Brotherhood-affiliated movement, without paying heed to sectarian considerations.[10]

## Saudi-Iranian Confrontations

While sectarianism may be an "invented conflict", as Rima Majid has asserted,[11] the fact remains that Saudi Arabia and Iran are presently using it as a powerful tool for mobilisation and political competition.

In Saudi Arabia, sectarianism has been a significant factor in defining the domestic political order. The Saudi royal family, the Al Saud, that has ruled the country in modern times for over 100 years, is affiliated to an 18th century reform movement referred to as Wahhabiya. In fact, the Saudi state order obtains its legitimacy from this affiliation and in turn utilises state machinery and institutions to enforce political, economic and cultural codes that are said to be based on the tenets of this movement. This affiliation with Wahhabiya has made the Kingdom a unique politico-religious entity in the Arab world that asserts its monopoly hold on state power on the basis of religious sanction, with its authority not being questioned at any national platform or in domestic competitive politics. The Al Saud-Wahhabi order gives central importance to the sectarian identity. It has institutionalised discrimination on sectarian basis, has failed to implement promised reforms, and has tended to view Shia aspirations as being linked with Iran's interests and thus as a possible security threat. Attempts made by the Shia to mobilise domestic cross-sectarian support against authoritarian rule rather than for purely sectarian advantage have been forcefully thwarted, so that over time cross-sectarian agitations have weakened and a sharp sectarian cleavage has come to define the political order.[12]

Like most powerful neighbours, Saudi-Iran ties have been marked by uneasy truce and fierce competition, with short-term accommodations giving way to deeper contentions. But, never have their relations been as sharply competitive or destructive as they are today. During the rule of the Shah, the two countries were on the same side in the global cold war divide and cooperatively supported the US's strategic interests in the Gulf. This period of uneasy camaraderie ended with the Islamic revolution in Iran in 1979. From the Saudi perspective, the revolution altered the regional scenario to its disadvantage. Revolutionary Iran parted from the US alliance with the US embassy hostage crisis, with its anti-West posture more in tune with Arab popular opinion than that of the Gulf leaderships which were robustly pro-West. Again, Iran's Islamic government challenged Saudi Arabia's de facto leadership of the Muslim world, exposing the numerous ways in which the Saudi monarchy had deviated from the straight and narrow path of Islam and accommodated Western-style norms and practices in contrast to the "authenticity" of Iranian adherences. The Saudi position was further complicated by its own home-grown challenge—the occupation of the Haram Sharif in Mecca in October 1979 by messianic zealots who came from the heart of the Wahhabi establishment and condemned the Al Saud for its venality and corruption and for abjuring the stern tenets of Wahhabiya.

The Saudi response to the Iranian challenge was quick and comprehensive. First, it asserted its lead role in Islam by backing the anti-Soviet struggle in Afghanistan, in tandem with Pakistan and the United States. This decade-long effort mobilised Muslims from across the world in a "global jihad", the world's first after the Great War. Though not emphasised at that time, this was a "Sunni" effort and in fact had the unintended consequence of preparing the ground for the jihadi cadres that came together under the rubric of Al Qaeda after the successful end of the Afghan mujahideen struggle.

Second, Saudi Arabia and the other Gulf monarchies encouraged and funded the Iraqi attack on Iran to stem the tide of the revolution that, in the view of the Arab rulers, threatened to overwhelm the region militarily and ideologically. This, fierce eight-year struggle, running in tandem with the Afghan conflict, succeeded in confining the ardour of the Islamic revolution to the borders of Iran. However, the viciousness of the struggle, including the use of chemical weapons against Iran and the shooting down of its civilian aircraft, left a long legacy of bitterness and laid the basis of a sectarian divide, which, though moderate in the early years after the war, would gain considerable resonance at a later stage.

After the war itself, economically exhausted Iran pursued the pragmatic approach of engagement with the Kingdom and the Gulf monarchies. However, developments outside the bilateral space ensured that this mutual accommodation through the presidencies of Rafsanjani and Khatami would give way to a more competitive scenario. This was caused by regime change in Iraq following the US assault of 2003, and the systematic dismantling of the old Sunni-governed state order in favour of Shia empowerment in Baghdad. Though Saudi Arabia had for long been very uneasy about Saddam Hussain's aggressive postures and expansionist designs in the region (affirmed indeed by the occupation of Kuwait in 1990), the Kingdom in his demise believed it was placed at a grave strategic disadvantage vis-à-vis Iran. This was obviously a sectarian perception since it had little basis in the Kingdom's own experience with the departed leader or the ideology and state-order he had commanded. Whatever the objective merits, the fact remains that Iraq set the stage for a Saudi-Iran regional rivalry that, although a competition for influence and power, in fact came to be increasingly defined within the framework of a sectarian zero-sum calculus.

From the Saudi point of view, other developments contributed to the strategic setback it had experienced in Iraq. Syria under Bashar Al Assad remained a staunch Iranian ally in spite of strong Saudi (and US) efforts in 2009-10 to persuade him to snap his links with Iran and return to the Arab mainstream. In Lebanon, the advantage gained by the Kingdom in the forced withdrawal of Syrian troops in 2006 was neutralised by Hezbollah's ascendancy after the Israeli invasion in July-August 2006. In Palestine, the Hamas moved close to Iran not on sectarian but on political basis, in spite of Saudi-sponsored attempts to bring Fatah and Hamas together in Mecca in 2007. Yemen, with which the Kingdom shared a 1400 km border and where the Kingdom enjoyed considerable influence, now became a security concern: Saudi influence on the president and the various tribal chiefs and political groups was perceived by the Zaydi (Shia) community to have empowered "Wahhabi"-oriented elements in the country at the expense of the majority Shia. These disgruntled elements, collectively referred to as Houthis, set up armed militia that attacked not only government troops but also the Saudi armed forces across the border. In a major conflict in 2009, several hundred Saudi troops were killed by this rag-tag bunch. The Kingdom immediately saw an Iranian hand, on sectarian basis, in the proliferation of Houthi power and influence. Thus, at the end of 2010, Saudi Arabia saw itself at the losing end of the regional balance of power. The Arab Spring only served to exacerbate Saudi security concerns.

## The West Asian Security Scenario

While Saudi Arabia was surprised at the swift collapse of Zine El Abidine Ben Ali's regime in Tunisia in January 2011, the fall of Hosni Mubarak a little over a month later came as a shock, since at one stroke Saudi Arabia saw the fall of a strategic partner that had given it some parity in its competition with Iran. Within a week or so of this setback, a more immediate challenge manifested itself—the public demand for reform in Bahrain, with gatherings of hundreds of people at the iconic Pearl Square. The Kingdom's leaders watched with dismay the ongoing dialogue between the demonstrators and reform-minded members of the Al Khalifa family, with an agreement on constitutional monarchy and other reforms becoming a real possibility. In the Saudi view, reform in Bahrain would empower the Shia and place them in a pivotal political position in a Gulf Cooperation Council (GCC) member-country. The Kingdom feared the ripple effect of this reform agenda on its own Shia population in the bordering Eastern Province, and in sectarian terms, a further boost for Iran at Saudi Arabia's very door step!

In response, Saudi Arabia abandoned its hitherto moderate and restrained approach in regional affairs and embarked on a pro-active competition with Iran, bilaterally and across West Asia. The sectarian mindset and mobilisation are central to the Saudi approach in this competition, emerging from a profound sense of being besieged by a cohesive, monolithic hostile Shia force. Even the avowedly liberal Saudi commentator, Jamal Khashoggi, reflected these fears; writing in June 2013, he said:

> The guide of the Revolution...Ayatollah Khamenei will fulfill his dream of delivering a sermon from the pulpit of the Umayyad Mosque [in Damascus] to announce that he [has] achieved Islamic unity, which he has long promised. He will descend from the pulpit with much pomp to wipe the head of a poor child to show the 'tolerance of the powerful' [towards Sunnis].[13]

A year later, this sectarian perception was reflected in a similar comment by Ghassan Charbal in August 2014 said, "The tipping of the [strategic] balance [in favour of Iran] has sparked regional tensions and a clear decline in relations between Sunnis and Shias." Charbal then went on to note Iran's influence in Iraq, Lebanon and Syria.[14]

In a recent paper, F. Gregory Gause III has described the West Asian scenario as a "cold war" in which Iran and Saudi Arabia are competing for power and influence "in the domestic political system of the region's weak states", with the principal aim of "determining the direction of West Asia's domestic politics."[15] Saudi activism is a response to the challenge posed by the Arab Spring which relates to "the proper role of Islam in the (Sunni) political order."[16] Specifically, this pertains to the accommodation of popular aspirations in the polity so that it obtains its legitimacy from the coinfluence of 'Islam' and 'Democracy'. For Saudi Arabia this is an "existential challenge" since it threatens its order both domestically and regionally. Domestically, it challenges the Saudi monopoly on power by promoting ideas of a constitution, political parties, elections, responsive governments and full transparency and accountability, in short a political system promoted by its arch political competitor in the Arab world, the Muslim Brotherhood and its various national affiliates.

Regionally, of course, the Kingdom is convinced that the Arab Spring, if allowed to run its normal course and embrace extensive political reform, will only redound to the advantage of Iran, which has accommodated a degree of public accountability in its own Islamic order and, eschewing sectarian alliances, has built up ties with the Brotherhood and its affiliates across West Asia and North Africa, while wielding considerable political influence across the Arab world. It is from these concerns that Saudi Arabia has embarked on sectarian mobilisation to confront Iran in different theatres—Bahrain, Syria and Iraq.[17]

### *Bahrain*

Most observers agree that the demonstrations in Bahrain in the early days of the Arab Spring were not fomented by Iran; in fact, these agitations were largely non-sectarian in character, with a long history of engagement between the royal family and activists gathered at Pearl Square in 2011.[18] Saudi military intervention, under the umbrella of the Gulf Peninsular Shield force, and the government's harsh crackdown on the agitators have encouraged the emergence of sharp sectarian cleavages in Bahrain, with both sides increasingly resorting to sectarian mobilisation. The government has painted the calls for reform as immutably "Shia" in character and supportive of Iranian interests. The mainstream Shia party, Al Wefaq, has been delegitimised and its leaders incarcerated. Attacks on Al Wefaq have been provocatively sectarian. Thus, Frederic Wahrey has quoted a Bahraini government officer rejecting dialogue with Al Wefaq in these words: "…there is an Iranian agenda in the dialogue that will be promoted ….I demand [Shia parties] to put down their weapons and guerilla training in Iraq, Iran, Lebanon and Syria."[19] Wehrey notes that there is "mounting evidence that sectarianism was seeping into Bahraini society—in some cases with regime hardliners' tacit encouragement."[20] At the same time, there is increasing inter-sectarian violence, along with the strengthening of hardline elements within Shia groups at the expense of mainstream parties.

## *Syria*

Iran's approach to regional security has been to pursue ties with its Arab neighbours, giving preference to Islamic rather than sectarian identity. Thus, Iran's ties with Syria were built on the basis of shared strategic interests; Gause points out that the ties were "not based on common values...but on common enemies, Israel and Saddam Hussain's Iraq".[21] Mohammed Ali Shaibani agrees, saying that "the affinity between the Iranians and Syrians is due to the imprint of the historic memory of the war with Iraq (when) Syria was Iran's only Arab ally."[22]

Syria felt the impact of the Arab Spring from the earliest days, when the first uprisings took place in Damascus in January 2011, and then spread rapidly to other towns across the country over the next six months. In the face of these challenges, the regime used disproportionate force and then mobilised support from its core Alawi bastion against what it saw as one more confrontation with Brotherhood-affiliated forces. As Heiko Wimmen has pointed out, the Assad regime ingrained into its co-sectarian support-base "a collective threat perception that equated any return of Islamism with impending genocide."[23] Thus, an uprising which in its early weeks was a call for reform soon acquired a sectarian character, enhanced by mutual sectarian vituperation, destruction of shrines and increasing violence on both sides. In this environment, attempts by activists and the government to appeal to cross-sectarian solidarity and national pride had little impact. The government increasingly resorted to mobilising Alawi militia and using Alawi army units and Special Forces to mete out collective punishments which led, on the Sunni side, to heightened radicalisation. When the Assad government spoke of cross-sectarian coexistence, its critics saw it, in Wimmen's words, as "a conscious and cynical strategy of turning civic contestation into sectarian conflict to prevent the wave of solidarity with victims of state violence..."[24]

The Syrian conflict had regional ramifications from the outset that further aggravated the sectarian divide. Qatar and Turkey collaborated to back Brotherhood-affiliated militia, providing weaponry, training and sanctuary. Saudi Arabia initially avoided sectarian mobilisation and instead backed the "secular" Free Syrian Army (FSA), made up of renegades from the national forces. However, separate from the efforts of the principal regional players, jihadis from Iraq came into Syria to join in the conflict, further strengthening its sectarian character. The principal jihadi group was Jabhat Al Nusra, set up in 2012, that by the end of the year had become the most powerful militia against the Assad government.

In 2013, being alarmed at the successes of Brotherhood and jihadi fighters compared to the relative feebleness of the FSA, Saudi Arabia asserted a lead role in the conflict, demanding that Qatar reduce its support for the Brotherhood while it brought all the Salafi militia together in the Islamic Front (IF). By early 2014, IF and Jabhat Al Nusra had ensured the Iraq-based jihadi group, the Islamic State of Iraq and (Greater) Syria (ISIS), was evicted from most of Syria. This Saudi activity was encouraged not just by its animosity for the Brotherhood but also because it saw the overt sectarian backing being given to the Assad regime by Iraq and Iran which provided supplies, weaponry and even militia to the government, while also encouraging Hezbollah fighters to fight on Assad's side.

### *Iraq*

Iraq, which emerged with its current borders after the First World War, was for several decades a pluralistic society. The situation changed after the 2003 war when the US occupation forces systematically dismantled the very pillars that had held the country together by disbanding the Iraqi armed forces and enforcing the policy of de-Baathification to exclude Baath party members from employment in government services. At the same time, the US authorities made sectarian identity the key to the Iraqi political order that privileged the majority Shia community.

As a mark of their dissatisfaction with the US occupation and the systematic marginalisation of the Sunni community, the latter refused to participate in the governmental machineries set up by the occupation and boycotted the elections of 2006. Thus, the Iraqi Sunni made almost no contribution to framing the constitution of 2005, which was largely done by Shia and Kurdish members working together. The Iraqi insurgency against US occupation also got organised on sectarian basis through 2005-08, so that Sunni extremists attacked occupation targets with the same ferocity they directed at Shia community members and institutions. Throughout this period, there were reports of Saudi and GCC funding for the Sunni insurgents, as also of large numbers of GCC citizens joining the Sunni militia.[25] However, in spite of this unpropitious environment and though alienated from the political process, most Sunnis remained committed to the idea of a united and pluralistic Iraq. This commitment found expression in the *Sahwa* (Awakening) movement that was mobilised among the Sunni tribes of Anbar province and used effectively against the jihadi group, Al Qaeda in Iraq (AQI) between 2007-09.

Sunni alienation from the Baghdad government got aggravated by the withdrawal of US from Iraq in 2011 when Prime Minister Nouri Al Maliki, fearing a threat from the non-sectarian armed forces, systematically removed Sunni and Kurdish officers and other personnel from the military so that the army now became almost exclusively a Shia force. Confident in the support being extended to him by Iran, Maliki then turned against his Sunni political allies, accusing the finance minister and the vice president of consorting with terrorist elements.

Still, the first agitations against Maliki in 2011 were cross-sectarian. As Heiko Wimmen has pointed out, the wave of protests that began in February 2011 originally started in the Shia-majority south, and was directed against all political parties in the ruling power structure headed by Maliki. The activists articulated explicitly anti-sectarian slogans, highlighting corruption and the use of the sectarian divide to promote divide-and-rule policies. In Baghdad, the agitators gathered at Tahrir Square, projecting that their movement could serve as a "model for public responsibility and co-existence alike."[26]

The government adopted harsh measures to disperse the gatherings, which not only broke up the public agitations but also over time deprived them of their cross-sectarian character; in fact, counter-mobilisation on sectarian basis effectively ended the unity agitations of 2011. The anti-government agitations that took place in 2012, after the arrest of the bodyguards of the finance minister, were largely Sunni in character, made up of clerics, tribal leaders, and Baathists and anti-occupation insurgents.[27] These agitations, which took the shape of sit-ins in different towns of Iraq, were broken up by government forces, with a violent attack on demonstrators in Hawija in April 2013. Separately, the jihadis of the Islamic State of Iraq (ISI), led by Abu Bakr Al Baghdadi, increased their violence, and a large number of Iraqis were killed. These killings, the government's counter-measures, and social media filled with hate speeches on sectarian basis further consolidated the sectarian divide.[28]

## The Challenge of the Islamic State (IS)

Just as the West Asian security scenario appeared to have reached its nadir in terms of the violence in Syria, the deepening sectarian cleavage across the region, and Iran and Saudi Arabia continuing to be deeply estranged, a new phenomenon emerged that thoroughly confounded the regional and extra-regional role-players and compelled them to take a fresh look at the political and military confrontations pursued by them over the past decade. This was the dramatic territorial expansion of the ISIS from June 2014 onwards. ISIS, which had been consolidating itself in Anbar province after its expulsion from Syria by the Islamic Front and Jabhat Al Nusra in early 2014, on June 10 captured Mosul, followed by towns across west and northwest Iraq, so that by the end of the month it was just 30 km from Baghdad.

On June 29, ISIS re-christened itself as the "Islamic State" (IS) and announced that the territories held by it were a caliphate and that its leader, Abu Bakr Al Baghdadi, would be the caliph. In June and July, the IS also expanded its control across the border into Syria, capturing a number of border posts, taking the important town of Deir el Zor, consolidating itself in Raqqa, and threatening to take Aleppo. From mid-July onwards, it also attacked towns and military bases in the Homs Governorate, and bases in Raqqa, Hasakh and Aleppo. It acquired considerable weaponry from these bases, including tanks, military vehicles, artillery systems, and truck-mounted multiple rocket launchers.[29]

In August 2014, exhibiting remarkable military alacrity, the IS forces took the historic Yazidi town of Sinjar on August 2; the towns of Zumar, Wana and Ain Zakh, with its oilfield and refinery on August 3; and on August 7, Qarakosh, Gwer and Makhmur. These successes in Iraq were particularly surprising since these territories were supposed to be under Kurdish control, where the Kurdish forces, the Peshmerga, enjoyed a good reputation as fighters. While the latter have since taken back Gwer and Makhmur and established control over the Mosul Dam, Kenneth Pollack, in a detailed analysis of the Peshmerga debacle, suggested that there was good reason to be concerned about Kurdish military capabilities, including its lack of recent battle experience and poor weaponry, as against the IS which has good equipment and high morale.[30]

The military successes of IS have had a number of immediate political consequences in Iraq and regionally. They doomed Maliki's aspirations for a third term as prime minister: almost all sections of Iraqi opinion now blamed him for the ongoing violence and divisiveness and for debilitating the Iraqi armed forces. The cry went out for an alternative candidate who would set up a "unity" government that would accommodate Iraq's different communities and bolster the armed forces so that the IS could be defeated. Haidar Al Abadi emerged as the new consensus candidate. Abadi succeeded to become a consensus candidate due to a number of regional parties coming together. Abadi promised to consolidate Iraqi nationhood and combat IS which prompted some Sunni tribes in Anbar to take up arms against the jihads.[31] It is clear that Iran and the US agreed on Abadi; Saudi Arabia might have been consulted as well. The Kingdom welcomed the change, while Iran supported the US air strikes on IS positions and its arming of the Kurds. There was possibly Saudi-Iranian coordination in regard to some other recent regional developments as well, such as their agreement on Egypt playing a lead role on the Palestine issue, suggesting that Palestine should not be a divisive issue between them. Again, Iran seemed to be backing the Saudi role to stabilise Lebanon: perhaps, it did not wish to see a new front being opened for the Syrian jihadis to disturb Lebanon's fragile unity.

## Prognosis

The Saudi-Iranian competition has convulsed West Asia in the flames of discord and war so that nations that were till recently robust and influential are now torn in fratricidal contentions. The sectarian divide today is now so deep and pervasive that it threatens to define West Asian politics for several decades to come, just as jihad has done for the last 35 years. The sectarian divide has not replaced jihad; in fact, its theatres of combat have provided new battlegrounds for jihadi veterans and new recruits. Present-day jihadi forces actually buttress the sectarian divide represented by the two giants of Islam, but are now themselves the lead role-players in ongoing regional contentions.

Jihad is manifesting itself in three forms: the Salafi groups in Syria, patronised by Saudi Arabia and consolidated in the Islamic Front; the Jabhat Al Nusra affiliated with Al Qaeda, a major force in Syria against the Assad regime, and working closely with the Islamic Front; and the IS, independent of Al Qaeda and even a challenge to it, that occupies territories across Iraq and Syria which it rules as a caliphate. The last force is perhaps the most dangerous: it is not only well-armed and well-funded, its successes have seduced jihadis from other groups so that there is every possibility that the Islamic Front and Jabhat Al Nusra could lose their cadres to the caliphate. The Islamic State is a real game-changer in regional affairs for the threat it now poses to the designs and interests of both the Islamic giants, compelling them to confer directly on regional security and mobilise their resources not for internecine conflict but to contend with their common foe.

The political prospects of the region remain uncertain: Is West Asia condemned to prolonged sectarian conflict in which the jihadi groups will be the principal players on the Sunni side? In this scenario, it is difficult to see how the existing national boundaries and political systems can survive unscathed, since the Islamic State will consolidate its territorial control and expand its authority across the Levant at the expense of the Salafi groups and Jabhat Al Nusra. This will condemn Bashar Al Assad and his Alawi support base to a remote corner of Syria, with the bulk of the country given over to fierce contentions among various Sunni Islamic groups affiliated to the Brotherhood, Salaf, Al Qaeda and IS.

This scenario could be replicated in Iraq as well, with the added complication that here the IS and its cadres will have to contend with Shia militia, with increasing involvement of armed elements from outside, mainly Iran. Yezid Seyigh has suggested that, regardless of its claim to pursue a universal caliphate, the IS is likely to consolidate itself in the territories in Iraq it presently occupies which are its "natural habitat" and where it has deep roots in local society; it is here that it will "tighten and deepen its rule of its mini-Islamic state."[32] In this situation of national breakdown, the Kurds will almost certainly declare independence and face the jihadis at their 1200 km long border. Armed competition with the caliphate will almost certainly engender cross-border connections among the Kurds in Iran and Syria; though a unified Kurdistan may not emerge, the Kurds will certainly be a new and powerful geopolitical force in the region.

With the Kurds being independent and IS in control of the north and west, what will be left of Iraq will be a rump Shia-dominated territory from Baghdad to the south, with an 800 km border with Saudi Arabia. The security concerns the Kingdom has had for the last few years will finally become a living and persistent nightmare from which there will be no escape. At the same time, Iran will remain a strategic competitor. In fact, though the Kingdom could have a rump Shia state on its borders, it will have every reason to worry about the threat from the Islamic State as well, given the jihad's long history of animosity for the Saudi Kingdom.[33]

These scenarios are quite realistic and would flow naturally from the present-day contentions of the principal players in the region. There is only one way out and that is for Iran and Saudi Arabia to set up platforms and institutions for dialogue and promotion of confidence building measures, and to address divisive issues face-to-face. This is already being increasingly advocated in the region. The normally restrained Saudi commentator, Abdulrehman Al Rashed, has emphatically stated that, "there is no room for ISIS (in the region)…ISIS, the common enemy, has now become a red line, regardless of the differences and goals of each party in this regional game."[34] Another Saudi writer, Tariq Al Homaid, has asked the Sunnis of Iraq to learn from their earlier mistakes, forcefully distance themselves from ISIS and participate in the new government.[35]

Reflecting the anxieties in the region, the Dubai-based *Gulf News* on August 16, 2014, published two articles on the same page—one by a Saudi commentator and the other by an Iranian—both urging Saudi-Iranian engagement. Under the headline, "A relationship of global significance", the Saudi writer Tareq Al Maeena said that, while there were still some differences between Iran and Saudi Arabia, "regional realities should encourage more cooperation between the two countries for a safer and more secure Middle East."[36] Echoing this view, the Iranian diplomat and academic, Seyyid Hossein Mousavian, admitted that both Iran and Saudi Arabia "have vested interests in conflagration in Syria, Yemen, Lebanon and Iraq." However, he insisted on the need to change the relationship: "It is no longer an option but an urgent necessity to talk and reverse the current trajectory towards further sectarianism, extremism and terrorism, spreading throughout the region."[37]

The hot winds of shared fear of violence and destruction generated by the nascent caliphate have compelled Islam's two principal leaders to confront unitedly the foe that threatens to overwhelm them both. Though the long years of sectarian animosity will not be wiped away quickly, the process has to begin immediately; for, as Chaim Kaufmann, an authority on ethnic civil wars, has noted: during ethnic wars, "hyper-nationalist rhetoric and real atrocities harden ethnic identities to the point that cross-ethnic appeals are unlikely to be made and even less likely to be heard."[38] The body blow inflicted on West Asia by the Islamic State should not put on the back-burner the original causes of the present-day sectarian divide: the challenge of political reform placed before the region by the Arab Spring. While the aspirations of the Arab world have been swept aside by vicious sectarian-based civil conflicts and in Egypt, by the restoration of the military dictatorship and the incarceration of the Brotherhood, the fact remains that across the Arab world, as Wimmen has noted, "divided societies harbour a potential for pro-democracy mobilisations that cut across the dominant cleavage lines."[39] She has pointed out that to dilute the appeal of these pro-democracy aspirations, Arab state powers "took concrete political decisions" to appeal to primordial faultlines that had been suppressed during authoritarian rule. She goes on to say:

> A historical perspective shows that (the) dispositions and dynamics [of sectarian mobilisation] are grounded in authoritarian, non-democratic, and violent practices of rule, leadership, and power maintenance applied by or on behalf of political rulers and leaders... Divided societies remain divided and indeed become more so as the result of strategies and practices devised by rulers and leaders defending positions of political power...[40]

The Arab Spring not only was an indictment of authoritarian order and dramatically exhibited the pervasive aspirations for freedom, democracy and dignity, it also exposed how fragile the authoritarian states actually were. Much earlier, in 1995, Nazih Ayubi had already alerted us to this reality when he had pointed out:

> Although most Arab states are 'hard' states, and indeed many of them are 'fierce' states, few of them are really 'strong' states. Although they have large bureaucracies, mighty armies and harsh prisons, they are lamentably feeble when it comes to collecting taxes, winning wars or forging a really 'hegemonic power' block or an ideology that can carry the state beyond the coercive and 'corporative' level and into the moral and intellectual sphere.[41]

Across the Arab world, the popular challenge to dictators (and their departure in some cases) has created power vacuums in which forces representing domestic primordial faultlines have asserted themselves. Saudi Arabia, as Wehrey has pointed out, "has intitutionalised sectarianism in virtually every aspect of political, social, and economic life" even as there are strong ideological affinities between its mainstream clergy and jihadi groups across the region. Domestic fragilities have also attracted external interventions by extremist elements, whose sectarian mindset has aggravated the domestic divide and further enfeebled the state order, as in Syria, Iraq and more recently in Yemen.[42] Now, while the challenge from the Islamic State could promote some dialogue and coordination among Islam's two giants, the Arab world will still need to address the deeper causes of regional turmoil—the absence of popular participation in domestic governance. The battle against the caliphate will not be won until transparency and accountability become the hallmarks of national governance.

## NOTES

1. Fatima Ayub, "The Gulf and Sectarianism", European Council on Foreign Relations, 2013, p. 2, at http://www.ecfr.eu/page/-/ECFR91_GULF_ANALYSIS_AW.pdf.
2. For a succinct account of the early years of the schism see Asma Afsaruddin, *The First Muslims—History and Memory*, One World Publications, Oxford, 2007, pp. 19-58. For a more detailed narrative see S.H.M. Jafri, *The Origins and Early Development of Shia Islam*, Oxford University Press, Karachi, 2000.
3. Elie Elhadj, "The Shia Crescent's Push for Regional Hegemony and the Sunni Reaction", *Middle East Review of International Affairs*, 18(1), Spring 2014, pp. 38-45. Population figures in West Asian countries are imbued with considerable political sensitivities, with authentic figures being rarely available in the public domain. Hence, different writers depending on different sources tend to provide a variety of figures. Thus, with regard to Iraq, the Pew Research Centre, basing itself on surveys in 2011, has estimated that 51 percent of Iraqis were Shia and 42 percent Sunni. A survey by *ABC News* in 2007-2009 found that 47-51 percent of the Iraqis were Shia. Also see Michael Lipka, "The Sunni-Shia Divide", Pew Research Centre, June 18, 2014, at http://www.pewresearch.org/fact-tank/2014/06/18/the-sunni-shia-divide-where-they-live-what-they-believe-and-how-they-view-each-other/.
4. Mari Luomi, "Sectarian Identities or Geopolitics? The Regional Shia-Sunni Divide in the Middle East", Finnish Institute of International Affairs, Helsinki, 2008, p. 4, at www.fiia.fi/assets/publications/WP56.pdf.
5. Murtaza Hassan, "The Myth of the 1400 year Sunni-Shia War", *Al Jazeera*, July 9, 2013, at http://www.aljazeera.com/indepth/opinion/2013/07/2013719220768151.html. Again, Gause has noted, the particularities of current politics, not "centuries-long hatreds", have sparked the latest round of Sunni-Shia tensions, and these particularities are subject to change, see F. Gregory Gause III, "Beyond Sectarianism: The New Middle East Cold War", Brookings Doha Centre, Analysis Paper No. 11, July 2014, p. 5, at http://www.brookings.edu/research/papers/2014/07/22-beyond-sectarianism-cold-war-gause.
6. Laurence Louer, "The Myth of the Shia Crescent", *Lebanon Wire*, November 19, 2013, at http://www.lebanonwire.com/1311MLN/13111905MJL.asp.
7. Frederic M. Wehrey, *Sectarian Politics in the Gulf—From the Iraq War to the Arab Uprisings*, Columbia University Press, New York, 2014, pp. 207-11.
8. See Luomi, n. 4, p. 19, Mari Luomi has quoted the distinguished writer on Iraqi history Charles Tripp as pointing out that "there is no more a single Shia narrative in Iraqi politics than there is an Iraqi one itself."

9. Samuel Helfont, "The Geopolitics of the Sunni-Shia Divide in the Middle East", *Lebanon Wire*, December 18, 2013, at http://www.lebanonwire.com/1312MLN/13121816FPRI.asp.
10. Frederic Wehrey et al., "Saudi Iranian Relations since the Fall of Saddam", National Security Research Division, RAND, Santa Monica, 2009, p. 22.
11. Rima Majed, "Did Arab uprisings deepen the Sunni-Shia divide"?, *AlJazeera*, December 18, 2013, at http://www.aljazeera.com/indepth/opinion/2013/12/did-arab-uprisings-deepen-sunni-shia-divide-2013121729.
12. Andrew Hammond, "Saudi Arabia: Cultivating sectarian spaces", European Council on Foreign Relations, 2013, at http://www.ecfr.eu/page/-/ECFR91_GULF_ANALYSIS_AW.pdf. Hammond has explained the Saudi situation thus: "Sectarianism of an ideological nature is an entrenched element of Wahhabi thought...Particular animus has been reserved historically for Muslims within the immediate range of the Saudi-Wahhabi heartland in the Najd, especially Shias who remain the most numerous 'other' who are resistant to orthodoxy".
13. Quoted in Alain Gresh, "Syria's Proxy War", *Le Monde diplomatique*, July 5, 2013, at http://mondediplo.com/2013/07/05syria.
14. Ghassan Charbal, "Sea of darkness", *Al Hayat*, English translation in Mideast Mirror, August 12, 2014.
15. Gause, n. 5, p. 3.
16. Ibid, p. 2.
17. Hadeel Al Sayegh, "Iraq: the ongoing perils of sectarian conflict", European Council on Foreign Relations, 2013, at http://www.ecfr.eu/page/-/ECFR91_GULF_ANALYSIS_AW.pdf. Hadeel Al Sayegh has pointed out: "The process of de-Baathification, the post-2003 purge of high-ranking Sunnis and most of the army that had enjoyed power under Saddam Hussain's rule, is the root cause of Sunni disenfranchisement."
18. Wehrey, n. 7, p. 73.
19. Ibid., p. 89.
20. Ibid., p. 92; For a summary of the sectarian scenario in Bahrain, see Heiko Wimmen, "Divisive Rule-Sectarianism and Power Maintenance in the Arab Spring: Bahrain, Iraq, Lebanon and Syria", German Institute for International and Security Affairs, Berlin, 2014, p. 22, at http://www.swp-berlin.org/fileadmin/contents/products/research_papers/2014_RP04_wmm.pdf.
21. Gause, n. 5, p. 5.
22. Mohammed Ali Shaibani, "Iran: strategist sectarian", in "The Gulf and Sectarianism", n. 1, p. 20.
23. Wimmen, n. 20, p. 22.
24. Ibid., p. 24.
25. Abu Musab Zarqawi, tutored in jihad in the battlefields of Afghanistan in the 1990s, was active against the US-led occupation in Iraq. In September 2005, he declared "all-out war" on the Shia and led attacks on a number of high profile targets. His followers in Al Qaeda in Iraq (AQI) attacked the Al Askari mosque in Samarra in February 2006. His intellectual mentor in developing his sectarian mind-set was, among others, the Syrian origin cleric, Mohammed Surur Zainul Abidin, who was resident in Saudi Arabia in 1965-73. He was later an influential role-player in the Saudi Sahwa movement of the 1990s. For an elaborate discussion on this issue see Fredric Wehrey et al., n. 10, p. 15.
26. Wimmen, n. 20, p. 14.
27. Ibid., p. 15.
28. Hadeel Al Sayegh, n. 17, p. 16.

29. Charles Lister, "Not Just Iraq: The Islamic State is also on the March in Syria", Brookings, August 7, 2014, at http://www.brookings.edu/research/opinions/2014/08/07-not-just-iraq-lister.
30. Kenneth M. Pollack, "Iraq: Understanding the ISIS Offensive against the Kurds", Brookings, August 11, 2013, at http://www.brookings.edu/blogs/iran-at-saban/posts/2014/08/11-pollack-isis-offensive-against-iraq-kurds.
31. "Iraq Sunni tribes takes up arms against jihadists", *Lebanon Wire*, August 16, 2014, at http://www.lebanonwire.com/1408MLN/14081603AF.asp.
32. Yezid Sayigh, "ISIS: Global/Islamic Caliphate or Islamic Mini-State in Iraq?", Carnegie Middle East Centre, July 24, 2014, at http://carnegie-mec.org/2014/07/24/isis-global-islamic-caliphate-or-islamic-mini-state-in.
33. "Islamic State defector says Saudi Arabia next stop for group", *Al Monitor*, July 31, 2014, at http://www.al-monitor.com/pulse/security/2014/07/syria-opposition-is-saudi-arabia.html.
34. Abdulrehman Al Rashed, "ISIS: The new Red Line", *Al Arabiya News*, August 16, 2014, at http://english.alarabiya.net/en/views/news/middle-east/2014/08/16/ISIS-The-new-Red-Line.html.
35. Tariq Al Homaid, "Sunnis must learn from their mistakes in Iraq", *Asharq Al Awsat*, August 17, 2014, at http://www.aawsat.net/2014/08/article55335528/print/.
36. Tariq Al Maeena, "A Relationship of Global Significance", *Gulf News*, August 16, 2014, at http://gulfnews.com/opinions/columnists/a-relationship-of-global-significance-1.1372818.
37. Seyed Hossein Mousavian, "Urgent need for improved Saudi-Iran relations", *Gulf News*, August 16, 2014, at http://gulfnews.com/opinions/columinsts/urgent-need-for-improved-saudi-iran-relations-1.1372819.
38. Quoted in Liam Anderson, "The Non-ethnic Regional Model of Federalism: Some Comparative Perspectives", in Reidar Visser and Gareth Stanfield (eds.), *An Iraq of its Regions—Cornerstones of a Federal Democracy?*, Hurst & Co., London, 2007, p. 213.
39. Wimmen, n. 20, p. 27.
40. Ibid, pp. 27-28.
41. Nazih Ayubi, *Overstating the Arab State: Politics and Society in the Middle East*, I.B. Tauris Publishers, London, 1995, p. xi.
42. Frederic Wehrey, "Everyday Sectarianism: The Paradox of an Anti-Islamic State Ally", Carnegie Endowment for Internal Peace, December 3, 2014, at http://carnegieendowment.org/2014/12/everyday-sectarianism-paradox-of-anti-islamic-state-ally/hvz7; and Frederic Wehrey, "The Saudi Thermidor", *Current History*, December, 2014, pp. 344-349.

# 7

# The Dynamics of Regional Security in the Middle East: A GCC Perspective

*Muhammad Abdul Ghaffar*

The fundamental shifts occurring in the West Asian region today will have profound impact on the strategic and security equations in the Arabian Gulf region. There are three main players in the equation that comprise States, (including great powers and regional states) radical, armed non-State actors and social movements. This paper will argue that social movements will continue to grow as a result of the havoc and destruction inflicted on the people of the region, caused mainly by radical non-state actors and the states that support them. Developments in the Middle East, particularly the Gulf region, can therefore be seen to encompass state actors, non-state actors and social movements, with an absence of clear coordination mechanism.

Barry Buzan & Ole Waever in their book, *Regions and Powers: The Structure of International Security*, argue that one of the more relevant scenarios to analysing regional security comprises a regional security system with the great powers as central.[1] There is potential for an integration of interests but following the US invasion of Iraq in 2003, a number of important elements can be noted:

I. Iraq has been transformed from a "buffer state" into a "state arena", in which the interests of regional players are played out along sectarian and ethnic lines.
II. A strategic triangle has developed that comprises the Gulf Cooperation Council (GCC) states, Iran and the United States.
III. There has been a significant growth in the role of non-state actors.

## Major Players in the Region

The political, security and strategic scenario in the Middle East involves a dynamic set of state players, regional and international, and the interplay between these state actors, non-state actors and social movements creates a constant cycle of tension and respite.

### *Regional Actors*

There are two principal players in the regional strategic game, the GCC states, mainly Saudi Arabia, and Iran. The former relies primarily on state-to-state engagement, adhering to recognised borders drawn up in the 1916 Sykes-Picot agreement.[2] In contrast, it can be said that the latter relies on more unconventional methods.

Iran: Iran utilises non-state actors to expand its regional influence and interests.[3] This undermines the sovereignty of nations within West Asia, as non-state actors operate on a transnational basis. The US invasion of Iraq has further unsettled the balance within the region, yielding a power vacuum, which Iran has been able to take advantage of.[4] Iran's reliance on the non-state actors has given it a prominent role within the region, spanning multiple borders that extends to the Mediterranean coast. In late 2010, the Arab upheavals (popularly known as Arab Spring) further altered the regional security equation and a race emerged to form regional alliances in what Malcom Kerr has called the 'Arab Cold War'.[5] The nuclear negotiations between Iran and the P5+1 and its outcome seem to decelerate Iran's nuclear ambitions with potential regional bargaining on the table. However, any regional advantages to Iran could further destabilise the region, and so, it is of utmost importance that other key players within the regional security equation are involved.

Saudi Arabia: Saudi Arabia currently faces three major challenges: a volatile situation in the region, deteriorating relations with Iran, and terrorism. Riyadh seeks to maintain a traditional security balance that can facilitate long-term stability and has played a major role during the recent regional crises maintaining oil prices in global markets, in negotiating peace in the Yemeni crisis and defusing tensions in Lebanon.

The United States: The events of 9/11 altered the United States strategic position towards eradicating global terrorism and resulted in the invasions of Afghanistan and Iraq. The disintegration of Iraq as a nation-state was replaced by sectarian affiliations that reverberated through the region and catalyzed sympathy for the non-state actors such as Hezbollah and the Islamic State (IS). This has instigated an era of disorder that seeks to destroy old boundaries and reconstruct new ones based on sectarian and ethnic lines.[6]

### *Armed Non-State Actors*

Armed non-state actors have always existed in the region since the past. They are not new to the region but the influence they wield has exponentially increased following the Arab uprisings. They have evolved into serious regional players with substantial finances, weapons and man-power and have gained control over large areas in the region. Armed non-state actors can be described as any organised group that operates outside state control and that uses force to achieve its objectives. Armed non-state actors can be divided into two categories, state affiliated groups such as Hezbollah, the Houthis and Asaib Ahlul Haq and those groups which have no direct links to states, such as Al Qaeda and the IS. State affiliated actors are those groups who either do the bidding of a state or are supported—financially or materially—by a particular state. The best example of such a non-state actor is Hezbollah and it is estimated that Hezbollah receives close to US$ 200 million a year from Iran.[7]

On the other hand, there are non-state actors who are not directly affiliated to any particular state and some of those have emerged after the unrest started in the region. The rise and spread of the IS can be taken as an example of such groups. The appearance of IS has been associated with the instability and lack of security in Iraq since 2003. The IS is currently the most multi-cultural non-state actor in the region, with its members coming from all over the world, and estimates of its size range from 10,000 to 20,000 combatants.[8] It is one of the richest non-state actors in the world, generating finances through illegal activities, the sale of captured oil and gas refineries and donations.

The emergence of social media platforms such as Facebook and Twitter has greatly benefited groups such as the IS. Their media and internet savviness has led to some people especially young men and women from different parts of the world to get their message and rally for their cause. Violent non-state actors in the modern world have also become adept at playing on social, economic and sectarian tensions, especially in the Middle East. It is their ideas that need to be contained, and this requires long term national and regional strategies to tackle religious extremism and sectarianism at the grassroots level.

### *Social Movements*

The emergence of social movements in Arab countries, particularly in Egypt, did not provide a new political alternative to the existing government, Some of the most important of these social movements include: The Kifaya (Enough) Movement (2004), The April 6 Movement (2008) and The Tamarrod Movement

(2013) which successfully garnered support from millions of citizens and inspired a number of similar movements throughout the Arab world that are generally independent youth movements, with no specific political allegiances.[9]

## Interpreting the Transformations

In analysing these transformation the following points can be observed:

I. The absence of a driving or dominant force in the region has created chaos.
II. After the collapse of the Soviet Union, the United States has become the sole superpower with no other regulatory force.
III. The role of international powers, especially the United States, in the conflicts in the Middle East is dominated by the decision to limit engagement in the region.
IV. The current regional and international landscape: Questions for the Future.

Thus, there are three important points emerging in the current regional and international landscape. Firstly, after withdrawal from Iraq in 2011, the United States did not have a comprehensive strategy for dealing with the aftermath. This opened the way for former Iraqi Prime Minister, Nouri Al Maliki, to build a sectarian state especially with regards to the army, the security apparatus, and the oppression of his adversaries and other groups. This significantly impacted the political and security political landscape in the Middle East.

Secondly, there has been an increase in Iranian influence after the United States' withdrawal from Iraq, especially in the Iraqi security apparatus. These two factors, namely the vacuum created by the withdrawal of the United States and the sectarian policies of Maliki, have led to the emergence of the IS.

Thirdly, there is a lack of trust between the Arabian Gulf countries and their neighbors, especially after Iran began to deploy military force directly in Syria, Lebanon, and Iraq via its militias. The threads of cooperation between Iran and the GCC countries—Saudi Arabia in particular—began to unravel and trust has reached an all-time low.

This situation raises an important question: How does the strategic landscape across West Asia starting from Syria, extending through Iraq and ending in the Islamic State, currently look?

To answer this question, one can make five general points:

(i) Religion will remain the main factor in current transformations; it will be used by various movements, leading to the erosion of the concept of a civil state.

(ii) The concept of a state has been receding, which works to the advantage of non-state actors.

(iii) There is a state of uncertainty regarding current regional transformations and what might come as a result of the expanding role of various countries in the region.

(iv) Strategic transformations in great power policies, such as the United States, and in international organisations, such as North Atlantic Treaty Organisation (NATO), will have far-reaching repercussions for the current regional security equation.

(v) The GCC countries face unprecedented threats in the wake of the current climate of regional and international polarisation.

These issues raise a pivotal question regarding the future: what will be the strategic behavior of the great powers, regional countries, and non-state actors? First, the new alliance that the United States is attempting to forge to fight IS, with the approval of NATO members, apparently involves its leaning towards cooperating with Iraqi forces and Iranian militias in Iraq, with the latter two operating on the ground in the battlefield. This is the result of the majority of NATO members refusing to deploy ground forces.

Second, all the countries of the region and the great powers agree that IS represents a national security threat; in fact these countries have declared their intent to enter the alliance that includes the USA as well as some regional countries. However a vision is yet to emerge around how to manage the alliance in its fight against IS. The question is: what are the United States and Western countries' plans for the alliance? Is it to exterminate IS and its state in Iraq? Or to confine it to a small area in Iraq and Syria and limit its expansion to other areas?

Third, will the Iraqi tribes cooperate with the alliance under the leadership of the United States? In other words: will the awakening (*Sahwa*) experiment repeat itself?

Fourth, how will these countries with so much distrust among themselves agree upon fighting IS while at the same time preserving the militias that have previously acted violently and remain in Iraq? It is worth noting that this problem also affects the Syrian crisis because IS extends from Iraq to Syria. The alliance's fate depends on how it will deal with the Syrian issue—a matter that requires a decisive, comprehensive, and clear strategic American presence. However, another important question is how can the United States cooperate with Iran to combat IS while simultaneously supporting the principles of a Syrian revolution that aims to bring down Bashar Al Assad's regime?

In the end, one can say that if the international alliance succeeds in realising some sort of victory over IS, it will unleash other polarising forces due to the dependence on militias as partners in the alliance. The people of the region will no longer tolerate further displacement, destruction, and slaughter than they already have. It is social movements, with nationalistic loyalties, that will emerge to challenge and counter the region's sectarian propensities.

## NOTES

1. Barry Buzan and Ole Waever, *Regions and Powers: The Structure of International Security*, Cambridge University Press, Cambridge, 2003, pp. 42-62.
2. For more information regarding the Sykes-Picot Agreement of 1916 please refer to BBC at http://www.bbc.com/news/world-middle-east-25299553.
3. Addis L. Casey et. al., *Iran: Regional Perspectives and U.S. Policy*, Congressional Research Service, Washington D.C., January 2013, at https://www.fas.org/sgp/crs/mideast/R40849.pdf.
4. Anthony Cordesman, *Winning the War in Iraq: Creating and Funding a Strategic Partnership*, Center for Strategic and International Studies, Washington D.C., 2011, P. 5.
5. Ryan Curtis, "The New Arab Cold War and the Struggle for Syria", The Middle East Research and Information Project (MERIP), April 2012, at http://www.merip.org/mer/mer262/new-arab-cold-war-struggle-syria.
6. Osama Al Sharif, "Creative chaos in action!", *Al Arabiya*, January 5, 2011, at http://www.alarabiya.net/views/2011/01/05/132259.html,
7. Matthew Levitt, "Hezbollah Finances: Funding the Party of God", The Washington Institute, February 2005, at http://www.washingtoninstitute.org/policy-analysis/view/hezbollah-finances-funding-the-party-of-god.
8. Mark Gollom, "ISIS by the numbers: How big, strong and rich the militant organization may be", *CBC News*, August 26, 2014, at http://www.cbc.ca/news/world/isis-by-the-numbers-how-big-strong-and-rich-the-militant-organization-may-be-1.2746332.
9. Ahmed Zakaria Basosy, "Why did the Tamrrod movement spread so quickly?", Regional Center for Strategic Studies, Cairo, 2013.

# 8

# The Present State of Affairs in Iraq: Islamic State and Prevailing Political Disorder

*Abdulwahab Al Qassab*

Arguably, the worst impact which the US occupation had on Iraq was the deliberate fragmentation of the country's population into sub-national, previously "secondary" identity groups. With time, individuals were identified primarily as members of communities based on religious confession/sect and ethnicity, such as Kurdish, Chaldean-Assyrian, Shia or Sunni Muslims, and not as citizens of Iraq. The occupying power, however, found willing accomplices in the shape of Iraqis who were predisposed to their vision, and who were willing to do the handiwork of Iraq's long-standing foe and neighbour to the East, Iran. The problems Iraq faces today on account of too much focus on the role played by the external actors, and ignoring that played by wide–scale political sectarianism and ignorance. An inspection of the collective actions that made Iraq's present-day fragmentation possible follows below.

In a remarkably candid preamble to their research paper titled "A Case of Soft Partition in Iraq", and published by the Brookings Institution's Saban Center, Edward P. Joseph and Michael O'Hanlon provide an argument for what they describe as an inherent predisposition for the fragmentation of Iraq into its three major constituents: Sunni, Shia and Kurdish. Joseph and O'Hanlon cite various examples that illustrate this tendency towards this susceptibility, including the conflict between Iraq's Kurdish and Shia Muslim communities for control of the country's oil wealth and the exclusivist policies of the government of then-Prime Minister Nouri Al Maliki against the country's Sunni community. Ultimately, the two authors recommend that the United States should not interfere directly to bring about the disintegration of Iraq rather that it should isolate itself and allow events on the ground to take their course.[1]

Another American political figure whose name has long been associated with plans for the partition of Iraq was US Vice President Joseph Biden, whose espousal of the idea of partitioning Iraq dates back to his time as a Senator. Biden's opinion was that the partition of Iraq was the most efficient way to resolve the disputes and conflicts which plagued the country's three main constituents none of which, he believed, wanted to achieve a modicum of co-existence. This paper shall not concern itself with multiple problems of this point of view, nor with the negative, immediate repercussions that a partition of Iraq would entail, such as the border disputes that would pit the Central Government in Baghdad against the Kurdish region as well as the Al Anbar Province and the Karbala Governorate. What this paper will seek to address, however, is the socio-political context which prevailed in Iraq's Arab communities, and which divided them into Sunni and Shia Muslim components, each of which claims a plurality of the population. This division manifested itself starkly through two distinct political phenomena. The first of these is the birth of Shia political parties, the existence of which stands in contradiction to the Iraqi constitution, which bans the formation of political parties on chauvinistic or sectarian grounds. The second such phenomenon is the rise of Sunni *takfiri* groups, typified first Al Qaeda and lately by the Islamic State of Iraq and the Levant (ISIL)/Daesh also known as the Islamic State of Iraq and Syria (ISIS), both of which have inflicted their terrorist and violent tactics on the civilian population of Iraq, the social fabric of which has been damaged through their actions.

Meanwhile, the Kurdish community, which comprises 17.5 percent of Iraq's population, has managed to effectively and deliberately seal itself off from the rest of the population. The Kurdish leadership believed that, by isolating their community from the rest of Iraq, they would insulate themselves from the negative fallout of the "constructive chaos" which was strayed in to the country by the US invasion. "Constructive Chaos" was originally proposed by the Austrian-American economist Joseph Schumpeter, before it was adopted and promulgated by individuals within the presidential administration of George W. Bush, including his Secretary of State Condoleezza Rice.[2] Eventually, Rice would describe the death and destruction which was visited upon Iraq as similar to the destruction of a crumbling building before a new one, and modernist example could be created for the rest of the Middle East to follow. This point of view, however, was discredited when ISIL made a push for the Kurdish enclave in the northern part of Iraq.

Al Qaeda and ISIL set a new and menacing precedent for the Sunni community of Iraq, which is not bound together through any kind of rituals or observations, or a cultural identity while Iraq's Shia community is bound together by a vigorous group identity and proximity to Iran. In addition, the vigor of Iraq's Shia community is bolstered by the large number of Shia seminarians from Iran, Afghanistan and Pakistan who study at Iraq's Shia Muslim shrines. These seminarians have also distorted Iraq's own Shia Muslim legacy, introducing practices which originate in Qajar and Safavid Iran, and are foreign to Iraq itself.

Most significant of these changes have been the rituals associated with the *Husseiniyat* passion plays which commemorate the slaying of the Shia martyr Imam Hussein Bin Ali in Karbala on the day of *Ashoura*, the tenth day of the Islamic lunar month of *Muharram*, during the 59th year of the Muslim calendar, after he rebelled against the ruling Omayad dynasty, buoyed by support from the people of Kufa, present-day Iraq. Hussein's martyrdom led the people of Kufa into a state of introspection which eventually gave rise to the rituals which eventually became the *Husseiniyat* passion plays. The Safavid and Qajari dynasties in Iran influenced these practices, gradually turning them into the markers of a broader Shia identity. Due to the spread of urbanisation, enlightened opinions and education, however, the more excessive self-flagellation involved in these rituals remained marginal, and in fact began to wither away until the US invasion and occupation in 2003. It is important to note that the reasons for this decline in popularity for these rituals were not due to any oppression by the previous ruling government of Iraq—deposed in 2003—but rather this was the natural resort of increased urbanisation, the spread of enlightenment and education and the growing realisation amongst Iraq's Arab Shia citizens that their earlier practices of excessive wailing were introduced by Persian zealots, and were not part of the "authentic" lineage of their past. Instead, they were tools used by successive Iranian dynasties to intensify the propagandising of Shia Islam in their own country, and the powerful rituals involved in the *Husseiniyat* passion plays provided an ideal vehicle to achieve these aims.[3] This ritualisation of the *Husseiniyat* was accelerated with the Wahhabi attack on the Shia shrines at Karbala in 1869.[4] Today, Shia political movements continue to exploit the *Husseiniyat* rituals to increase their support base, benefitting from the fact that Article 10 of the present Iraqi constitution elevates these practices to a protected status, and brings them under the auspices of the central government.[5]

With time, such sectarian rituals provided the bread and butter of Iraq's ruling Shia Muslim political parties, which would use their power and their hyperbolic devotion to the passion plays to bring all governmental work to a halt for longer periods of time, without any legal justification for doing so. Once these practices were embedded in society, Shia political groups began to spread the notion that the Shia religious community was under attack, something which accelerated after the defeat of the Iraqi government forces at the hands of ISIL in Mosul, on June 10, 2014. Only weeks before that defeat of the Iraqi armed forces, a procession of marching Shia pilgrims, en route to the Imam Mousa Al Kazem Shrine in North Baghdad, began shouting sectarian slogans and demanding the burning down of a much revered Sunni mosque and shrine as they passed through the Athamiya district in the Iraqi capital. The marchers burned the homes of ordinary Sunni Iraqi residents of the patrician suburb. The attack was allegedly retribution for the death by poison of the Imam Mousa Al Kazem in the goal of 9th century (Sunni) Abbasid Caliph Haroun Al Rasheed. Iran's deceased leader Ayatollah Khomeini had previously written about the value of such mass processions, such as the one which led to a riot and looting in Athamiya:[6]

> "These processions of self-flagellation are the evidence of our ultimate victory (in the battle of Karbala). The passion plays should be held throughout the towns and across all countries … the very survival of our (Shia) people is bound up with the preservation of this heritage."

More recently, Shia Supreme Leader Ayatollah Ali Al Sistani issued a fatwa promoting the action of a "Pre-emptive Jihad" to defend the sanctity of Shia shrines, in the wake of the ISIL defeat of Iraqi government forces on June 10, 2014. The Baghdad authorities quickly made use of this religious edict in order to build a volunteer militia to recapture the areas taken by ISIL. Lacking sufficient training, these unprepared volunteers died in large numbers at the hands of the rebels. The tragedy was that they died not in order to protect the shrines, as purported, but rather to defend the rule of then Prime Minister Nouri Al Maliki, after the government forces had been roundly defeated and its rank and file had deserted.

The people of Iraq's Arab Sunni community held civil, restrained protests where they demanded the restoration of their rights and an end to the discriminatory policies to which they were subjected which is contrary to the surreptitious use of religion by the Shia Muslim marchers. The Iraqi authorities, meanwhile, were quick to use force to crush and disband these protests, without responding to the demonstrators' demands. Throughout 2013, a year marked by protests within the Sunni community in Iraq, the Baghdad authorities used power against demonstrators in Mosul, Huwaija and the Saria Mosque in Baquba. Despite such pressures, the "Anbar Protests Movement" continued along its peaceful path throughout its first year, which ended in December 2013. Despite the fact that the protest movement proved unexpectedly popular within Iraq's Sunni Muslim community, and therefore alarmed the authorities in Baghdad, the demonstrators never became violent in asking for their demands, even as the forces loyal to Maliki attacked the demonstrators in the town of Ramadi in Al Anbar, following the expiry of a deadline which they had imposed. Eventually, however, the assault by Maliki loyalists, which also included the local governor of Anbar and former members of the US-backed Sahwa militia was met by armed resistance. Rebels forced the pro-government forces out of several quarters in Ramadi, and would prevent them from entering into the town of Fallujah. With time, ISIL would dominate the military council which had acted as the umbrella group for the armed rebel groups and the protesters.

From the very early days, the Anbar protest movements have faced a number of very serious challenges which impacted their credibility and their ability to achieve their goals. Most importantly, there was no sense of nation-wide consensus on the justice of their demands, all of which had a patriotic and non-sectarian tone. Perhaps, the only demand which was specifically focussed on the community which gave rise to the protests was the release of detainees held without charge by Iraq's intelligence service, many of them female prisoners held as hostages. The result of years of sectarian agitation which was overseen by the leading Shia political parties was that this protest movement was never capable of making inroads in the predominantly Shia South of Iraq, despite the relevance of the protesters' demands to the people in that part of the country: all of Iraq was oppressed by the Maliki regime.[7] This did not stop then Prime Minister Maliki from demanding, however, from suggesting that the protesters had more in common with the armies of Yazid—the Umayyad leader who assassinated the Imam Hussein—and identifying himself and his supporters with the backers of the Imam Hussein, at a special ceremony to commemorate the Karbala massacre, held on December 30, 2013.

## The Role Played by ISIL

Perhaps the worst humiliation suffered by the people of the six rebelling Sunni provinces in Iraq was the rise of ISIL and its intervention in the daily lives of Iraqis in those areas, which was reminiscent of the worst excesses of Al Qaeda and which, at the time, provided a justification for the fanatical sectarianism of Shia Iraq. Indeed, to the misfortune of the people of the rebellious provinces, this is exactly what happened: ISIL's actions provided the *casus belli* for a fatwa justifying "pre-emptive jihad" on the part of Shia Muslim Iraqis, which in consequence allowed Maliki to form the Popular Mobilisation Militia. Additionally, these actions led the Badr Organisation to reveal its true face as a violent, paramilitary organisation, following years of proclamations that it was in fact a non-violent, political group. Remarkably, most of ISIL's actions are carried out in majority Sunni provinces, and the Sunni community has borne the brunt of its violence; whereas any Shia victims of ISIL's actions have been purely coincidental.

In addition to this, ISIL has been responsible for promulgating and promoting a distorted interpretation of Islam which is completely alien to the institution of Sunni Islam being practiced in Iraq since long, and which prevailed up until the invasion of 2003. This puritanical, *Salafi* version of Islam began making inroads into the Iraqi community during the international sanctions regime: a time of unusual misery and hopelessness for Iraqis. One oft-neglected detail of history is that the former, legitimate government of Iraq, led by Saddam Hussein, was not tolerant of this foreign innovation and, while Salafis were not generally physically liquidated, many were imprisoned.

Another of ISIL's sins, of which it was guilty as a retaliatory measure, was the way it presented itself as the guardian of Sunni areas in the face of Shia militia, which ultimately secured the support and the sympathy of wide swathes of the Sunni community which had long suffered due to the policies of Maliki. The result of much of this is that the actions of ISIL might lead to the complete re-drafting of the broader map of the Middle East; as the following map shows.

**Map 1: Sectarian division and borders in Iraq and Syria**

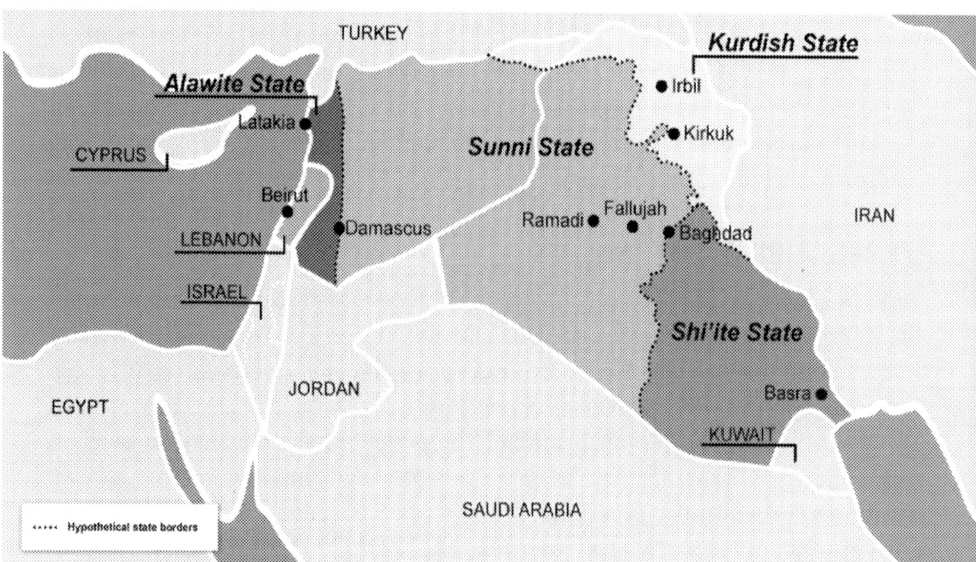


Sources: The Gulf/2000 Project (http://gulf2000.columbia.edu/images/maps/Iraq_Religions_lg.jpg, http://gulf2000.columbia.edu/images/maps/Levant_Ethnicity_lg.png) and Robin Wright, "New York Times" http://www.nytimes.com/interactive/2013/09/29/sunday-review/how-5-countries-could-become-14.html)

## The Sins of Occupation

Iraq's sectarian dualism was intensified due to number of sins committed by the country's occupying powers, and which were promoted by a number of Iraq's Shia Muslim political forces with long and deep-seated connections to Iran. There was a promotion of the idea that US forces entered Iraq as liberators, not as invaders. In this regard, the invasion forces further presented themselves as ending the oppression suffered by Iraq's Shia Muslim and Kurdish populations, ostensibly oppressed by the Sunni Arabs of the country. This further allowed the Americans to present all resistance to their occupation as being driven by terrorists, who were controlled by Sunni Muslim and Wahhabi states which, therefore, orchestrated attacks on predominantly Shia areas which were being victimised, allegedly, for the loss of authority from the Sunni community. The occupation also claimed that the rump of the former government was motivating the spread of terrorism in the wake of the invasion, thus justifying the de-Ba'thification efforts of the occupation regime led by American General Paul Bremer which begun in May 2003. That law was welcomed by the Shia political movements which were the self-appointed guardians of a putative confessional majority in Iraq. The assertion of a constitutional role for the Shia majority of Iraq, which was signaled by a visit of Paul Bremer to the seat of Shia religious authority in Najaf, even before the official drafting of the constitution.[8]

## Implications and Repercussions of the Politics of Fragmentation

The policy of fragmentation which began with the "Coalition Provisional Authority", set up by Paul Bremer to administer Iraq in the wake of the invasion has had tangible effects on Iraq as it exists today, in the time of ISIL. These are manifested in societal features which previously were not in evidence in Iraq. It led to a vertical division of Iraqi society into its Shia, Sunni and Kurdish segments. The expansion of the region in which the Kurdish population enjoys effective autonomy from the original area envisaged by Iraq's pre-2003 constitution, and presently includes disputed areas with non-Kurdish populations. The affected regions are populated mainly by Sunni Arabs. While this contradicts Article 140 of the present Iraqi constitution, events on the ground have already developed with armed Kurdish groups establishing their *de facto* presence in these areas, making use of the retreat of the Baghdad government's forces in the face of ISIL. There was an effective constitutional prohibition against the naturalisation of any Arab. A proposed federal system which would pave the way, in effect, for a complete fragmentation of Iraq, with the formation of a Shia enclave being only a small step from the existing Kurdish autonomous region. The beginning of large-scale "ethnic cleansing" operations which have seen the Sunni Arab populations in specific cities such as Baghdad, Samarra and in the South moved. The large Sunni community in the city of Basra, for example, was forcibly removed.[9]

Detailed and concrete plans for the dismantling of present-day Iraq are already in place, and have been hinted at by US Vice President Joseph Biden, and echoed by a number of Western think tanks. Shia militant groups have seized control of state institutions, with the support of both the United States and Iran. This has resulted in the exclusion of any Sunni Arabs from the political and decision-making process, in some cases extending to vilification, physical violence or threats. What happened to former Vice President Tariq Al Hashemi is an example of that. The expulsion of Hashemi allowed for the creation of a power vacuum at the top of the Iraqi government, one which was engineered by the Shia political forces: the pro-Tehran Dawa Party was able to appoint one of its operatives, Khudair Al Khuzaie, as Vice President while the Jaladin Talebani, a Kurdish potentate and the constitutional president, was absented due to health reasons.

The entire system of government in Iraq slipped into the dictatorship of Maliki whose orders could never be contested. This allowed Shia political groups to cement their grip on the levers of power. The breaking point came, however, when Maliki began to present himself as the only possible candidate for the leadership of Iraq, which ultimately drove him into conflict not only with Sunni Arab and Kurdish politicians, but with other Shia politicians, too. The ouster of Maliki, at that point, quickly became a matter for national consensus. The appropriation of the will and the demands of the protestors by unctuous and self-serving politicians whose careers were otherwise unrelated to the Sunni community of Iraq.

The maps (in this chapter) here illustrate the very intricate level of diversity within the boundaries of Iraq. While this population diversity does not necessarily lead to conflict, it has been used for the purposes of a conflict-by-proxy with, for example, Shia political forces making use of the Popular Mobilisation militia to fight against other sections of Iraqi society. It has also further served to bring Sunni Muslim forces under the ISIL banner, as well as to mobilise Kurds to fight with the Peshmerga and the Kurdish Regional Government. With these stresses and strains, the only thing between Iraq today and an all-out civil war would be the spark that activates ISIL sleeper cells in Baghdad, or perhaps the realisation of ISIL's self-appointed Caliph Abu Bakr Al Baghdadi's threat to attack the Shia holy sites in Karbala. With Iraq now being at the precipice, its society is faced with a number of pressing challenges, the resolution of which is of extremely significant. The alternative is to allow the dissolution of Iraq's national identity, which appears to have lost much of its original meaning

## The Multi-faceted Aspects of Disintegration

In addition to the negative practices which were introduced by the foreign occupation or which, at least, were exacerbated by the invading forces, there were the policies which were followed by Shia political forces. Exploiting the idea of an "oppressed majority" which they claimed to be under previous governments, these groups have mobilised their cadres and apparatchiks to put them into positions of power individuals who do not even enjoy a modicum of governmental skill. Sunni political movements also are guilty of the same, partly because of wide non-participation of Sunni Muslims in the political process, and a boycott of the first two elections to the national legislature and other bodies. A similar partisanship leading to the incompetence of politically appointed officials also prevails in Kurdistan, further leading to the state of widespread administrative corruption that exists in Iraq today.

A second feature related to this phenomenon is the multiplicity of media organisations that have served to add total confusion and ambiguity experienced by an average Iraqi citizen, who always remains unsure of the future direction of the country. One group which is trying to capitalise on this state of affairs is the wide group of tribal and clan chieftains who have begun to form a coalition to protect their interests, aimed at fighting against their dwindling power. Once parochialism is added to the mix, one can see the extent of the damage which the occupation has done to the social fabric of Iraq and to its overarching sense of national identity, with all sections of society clamouring for larger and larger pieces of the pie, ripe for the taking.

The following map gives a more detailed illustration of the tribal composition of Iraq. By examining the way that the same tribes extend from the north to the south of the country, and indeed extend across sectarian and even ethnic boundaries, we can see the extent to which tribal leaders have failed in their duty to bring the country together.

## The Tribes of Iraq

Arabs compose between 77 percent and 80 percent of the multi-ethnic population of Iraq, with Kurds dominating the remaining population. The result of this is that Arab culture has been the dominant feature of Iraq's identity beginning with the introduction of Islam to the country and throughout the rest of its history, while the history of Arab population living within Iraq can be dated to the first millennium BC. In fact, the vast majority of Iraq's population, whether they identify ethnically as Arabs, Kurds or Turkmen, can be traced back to one of a set of tribes and the heritage of which within Iraq's territory dates back to centuries.

Map 2: Tribes in Iraq

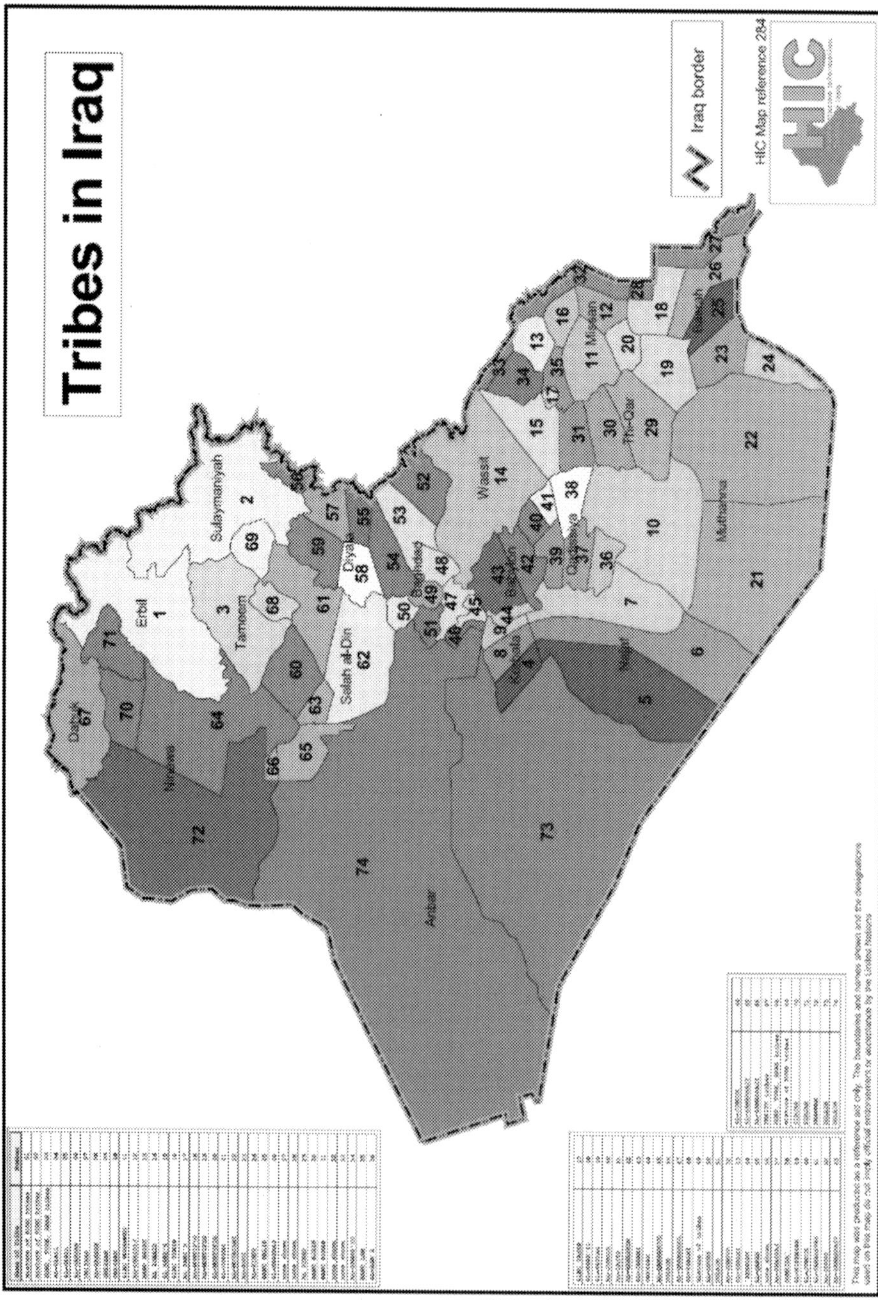

In the midst of this extensive diversity, however, the different components of Iraq's population lived in relative harmony throughout the ages. Tolerance and acceptance of the other, and non-violence, were the mainstays of Iraqi culture in the past, unlike the present state of affairs. History does not provide evidence of long-standing feuds and vendettas based on ethnicity or religious sect across these tribal lines.

One cannot underestimate the importance of tolerance and acceptance as features of Iraqi society throughout history. While the author acknowledges that Iraq's Muslim Arab population was divided between Sunni and Shia Muslim groups, largely equal in proportion, this was, historically, not a factor which led to outright violence between the two groups. Indeed, inter-marriage across confessional lines of Shia and Sunni families was fairly widespread before the American invasion, notwithstanding the Shia community's deep-seated sense of oppression and disenchantment.

The earlier era of Iraqi history which dates back to the Ottoman-Safavid rivalry shows that the repeated and incessant Iranian attempts to infiltrate into the affairs of its next door neighbour, Iraq, by way of leveraging influence over the Shia community have been thwarted. Indeed, Iran has found Iraq's Kurdish population to be a more useful ally in the struggle to dominate Mesopotamia.

The earliest evidence of this coexistence, between various Arab and Kurdish groups, dates back roughly 3,000 years, with a stone inscription attributed to the Assyrian King Sennacherib which refers to both the "Kordo" and "Aribi" people. Such long-standing diversity falsifies the suggestion that Iraq is merely a composite of provinces forced together by the British colonial forces in the 20th century.

Following the occupation, malicious actors were able to exploit this confessional diversity in Iraq, which had previously been understood merely as a difference of theological opinion and not as the hallmark of a cultural identity. Even the elaborately ritualised practices of Shia Muslims were not able to overcome the kinship bonds which existed between inter-sectarian Arab ties, while Islam was able to provide a framework for the coexistence of Arabs and Kurds. This is what allowed a Kurdish man, Sheikh Abdul Karim Al Mudaress, to rise to the highest place of theological authority amongst Iraq's Sunni Muslim community, and become famed for his Koranic commentaries.

Ultimately, such diversity was a process not for friction, but for a sense of social peace and harmony, and a kind of power-sharing. One can clearly view this in the way that members of one of Iraq's largest tribes, the Al Bayyat, identified as Sunni Muslim Arabs in one part and Shia Muslim Arabs in other, while the other members are free to be identified as Turkmen or Kurdish. This diversity has never been taken as a way for internal strife within Iraq.

The question which raises itself at this point is: will a democratic transition be possible in Iraq, through its restoration as a country of all of its people and citizens, regardless of ethnicity and creed? Before providing a concrete answer, it would be necessary to give a more detailed description of the nature of the democratic transition which the author hopes for in Iraq. Given the exposition above, what conditions exist in Iraq and could allow for a democratic transition there?

Such a transition, if it were to be successful must have an all-encompassing national identity of Iraq at its core. In other words, it must be unbiased towards any particular ethnic or confessional group. The alternative to this would be for ethnic and sectarian mobilisation leading to three separate political entities in Iraq each of which has its own, separate set of worldviews. A general description of what would happen can be found below:

### *The Shia Community*

In its political manifestation, the Shia camp will necessarily be tied to Iran which, through the system of *Vilayet-e-Faqih*, although a contentious ideology, continues to be a controlling factor within the Shia body politic. The Shia Muslim ecclesiastical authorities play a significant role in this. Notably, two distinct Shia movements that are sensitive to the risks inherent in this posture, and cognizant of the futility of attempting to rule Iraq without arriving at a consensus with the country's Arab and Kurdish Sunni communities, have arisen. These movements are led by: Sayed Ammar Al Hakim, of the Islamic Supreme Council of Iraq; and Sayed Muqtada Al Sadr. Despite the efforts of these two groups, however, the pro-Iranian faction amongst the politicised Shia classes remains ascendant. The latter bloc's control of a wide group of militias ensures that any positive, ameliorative effects of Shia politicians, free of Iran, will be limited. While there are intra-sectarian political movements and a tribal Shia political movement as well, these two remain subjugated by Iranian loyalists.

Iranian influence within Iraq's Shia community has itself developed and progressed. Tehran has moved beyond merely relying on the political class amongst Iraqi Shias, the survival of which can always be called into question, or who may opt to change loyalties in the present thawing of US-Iranian relations. Instead, Tehran has opted to form proxies which are directly loyal to it, along the same lines of Lebanon's Hezbollah, led by an Iraqi Hassan Nasrallah who affirms the *Villayet-e-Faqih* and displays outright allegiance to Iran.

The author has observed how such a Made-in-Iran movement has been able to seize power within Iraq's Shia community, under the leadership of Hadi Al Ameri and Abu Mahdi Al Mohanndas at the helm of the Badr Organisation, as well as Qays Al Khazaali within the Asaeb Organisation. Either one of these three men could possibly become "Iraq's Hassan Nasrallah", or the Iranian leadership may simply find another person willing to blindly carry out their plans for the Fertile Crescent.

### *The Sunni Arab Community*

Faced with a distorted political reality, the Sunni Arab community of Iraq has been forced to seek a "Sectarian Solution" of their own, for their protection. While the sectarian identity of Iraq's Sunni Arabs continues to develop fully, the process of the coalescence of a Sunni Arab identity is now well under way. This was made patently clear by the demands for greater regional autonomy which were made by the Sunni Islamic Party of Iraq, during the protests which preceded the Maliki crackdown in the Sunni provinces. Despite not being the most populous region for Sunni Arabs, some of the Islamic Parties of Iraq bureau continues to demand the formation of an autonomous zone for the Sunni Arab community in the six provinces.

With one member of the Islamic Party of Iraq, Salim Al Jabouri, now serving as the Speaker of Iraq's Parliament, suggests that this particular group now has the opportunity to present its worldview to a wider audience. Their call to establish a Sunni enclave may find acceptance due to the injustices suffered by the country's Sunni community. The violence and vengeance visited by the Popular Mobilisation militia upon the Sunni Arabs living near Diyala and Tikrit have made the Sunnis across Iraq very suspicious of this group, but the defeat of the Iraqi army at the hands of ISIL, led many living in Sunni areas to drop their opposition to the Popular Mobilisation militia and to even welcome them as liberators.

Added to this was the capture of the district of Al Nakheeb, in the Anbar Province, by Popular Mobilisation forces and its linking to Karbala. This effectively allows Iranian proxies a chance to sit at the border with Saudi Arabia, and indeed a visit by General Qassem Suleimani is a worrying harbinger of the ability of Iran to pressure Saudi Arabia, especially via its predominantly Shia Eastern Province.

### *The Kurdish Community*

There are four main political movements which account for Kurdish political opinion:

First, the Patriotic Union of Kurdistan (PUK) is led by Jalaledin Talebani.

This group has long been a bastion of nationalist sentiment, and takes the region of Suliemaniya as a stronghold. The same area is one which has long been coveted by Iran, which has used a number of ulterior motives to try and dominate it. The PUK has traditionally had a strong following amongst educated, left-wing Kurdish individuals. The party has suffered, however, as a result of defections by some of its old guard disenchanted with the nepotism and financial and administrative corruption which is reportedly widespread throughout the PUK. The PUK is locked into a love-hate relationship with a second group, the Kurdistan Democratic Party.

Second, the Kurdistan Democratic Party (KDP), which is active in the regions surrounding Dohuk and Erbil, has survived as the single most important political formation amongst Kurds in Iraq, despite its reliance on tribalism for legitimacy, and the power of its former leader, the late Mullah Mustafa Barzani. Barzani's son Masoud is now at the helm of the KDP, and further serves as the President of the Kurdistan Regional Government. So great were intra-Kurdish threats against the KDP that, in 1996, it was forced to seek the aid of the Saddam Hussein-led central government in Baghdad.

Third, the Gorran—The Movement for Change is a rising star on the Kurdish political horizon which is composed largely of defectors from the PUK. The group's *raison d'etre* is a disillusionment with the monopolisation of political power in Kurdistan by the two main parties, the PUK and the KDP.

Fourth, the Islamic Union of Kurdistan is today one of the most significant political movements active in the country. It may, in fact, be the only Kurdish political movement with the strength to challenge the PUK-KDP grip on power. Although the Islamic Union of Kurdistan is an ideological imprint of the global Muslim Brotherhood, local specificities have their input on daily politics, and thus push the Islamic Union into the Kurdish consensus on such issues as federalism in Iraq. Several other Islamist groups operate in Iraqi Kurdistan, including the Gamaa Islamia led by Sheikh Ali Babir, as well as local franchises affiliated with Al Qaeda.

Smaller, ethnic and religious groupings active within Iraqi Kurdistan include organisations representing Turkmen and Arab populations residing in Kurdish areas. The effectiveness of these groups remains to be seen however, and in fact, what used to be called the Turkmen Front has largely disintegrated, with most of the ethnic Turkmen members coming under the leadership of Shia Arabs, and with most of the Sunni Arab members being absorbed by Kurdish movements. Meanwhile, Assyrian activists have tried to unify and bring under their auspices all of Iraq's Christian communities, even ushering in a novel ethnicity in the guise of the "Chaldeo-Assyrians".

The way in which PUK and the Gorran movement side firmly with Iran, a long-standing feature of life in Suliemaniya, and their refusal to back an extended term in the Presidency for Masoud Barzani, foretell a possible civil war-like split in Kurdistan, reminiscent of the 1990s, when the region was effectively divided into two separate enclaves, with competing capitals in Erbil and Suliemaniya. Such an outcome would only further entrench the internal discord of Iraqi society.

The Kurdish region has suffered the indignities of ISIL to the same extent as the Sunni Arab districts. The defeat of the Peshmerga militia at the hands of Sunni extremist group destroyed the previously high levels of confidence which the average Kurdish citizen had in this organisation, dedicated to his protection. It was only with massive international support for the Kurdish regional administration and the Peshmerga, the then militia, which Kurds see as a guarantor of their future independence, would have been consigned to history. This has not prevented the political leadership of the Kurdish Regional Government from making grandiose claims of never surrendering the territories which the Peshmerga, along with fighters from the PKK in Syria and the Western militaries, secured. The problem is that the Kurds do not form a clear majority in these "contested areas", but rather form one part of the fabric, alongside Arabs and Turkmens. This is a ticking time bomb which needs to be investigated closely.[10]

## Outcomes and Repercussions of a Sectarian or Ethnic Division of Iraq

The sectarian and ethnic division of the country has resulted in a total and complete Iranian control over Iraq. Indeed, Iranian control over Iraq has already surpassed previous expectations, and greatly so, with the formation of the Popular Mobilisation militia, giving Tehran outright control of the security and military affairs of Iraq. The formation of this organisation was blessed by Ayatollah Sistani, a leading Shia cleric. Here, the existence of ISIL has provided Iran and the Shia clergy with the justification it needed to try and solidify its gains.

Further, there is an increased power and influence of (Sunni) extremist and Salafi groups, leading ultimately to greater power for Al Qaeda. The meteoric rise to power of ISIL is a great example of this. This paper has previously discussed some of the negative results that ISIL's ascendancy in the North and Northwest of Iraq has had on the country.

An exacerbation of the present state of ethnic/sectarian cleansing seems to be a deliberate policy aimed at the future fragmentation of Iraq. The role played by the Popular Mobilisation militia in Diyala and Tikrit, was an indication of the primacy of vengeance as a motivator for the actions of Iranian-backed Shia paramilitary groups active in Iraq. The deterioration of Iraq's national character and of its global geostrategic vantage points are clearly visible throughout the country. In short, this means the transformation of the country from one of a geostrategic pivot into a trans-national catalyst of fragmentation. The rise of Kurdish national identity, at the expense of the over-arching national belongingness of Iraqis within the Kurdish regions of Iraq has also been witnessed in the country.

## Preparing to Rebuild: Causes for Hope

The description above give observers cause for disenchantment and perhaps even hopelessness. The status quo is not an easy one, and the amount of damage done to individual Iraqis and their worldviews is not modest. There remains a glimmer of hope, however, in the ability of Iraqis to begin reforming themselves; which must significantly begin with the reform of the individual. The grand challenge is to persuade individual Iraqis of the value of a reunified Iraq, as opposed to the fragmentation of the country. This paper aims to explore the means by which such a reunified, healed Iraq can be brought into existence. Formulating such a plan requires an understanding of the positive characteristics of Iraqi society.

With Maliki removed from power, despite having won a majority of parliamentary seats in the 2014 legislative elections, Haidar Al Abadi came into power with a promise to resolve some of the injustices suffered by citizens in the restive Sunni provinces. These promises were not realised, however, with the result being an intensification of the conflict in Iraq and ISIL capturing more than half of the country's territory. The absence of a genuinely patriotic Iraqi resistance movement has inflamed tensions and worsened sectarian fragmentation. In discussing the future prospects for Iraq, the factor of time cannot be ignored: allowing the status quo to fester unchecked will create irreversible change and the ultimate redrawing of community boundaries within Iraq. Examples of this include the adoption of Shia Islam by previously Sunni tribes in the South of Iraq and the adoption of a Kurdish ethnic identity by Arab tribes settled in the North of the country. Parties interested in improving Iraq must also act on a number of various axes, in parallel, in order to make the best possible use of time.

At a societal level, this includes tribes/clans, civil society organisations and professional/trade/labour organisations. It is imperative that the tribes be freed of the self-serving motives which lie behind their actions in the midst of the presently prevailing sectarian regime. In terms of more formal civil society organisations, special care needs to be given to those which were set up and financed by the CPA. Action on this front requires the promotion of the values of volunteering among the youth and in the educated classes. There is also a need for the formation of a "tribal council" which would bring together the clan chieftains of Iraq, across ethnic lines, thus bringing in Arab, Kurdish, Turkmen and Chaldeo-Assyrian tribal leaders. Such a body would serve to inhibit the presently inflamed tensions between the various components of Iraqi society. This approach calls for the strengthening of the shared heritage of all of these tribal groups.

One of the essential elements for the success of such an institution is the spread of tolerance and acceptance of the other. In other words, Arab tribal leaders must accept that Kurds will not be transformed into Arabs, and vice versa. Previously, such toleration and acceptance of others was the hallmark of social peace in Iraq, leading the way to shared marriages and coexistence. Here, cities must be celebrated and their roles as urban spaces for cross-sectarian coexistence strengthened. This would be merely a return to the state of affairs prior to the 2003 invasion. Here, Baghdad, Basra and other cities can play a crucial role. Iraq's educational system also has a vital role to play here. The damage done to it since the invasion has of course played a large role in the deterioration of intra-sectarian relations. Similarly, the role of trade unions and professional guilds needs to be utilised to assert the dignity in honest work and labour.

At the political level, in the past, attempts to create political parties which transverse sectarian and ethnic boundaries have met with dismal failures. This proposition, despite its attractiveness, lacks a certain level of realism and practicality. It should be noted, however, that such political parties which cross ethnic and sectarian lines, have existed during various periods of Iraq's history. The Baath and Communist parties have such a pedigree as did, to a lesser extent, the Muslim Brotherhood. In today's world, it would be necessary for such a political movement to deliberately and vociferously demand the implementation of non-sectarianism.

Security wise, this is possibly the most critical level which needs to be engaged in order to achieve the aims which this paper seeks to accomplish. Today, while the central government has nominal control of all aspects of the security situation, Iranian-controlled militia and ISIL represent serious hindrances to the rule of law. It is important that specialists in the fields of security, sociology and politics prepare detailed studies of what needs to be accomplished in order to deal with the negative effects which Iraq has suffered for so long.

By addressing religious issues, Iraqi national cohesion can be restored. Religious affairs are not of concern for the author of this paper, but one thing which should be made clear is that the finances of religious trusts (*Awqaf*) can be better administered. The funds can be used to build credit unions, hospitals or educational establishments or even residential complexes. It is important here to note the positive role being played in the religious sphere by one theologian in particular: Sayed Mahmoud Hassani Al Sarkhi, who is leading a revival of Arab Shia away from Iranian influence. Given the previously mentioned role which Iraq's cacophonous media has played in disrupting the country's stability, any serious attempt to reform Iraq and restore a semblance of normalcy, must involve addressing the negative aspects of Iraq's media.

At present, Iran is the singular regional player that is active in Iraq. Regardless of what people may or may not claim about the power of the occupation forces, their potency remains limited relative to Iran's. In turn, efforts must be made to contain Iran's unreasonable influence over Iraqi affairs. This necessitates a similar effort must be made on the global stage, with the involvement of the European Union and the Arab League, as well as the Organisation of the Islamic Cooperation (OIC). The precedent set by the European Union's ban on research funding on illegal Israeli settlements is an inspirational background here.

## NOTES

1. Edward P. Joseph and Michael O'Hanlon, "A Case of Soft Partition in Iraq", The Saban Center for Middle East Policy, Brookings Institution Analysis Paper No. 12, June, 2007, at http://www.brookings.edu/research/papers/2007/06/iraq-joseph.
2. "Creative destruction", July 2013, at whatis.techtarget.com/definition/creative-destruction.
3. See the discussion by Ali Al Wardi in his encyclopedic work, *Excerpts of the Modern History of Iraq*, Dar Al Warraq publishers, London, 1991-1992, pp. 69-88.
4. An authoritative text on the influence of Iranian theologians on the development of Shia Islam in Iraq see Isaac Naqqash, *The Shia of Iraq*, Princeton University Press, Princeton, 1994.
5. The full text of the Iraqi constitution is available online in Arabic at http://www.krp.org/uploadedforms/IraqConstitutionA.pdf.
6. See Abdullah Ben Abdelaziz, "*Husseiniyat* Rituals Nothing to Do with the Imams", link in Arabic at http://www.alrashead.net/index.php%3Fpartd%3D3%26derid%3D1785.
7. One important exception was the role played by Iraqi patriot Uday Al Zaidi and his comrades in the Governorate of Dhi Qar.
8. See the preamble of the Iraqi constitution, as well as Article 41 of the same document.
9. Basra has historically a predominantly Sunni Muslim city, before the success of urban regeneration projects attracted people from the largely Shia rural hinterlands to settle within the city limits. This is borne out by the overwhelmingly Sunni sub-districts which surround Basra, such as Al Zubair, Abu Al Khaseeb, Al Seeba and Al Faw.
10. "Kurdish official: We will not withdraw from the areas which we captured", *Asharq Al Awsat*, June 8, 2015, p. 8.

# 9

# Gulf Security Architecture and the GCC: Time to Shed Past Baggage and Start Anew

*Rajeev Agarwal*

The West Asian region has been in turmoil for around five years now. What started off as a local incident in Tunisia in December 2010 engulfed the entire region of North Africa and West Asia in what has been popularly termed as 'Arab Spring'. Five years down the line, some of the countries are still trying to grapple with the changed political dynamics (Tunisia, Libya, Egypt and Yemen) while others have prevented it from taking an ugly turn (Saudi Arabia, Jordan, Morocco etc.). Then, in case of Syria, the country is in a state of civil war, and the most recent case of Iraq which seems to have imploded under the pressure exerted by the Islamic State of Iraq and Syria (ISIS).

Initially, the Arabian Peninsula was by and large left unaffected by the protests. Though there were incidents of protests and clashes in Bahrain and Saudi Arabia none of those were on the same scale as what transpired in the rest of the region. The Gulf monarchies survived. What is however affecting the Arabian Peninsula and particularly the six countries of the Gulf Cooperation Council (GCC), is the rapidly changing political dynamics in the region. On one hand, it can express apprehension in the region over the rise of Iran in recent past, and on the other hand, it is the intra-GCC rivalry which is threatening to alter the fragile balance within the GCC. The emergence of Qatar-Saudi Arabia competition is one such major issue. The concern over progressive shift in US policy away from the region towards the Asia Pacific as a part of its "rebalancing" is another major fear as it threatens to deprive and dilute the decades long US pledged security guarantees in the region.

In addition, the ongoing conflicts in Iraq and Syria have highlighted the total lack of consensus, unity and common goals with regard to not only GCC but the entire Arab world at large. These conflicts have clearly highlighted the inability of an organisation like the GCC in its present form not only to take political decisions but also to take suitable collective actions to address serious security issues in the region. In a future scenario, where, devoid of US security cover, the region will have to address security concerns on a regional platform, GCC, the lone regional structure faces an existential threat.

The Gulf region, in fact, embodies and reflects the concerns of the entire West Asian and North African region. They contain majority of the crude oil and natural gas resources, employ a large number of emigrant workers in the region, are home to the most holy sites for the Muslims, harbour a bitter regional rivalry often drawn along sectarian lines between Saudi Arabia and Iran, and have a major role to play in all other issues effecting the enormous region at large. The Arab-Israeli dispute, Egypt-Israel peace treaty, US role in the region, question of Muslim and/or Arab unity and in recent decades, the threat of Islamic fundamentalism and terrorism through groups like Al Qaeda, ISIS etc., all have links through the Gulf region.

The Gulf region and its well-being is, therefore, crucial towards ensuring peace in the region and to coordinate and implement it, there is a requirement of a potent and effective regional organisation. Presently, GCC is the only such organisation, which too is grossly inadequate due to major structural fault-lines, especially the fact that it does not include two major nations north of the Persian Gulf; Iran and Iraq and is, therefore, largely ill representative of region. Consequently, it would be wrong to expect GCC to address and resolve major security concerns of the region. There is, thus, an urgent need for GCC to evolve into a new form which would be more inclusive and potent to bring the region together in facing rapidly evolving issues, especially in context of security.

This paper thus attempts to examine the evolution and role of GCC to examine past attempts at securing the Gulf region, study in brief some of the major security threats in the region, evolving geo-political and security dynamics in the region and finally, put forth possible options for a more robust security architecture for the region.

## Gulf Security and GCC: The Beginnings

The GCC was created in 1981, shortly after the 1979 Iranian revolution. The basic premise of GCC was to bring together countries of the Gulf region against the perceived threat from two enemies; Iran, an ideological enemy and Iraq, a belligerent power. The GCC thus chose to ignore the geographical and geopolitical realities of the region. Iran and Iraq, geographically cover almost the entire Northern coast of the Persian Gulf, are critical links towards the Levant, Central Asia and South Asia and are huge reservoirs of natural resources. Geo-politically too, Iraq and Iran with their civilisational histories, political evolution over centuries and significant economic and military powers could not be ignored. On the other hand, Saudi Arabia counted as the only major country in the GCC, others being much smaller states. The third pillar to lend critical support to GCC was the US which pledged to provide security guarantees to the member nations. GCC thus stood up as a structure almost on one leg with US support being its crutches. The organisation was deemed to fail as has been witnessed over the decades.

GCC, however, has not been the only attempt at forging a regional architecture for the Gulf region. Previously also, there were attempts to counterfeit various security structures in the region. For the first seven decades of the last century, Britain extended its security umbrella over the region. It kept a semblance of order and avoided major conflicts through plaint regimes and troops stationed in selected land and naval bases. However, the rise of Arab nationalism and a declining economy forced Britain to withdraw from the region in 1971. The role of 'security provider' was, thereafter, taken over by the US.

Even before formally taking over from Britain, the Gulf's importance to US strategic interests' became apparent with the articulation of the Nixon Doctrine in 1969. The Nixon Doctrine called on US allies to contribute to their own security with the aid of American security assistance. In accordance with the doctrine, the US opted for reliance on its regional allies for preserving the security of the Persian Gulf, avoiding direct engagement. The "Twin Pillars policy" was a natural outgrowth of it.[1] It incorporated twin pillars in the form of Saudi Arabia and Iran to ensure security of the Persian Gulf. US' reliance on the strategy of "local hegemony", which was in effect an "indirect" hegemonic dominance of the US, was meant to be an alternative for direct hegemonic presence in order to avoid a Vietnam-type crisis. This security pattern seemed to work for a while. Endowed with oil revenues and US support, Iran built up a modern military and was willing to counter any security disturbance in the region. In the early 1970s, Iran even sent troops to Dhofar and effectively crushed the leftist armed struggle that threatened the regime in Yemen. This security arrangement, however, fell apart when the Iranian Islamic Revolution toppled the Shah's regime in 1979.[2] At his 1980 State of the Union address, in reaction to the 1979 Iranian revolution, President Carter articulated his own doctrine:

> "An attempt by any outside force to gain control of the Persian Gulf region will be regarded as an assault on the vital interests of the United States of America,

and such an assault will be repelled by any means necessary, including military force."[3]

During the 1980s, the US, fearing Iranian revolutionary expansionism, turned to Iraq as well as to the newly formed GCC, to balance Iran. At the same time, given the military weakness of the GCC states and lacking the strong pillar previously provided by Iran, the US began to be drawn more directly into the region. After the Shah's fall, the 'Rapid Deployment Force', organised by the US Department of Defence, and growing US investment in regional military bases, such as Masira and Bahrain, highlighted this trend.[4] In August 1990, this US strategy of relying on Iraq along with the Gulf States too failed when Iraq attacked Kuwait. Thereafter, the US shifted from reliance on regional allies to an even more proactive and forward military presence of US forces in the region which included basing, prepositioning and military exercises to prepare for and support crises. Also, the end of Cold War meant that Russia was out of the picture and the Gulf region became the region of primary interest for the US.

After the Iraq war in 1991, Presidents George H.W. Bush and Bill Clinton also created a multilateral security framework known as the Madrid process. Within that, as regards the Gulf region, US pursued strategy of the containment and deterrence of Iraq and Iran, relying on military tools rather than a political framework to bring comprehensive peace to the region. The Joint Staff in the Pentagon outlined three main goals. The three goals were: 1) improving rapid US deployment capabilities; 2) strengthening local defence capabilities of GCC states; and 3) promoting intra-GCC cooperation and inter-agency cooperation between states. Unfortunately, only the first goal was consistently improved and the results were seen in the second war against Iraq.[5]

The failure of the twin-pillar strategy and Iraq's invasion of Kuwait also taught US two important lessons. First, empowerment of the regional powers can get out of control and turn into a major threat to the interests of the US. Second, the US cannot depend on regional states to provide security. US presence in this strategic region would, therefore, be inevitable. In 1999, the US introduced a new strategy to minimise threats posed by Iran and Iraq. The Cooperative Defence Initiative (CDI) was a plan for integration of the defence forces of the GCC, Egypt, and Jordan and coordinate intelligence sharing between them.[6] It identified Iraq and Iran as major security threats to the region. With the CDI in place, all GCC members even signed a joint defence pact in December 2000. This pact called for the pooling of GCC's defence resources and specified that an attack on any member would be considered an attack against all the states. Furthermore, the 'Cooperative Belt' early warning network too was inaugurated in late February 2001. It provided radar, early warning and secure communications links between the six GCC nations.[7]

However, the 9/11 incident and the resultant war on terror in Afghanistan along with the war on Iraq in 2003 once again changed the entire dynamics of security and US engagement in the region. Coupled with the discovery of 'covert' nuclear programme in Iran in 2002, US found itself deeply engaged in the security issues of the region. As the Iraq war ended with elections in 2005 and the Afghanistan war dragged on, the US had to take a serious relook at its engagement with the Gulf region. In May 2006, the US launched Gulf Security Dialogue (GSD). The dialogue served as the principal security coordination mechanism between the US and the GCC. The core objectives of the Dialogue were the promotion of intra-GCC and GCC-US cooperation to meet common perceived threats. The Dialogue provides a framework for US engagement with the GCC countries in the following six areas: (1) the improvement of GCC defence capabilities and inter-operability; (2) regional security issues such as the Israeli-Palestinian conflict and Lebanon; (3) counter-proliferation; (4) counter-terrorism and internal security; (5) critical infrastructure protection; and (6) commitments to Iraq.[8]

All these initiatives resulted in three important results: *firstly*, Iran felt completely excluded from the region; *secondly*, US got more and more engaged in the security issues of the region and *thirdly*, the GCC became totally reliant on the US for mitigating the perceived security threats in the region. Another important development that took place in the region in particular, and the world in general, during the first decade of 21st Century was the rise of non-state actors and extremist groups like the Al Qaeda. They threatened to challenge the very notion of state and state security. With support from some nations seeking to take on their adversaries through proxy methods, such groups rose to emerge as a trans-regional security threat, something that a weak regional organisation like the GCC was incapable of handling.

## Security Challenges in the Gulf Region and the Failure of GCC

In order to arrive at any sustainable security framework for the region, it is essential to understand major security concerns and threats in the region. Primary issue in the region is of legitimacy of existing structure. The fact that Iran, one of the leading regional powers is not part of the set-up does not instigate confidence. It, in fact, leads to mutual suspicion and ill perceived security threats. Iran feels that it has been unduly targeted on the pretext of its nuclear programme. Iraq, too, emerging from the shadows of Gulf wars, feels that it has a rightful place in the region, giving its economic and military potential and historical position in the region. In the post-Gulf War scenario where Iran and Iraq have become closely aligned, the effect becomes even more glaring. On the other hand, Saudi Arabia, has banked upon its leadership in the GCC and the security guarantees from the

US to project its role in the region. Hence, there is a structural imbalance in the region which gets even more compounded when we consider the existing and evolving security threats.

## Security Concerns in the Region

The Gulf region has always been an extremely volatile region. Most of the threats to security emerge from deep-rooted ideological disputes. The fact that there is no state with overwhelming power and all major regional powers vie for leadership role adds to the security challenge.

In terms of security threats, Iran is perceived to be the biggest threat to the region. The entire construct of GCC was based on the fear of post revolution Iran. In fact, Muhammad Abdul Ghaffar goes a step further wherein he states that the Iranian revolution created a strategic vacuum which resulted in a number of variables including the collapse of twin pillar strategy, Soviet invasion of Afghanistan, Iran-Iraq war, Iraqi invasion Kuwait and in some ways events like 9/11 too.[9] In addition, there are territorial disputes between Iran and a number of GCC countries.[10] Iran's nuclear programme often casts a shadow over the future security situation and there is an ideological conflict between the Shia majority Iran and the Sunni-ruled GCC countries.

Looking beyond Iran, security challenges to the Persian Gulf may be broadly divided into three categories. These include conventional security challenges emanating from balance of power dynamics; more recent challenges rising out of globalisation and economic development; and the third category of security challenges whose roots tend to lie in the domestic and regional political economies.[11]

Over the last century, the Persian Gulf has been witness to multiple, interlocking rivalries and competitions, many of which have, at one time or another, resulted into open conflict. Some of these have revolved around Iran's supposedly "revolutionary" posture toward its Arab neighbours, Iraq's hegemonic policies in the 1990s, Iran-Saudi Arabia rivalry for regional leadership, the threat of Shiite Crescent led by Iran, the suppressed and marginalised Shiite populations in Bahrain and Saudi Arabia and the more recent Saudi Arabia-Qatar rivalry. Also, US policies in the region, especially its military stance and anti-Iran alliances with the GCC have been provocative as well. The balance of power, while maintaining its stance, has shifted in past few years due to developments in the region, emergence of Turkey as a major player, marginalisation of the Palestine issue among the Arab world and also the neighbours Iran and Iraq coming together after US withdrawal from Iraq. This tussle has disturbed the fragile balance and is perpetuating security concerns in the region.

The second set of security concerns revolves around the Gulf's close connect with the global market economy. These concerns revolve around issues such as food security, cyber security, the issue of migrant workers, and the issue of preserving national identities in the face of ever-increasing expatriate populations especially in GCC countries. This, however, is more a domestic concern having regional ramifications.

The third category of security challenge is far more diverse in nature. Energy security which has domestic, regional and global ramifications forms one part of it. The Persian Gulf derives its primary strategic significance through energy security, both in terms of uninterrupted flow and access to open transportation routes. With the Strait of Hormuz as a chokepoint and Iran's influence over it, a potential of regional conflict is omnipresent which makes supply of oil and natural gas to global importer, a major security concern. The next challenge is the emergence of Jihadist groups inside states which are weak or those non-state actors who encourage such groups as a part of their regional strategies. The emergence of Al Qaeda and its affiliates in weak and collapsing states like Syria, Iraq, Yemen, and Afghanistan is a clear example of it while alleged support of Saudi-led countries to rebel groups in Syria and Iraq could be examples of state supported groups. The third challenge is in states which seek regime security through rentier bargains with other powers and rely on 'buying off the populations' in order to survive and govern. Most of the Gulf monarchies would fall in this category where the continuance and legitimacy of monarchies is derived from fear, money, foreign military presence and excessive control over the population. 'Arab Spring' in 2011 was a clear example of how such states bought off their political legitimacy through such means. This threat too, though domestic in nature, gives opportunities to rivals to create uncomfortable conditions in home nation leading to unrest and possible overthrow of regime.

The next security concern emanates from the threat of proliferation of nuclear weapons and Weapons of Mass Destruction (WMD). The geopolitical realm of the region would undergo a drastic change if Iran obtains a nuclear weapon. The Iranian effort to obtain a nuclear weapon could serve as the Shia axis's ultimate shield against any attempts to curtail its progress. The Sunni-ruled states of the Arab world, especially the GCC states, fear that if Iran acquires nuclear weapons, they are the ones who will be subject to pressure that will be difficult for them to counter. A nuclear-armed Iran would multiply the threat perceptions of the GCC countries.[12]

## Failure of GCC

The GCC in its structure and conduct has always been too focussed on the Iranian threat. The Iran factor has even overshadowed intra-GCC disputes and has helped Saudi Arabia to dominate the GCC and the US to dictate its security issues. Thus, other security issues, though equally important have been largely ignored by the GCC. Also, GCC in its construct is based primarily on Gulf monarchies. These monarchies shared common goals of not only warding off external threats but ensuring regime security. In such a structure, scope for countries like Iran, Iraq, Turkey or Egypt did not exist. Also, common interests like intra-GCC trade, common security arrangements with the US and shared political objectives in the region made it difficult for the GCC to see anything beyond Southern Gulf region.

The overpowering presence of Saudi Arabia and its dominance in GCC too made it an ill represented regional organisation where the smaller states were expected to push the stated line from Saudi Arabia. GCC has even failed to resolve intra-GCC issues including some territorial disputes. Although most of the territorial and disputes over islands have been resolved over time;[13] still mutual mistrust over recurrence of such issues remains. This manifests itself in prevailing military tension in the region.

Despite being formed as an anti-Iran alliance, the GCC has failed to rein in Iran or prevent its alleged nuclear programme. It also failed to foresee the after-effect of Gulf War in 2003. Although it succeeded in overthrowing Saddam Hussein by aligning with the US, but the resultant Shiite government in Iraq in close proximity with Iran presented an even bigger threat to the GCC.

As witnessed in the wake of 'Arab Spring' of 2011, there has been a large scale influx of Jihadist groups in the region. These groups are challenging the very concept of statehood in the region like the ISIS in Iraq and Syria. The GCC has once again failed to put up a united front or formulate a cogent strategy to take on this evil.

The security concerns in the Gulf region are thus wide in scope ranging from ideological dispute between Saudi Arabia and Iran, energy security, threat of Al Qaeda and other terrorist groups, threat of nuclear weapons and WMD, threat of Iran itself to the GCC and the primary concern of Gulf monarchies. GCC has however, failed to come up with satisfactory solutions to either of them. The failure can be partly attributed to the structure of the GCC and partly due to the mutual mistrust and suspicion which exists in the region, both within members of GCC as well as those outside of it. Any future security architecture in the region will, thus, have to factor in all such issues before evolving a new structure for the region which is more representative, inclusive and potent to address regional security issues.

## Options for an Alternative Security Framework

GCC was formed primarily as a defensive mechanism against post revolution Iran. More than three decades on, there is a need for relook. As discussed in previous sections, there cannot be any viable security solution to the region without Iran and Iraq. In a 2006 speech delivered at the annual Manama Dialogue, organised by the International Institute for Strategic Studies (IISS), Bahrain's Foreign Minister, Sheikh Khalid Bin Ahmed Al Khalifa, stated: "In the Gulf, no sustainable long-term regional security arrangement can be envisioned without Iraq and Iran acting as two of its pillars." Iranian and Iraqi officials have similarly argued that Gulf security is best advanced through cooperation and coordination among the littoral states.[14] In fact, the Gulf Region is the core of a larger region extending from the Levant upto Iran and could also include Afghanistan. On the other side, some parts of Maghreb including Egypt would need to be included too, the reason being that culture, economy and security issues in this larger region are closely interlinked and cannot be dealt in haphazardly. The ongoing civil war in Syria, the implosion of Iraq under the onslaught of Islamic State (IS), the Gaza conflict, the transition in Egypt and the struggle in Yemen clearly demonstrate that these conflicts cannot be resolved locally as also that the GCC cannot remain immune from such conflicts. There is thus a requirement to rework the regional dynamics in a comprehensive manner while devising a new regional structure.

Robert E. Hunter in his book on Gulf security[15] has highlighted eight major factors to be kept in mind while devising a new security architecture for the Gulf region. These are, the future of Iraq, Iran, asymmetric threats, regional reassurance, the Arab-Israeli conflict, regional tensions, crises, and conflicts, the roles of other external actors, and arms control and confidence-building measures. Iraq is important not only as a large nation in the Gulf region but also because of its continuing conflict and the interest and engagement of other regional countries in it. Iran is important due to its central location in the region, its size, influence right up to Levant and military-cum-economic capabilities and also the threat of nuclear weapons. The rise of asymmetric threats especially terrorism caused by Al Qaeda, ISIS, Kurds and other groups would be an important consideration in a new security structure for the Gulf region.

The impact of other regional tensions, crises and conflicts—which include sectarian issues across the region, Saudi Arabia-Iran rivalry, Kurdish issue across Turkey, Syria, Iraq and Iran, the threat of piracy, radical Islamism etc. would be important components of a new structure. The role of the US and other external players like Russia, China, EU and India too, would be critical in a future architecture. The Arab-Israeli conflict too would be important. Even if there is no direct linkage between Gulf security and the conflict, the cause of Palestine has strong connect in the people of the region. Arms-control measures and Confidence building measures (CBMs) too would be an essential part of a security structure that is effective because they benefit the security and political interests of the participants.

The future role of the US would also be one of the most important component in the future architecture. Robert E. Hunter discusses five such issues with regards US engagement in the region:[16] the withdrawal of US forces from Iraq, US policy and approaches regarding Iran, US forces in and near the region, formal security guarantees, and a US nuclear guarantee. In this the future role of the US, especially in context of its 'rebalancing to Asia Pacific' and its reluctance to get directly engage in region's conflict since 2011 would be an important factor.[17]

## Models for New Security Architecture

Many analysts believe that GCC is inadequate to address security concerns of the Gulf region and that a new arrangement needs to be devised. Also, any security arrangement should take into account the failures of the past and consider the strategic circumstances that exist today and should include all the actors involved. Such a 'common security framework' should be based on a 'cooperative security model' and based on a set of assumptions about the relative security stance of an actor vis-à-vis the others and in which the military endeavours are not the primary focus. In this respect, the main concern is development of structures to attain a comprehensive and positive vision of security which involves achieving proper measures to involve concerned parties in order to resolve hostilities before they turn into violence. The idea is that all states will find virtual security through commitments to limit military rivalries rather than through attempts to gain dominance. Such security architecture assumes that regional rivals that can be potential enemies will accept the same legal and offensive constraints on behaviour as friends, despite the existence of considerable mutual mistrust.[18]

Others argue[19] that the Gulf security system needs to be constructed from three interlocking elements: balance of power, reform, and multilateralism. Only such a combination will provide both the progress and the stability needed for enduring security, while also relieving the United States of excessive costs and exposure to risk as the sole security provider. They seek a local power equilibrium. Two important prerequisites of such an equilibrium are that no single power can outweigh a combination of the others and that the powers are all reasonably content with the status quo. For the foreseeable future, the balance of power in the Gulf will be underwritten by the US. As regards reform, they argue in favour of building a more stable regional system that will pose less of a burden to external powers and reverse the growth of extremism, reform of the region's political, economic, social, and defence structures is essential. Also, the task of Gulf security cannot be left either to regional actors or to the US alone. There would be a need for a multilateral engagement involving EU, Russia, and China too to pitch in.

Another recommended model seems to be based on the experience of Organisation for Security and Cooperation in Europe (OSCE). The argument is based on the premise [20] that Gulf security issues are somewhat similar to issues of Europe in 1970s. OSCE incorporated a broad array of issues defined within the purview of the organisation, but the cornerstone was the "indivisibility of security". Today, we would phrase this in terms of a win-win situation: that security is not a zero-sum game and that it must be established at no one's expense, rather to the benefit of all involved. OSCE required overcoming the deep set West-East mistrust and building a common perception and conviction that détente is a continuous process with the corollary of coexistence rather than vanquishing the enemy. In so many ways, this is similar to the situation in the Gulf. There are perceptions of existential threats, hegemonic aspirations and security is primarily defined in military terms.

Robert E Hunter too proposes models for Gulf security.[21] He argues that in the creation of a regional security structure for the Gulf, an important point to contemplate is whether there is value in creating formal political and security commitments among various countries in the region and perhaps even in requiring that this be done before other steps are taken. These commitments could take many forms. One common form is collective security, which is an "all-against-one" approach designed to provide incentives for all members to support what is agreed by all to be a common good in the interest of common security against any threat from any member. Such an agreement can impose high requirements in terms of discipline and willingness to act, as witnessed by the developments that led to the collapse of the most famous of all collective security pacts, the League of Nations. Another popular form of security commitment is collective defence, a key example of which is the NATO Alliance. In this form, all the parties agree to come to the aid of any member or members that are subject to some untoward behaviour (aggression is the most common trigger) that emanates from outside the pact. This is an "all-for-one and one-for-all" approach.

He then lays out various models like the NATO and EU. He proposes two models: Conference on Security and Cooperation for the Persian Gulf (CSCPG) and An Association of Persian Gulf Nations. CSCPG could be patterned on the Conference on Security and Cooperation in Europe (CSCE), which was designed to help reduce tensions during the Cold War, when different countries wanted to explore ways of cooperating even during a time of basic geopolitical and ideological conflict. Aspects of CSCE—basically, security cooperation—might be usefully adapted to a CSCPG in making possible a range of relations between Iran and the Arab States of the Gulf without any of the local countries to relinquish basic approaches or to compromise their interests. An Association of Persian Gulf Nations would be patterned on the Association of Southeast Asian Nations (ASEAN), and on ASEAN's Treaty of Amity and Cooperation in Southeast Asia, which incorporates 17 non-ASEAN members, including the US, Russia, China, and the EU. The advantages of this model are that it has developed slowly; it includes tension-reduction mechanisms; it does not require that all disputes be resolved before countries can join; and it relates politics, economics, and security together. The treaty also provides a role for external countries if and when regional countries see this role as beneficial.

## A Model for the Gulf Region

All the above models suggested have few things in common; need for the structure to be inclusive in nature (Iran, Iraq and some others therefore need to be a part of it), cooperative and confidence building mechanisms, recognise the role of external players, have a region-wide method of dealing with conventional and asymmetric threats, commence with a 'Common Minimum Programme' instead of a large structure and have a collective response mechanism. In case of the Gulf region, due to its geographical and geo-political linkages with the larger region in West Asia and North Africa as such, the structure would need to incorporate a much larger membership.

Graduated evolution of such a structure would be the key which Kenneth Pollack too suggests through the idea of a "security condominium" which would begin by establishing a regional-security forum at which relevant issues could be debated and discussed, information exchanged, and agreements framed. The members could then move on to confidence-building measures, such as notification of exercises, exchanges of observers, and information swaps. Ultimately, the intention would be to proceed to eventual arms-control agreements that might include demilitarised zones, bans on destabilising weapons systems, and balanced force reductions for all parties. In particular, the group might aim for a ban on all WMD, complete with penalties for violators and a multilateral (or international) inspection program to enforce compliance.[22] Ray Takeyh and

Steven Cook too recommend a similar approach that "could evolve gradually, beginning with confidence-building measures and arms-control compacts and, eventually, lead to a full security system that resembles institutions such as the OSCE." The need is, therefore, to recognise the role and scope of such a structure in future. Obviously, GCC in its present form would have to perish the moment Iran and Iraq are to be incorporated in the new structure. But the reality of the security requirements dictate such a step.

There is also the talk of converting GCC into a 'Gulf Union' as was discussed at the GCC Summit in Bahrain in December 2012,[23] but has yet to take any shape. This too would be grossly inadequate as there are no indications that the Gulf Union would have an expanded membership to include Iran, Iraq and others. Also, it is yet to find full support within the GCC leave alone outside of it. Oman dismissed it with its Foreign Minister Yusuf bin Alawi stating at the Manama Dialogue in December 2013, "We are against a union. We will not prevent a formation of union, but if it happens we will not be part of it."[24] Saudi Arabia seems, however, convinced that Gulf Union is the need of the hour. Prince Turki Al Faisal stated that, "people in the GCC want a closely-knit union and such a union has now become inevitable."[25] The tussle between Qatar and Saudi Arabia, primarily over Qatar's support to Egyptian Muslim Brotherhood is a matter of concern as it threatens to split the GCC down the middle. The recalling of ambassadors from Qatar by Saudi Arabia, UAE and Bahrain in March 2014 was a clear manifestation of this divide.[26]

The role of the US in any security structure in the region would be critical. The strategy adopted by the US towards the region in past three years, especially after the 'Arab Spring' has been a matter of concern for the region. Its reluctance in getting directly involved in the military campaign in Libya, its refusal to militarily intervene in Syria as well as the drawing down on wars in Iraq and Afghanistan are a clear indication of its loosing appetite for military conflicts in the region. Also, the discourse of the US 'rebalancing towards Asia-pacific' could also thin down US military involvement in the region. In addition, discovery of shale gas in the US could result in reduced reliance on region's oil. These issues are of grave concern to the region and are setting serious doubts in the minds of policy makers in the West Asian region on future US intentions.

Echoing these concerns, Abdulaziz Sager, Chairman of the Gulf Research Center said in a column in *Arab News*, "The US-GCC relationship appears to be at a crossroads. Despite a long history of relations and a clear common and mutual interest in the stability and security of the Gulf region, the GCC states and the United States look as if they are growing apart on an almost daily basis...the prevailing mood appears to be that the terms are beginning to change to such a degree that the GCC states have no choice but to act on their own and without consideration of US interests and concerns. This is bound to have consequences, real and unintended, for both sides, and the question should be asked whether such increased separation will not come back to haunt the region as a whole."[27] Even Leon Panetta, former Secretary of Defence of the US while speaking at the Emirates Centre for Strategic Studies and Research, Abu Dhabi said, "It is our hope that the GCC, can play an important role in the future providing security for this region. Across the board, Washington is urging allies to build local capacity. That's what we're doing for the UAE and that's what we're doing with other countries. Yes, we give them the help they need, we give them assistance, but the fact is that they have to help provide for their security."[28]

The ongoing turmoil in West Asia, however, could be an ideal opportunity for the region to rise above past mindsets and mutual suspicions to come together and find a viable solution for the future. Given the existing and evolving dynamics few things seem inevitable in the new structure:

I. Inclusion of Iran and Iraq, and Yemen in the new structure as core members.
II. Inclusion of Egypt too as a core member primarily due to four reasons: its historical and geo-political significance in the Arab world, its peace treaty with Israel, role in frequently brokering peace between Palestine and Israel and fourthly, the Suez Canal being the primary route for passage of oil and natural gas consignments from the Gulf region.
III. Participation of Syria, Jordan, Lebanon, Turkey and Palestine, in some form.
IV. Role for major external powers like the US along with Russia, China and India.

As discussed earlier, the new structure may not be all encompassing at the start. It could commence merely as a security dialogue; "Regional Dialogue for Cooperative Security in the Persian Gulf." Countries party to it could commence with the dialogue with simpler issues to build confidence like establishing political and military commissions to reduce the risk of conflict, establishing Military Cooperation Centers where military personnel posted from each of the member countries would exchange data on military exercises, naval movements, counter-piracy cooperation and sharing anti-terrorist intelligence. Establishing a Coordinating Secretariat and establishing of 'Hot lines' could also go a long way in dispelling doubts on military movements and intentions of others. Creation of a 'Rapid Reaction Force' could be a step in a later time frame which should involve near equal commitments from members. Military exercises across the region could be yet another confidence building measure. Arms-control agreements, demilitarised zones, bans on WMDs too are subjects which are desirable but could be put off for later.

The role of external powers would be crucial to the success of new structure and the 'Big Four' in form of US, Russia, China and India would need to be incorporated. This would facilitate downsizing of US military commitment; at the same time increasing the involvement of the other three. The basic role that these four could be given is the role of mediation, red-flagging any untoward incident developing in the region and helping the structure in integrating with the global security network.

## Conclusion

A right sized and well-intended security structure is the need of the hour not only for the Gulf region, but the entire West Asian region. Given the deep rooted mistrusts, ideological conflicts and regional rivalries, it looks a difficult task. However, the choice to ignore and move forward is simply not there as is evidenced in the ongoing turmoil in the region and the inability of the GCC to do anything about it. While the ultimate aim may be ambitious, the challenge is to select a very acceptable 'common minimum programme' which could at least bring all players to the table. Also, the inclusion of states like Iran, Iraq and Egypt would help dispel doubts of hegemonic designs of Saudi Arabia within the GCC and also act as counter balancing force in the region. Counter terrorism could be another unifying factor. If the members of the new architecture align closely, the space occupied by terrorist forces like Al Qaeda and ISIS could reduce.

The bottom line is clear. The present system of Gulf Security is grossly inadequate to meet regional security challenges. It is, therefore, time for the GCC as well as other major stake holders like Iran, Iraq and Egypt to rise above the usual rhetoric and forge a regional partnership. There will be teething problems, the framework might eventually fail, but an attempt needs to be made. It is not important how the structure evolves 10-20 years down the line, but what matters is the way a common platform is created where all stakeholders can shed their mutual suspicions and mistrust and come together to, at least, start a dialogue. It may, therefore, be just the right time for the "Regional Dialogue for Cooperative Security in the Persian Gulf" to take shape.

### NOTES

1. "The Gulf Security Architecture: Partnership With The Gulf Cooperation Council", A Majority Staff Report Prepared for the Use of the Committee on Foreign Relations United States Senate One Hundred Twelfth Congress Second Session, June 19, 2012, p. 7, US Government Publishing Office, at http://www.gpo.gov/fdsys/pkg/CPRT-112SPRT74603/html/CPRT-112SPRT74603.htm.

2. Kayhan Barzegar and Mohammad Reza Agharebparast, "Security Architecture in the Persian Gulf: A Comprehensive Appraisal", *Iranian Review of Foreign Affairs*, 3(3), Fall 2012, pp. 7-28.
3. "The Gulf Security Architecture: Partnership with the Gulf Cooperation Council", n. 1, p. 7.
4. Andrew Rathmell, Theodore Karasik and David Gompert, "A New Persian Gulf Security System", Issue Paper, RAND, 2003, at http://www.rand.org/content/dam/rand/pubs/issue_papers/2005/IP248.pdf.
5. Michael Kraig, "Assessing Alternative Security Frameworks for the Persian Gulf", *Middle East Policy*, 11(3), Fall 2004, pp. 147-148.
6. Patrick Knapp, "The Gulf States in the Shadow of Iran", *Middle East Quarterly*, 17 (1), Winter 2010, pp. 49-59.
7. "Allied Contributions to the Common Defence", A Report to the United States Congress by the Secretary of Defence, Chapter 2, Department of Defence, USA, March 2001, at http://archive.defense.gov/pubs/allied_contrib2001/index.htm.
8. Christopher M. Blanchard and Richard F. Grimmett, "The Gulf Security Dialogue and Related Arms Sale Proposals", CRS Report for US Congress, October 2008, at https://www.fas.org/sgp/crs/weapons/RL34322.pdf.
9. Muhammad Abdul Ghaffar, "Regional and International Strategy for Gulf Security", Bahrain Center for Strategic, International and Energy Studies, 2012, p. 3.
10. Rajeev Agarwal, "Security in the Gulf Region: India's Concerns, Vulnerabilities, Interests and Engagement Options" in Rumel Dahiya (ed.), *Developments in the Gulf Region: Prospects and Challenges for India in Next Two Decades*, Pentagon Press& IDSA, New Delhi, 2014, p. 41.
11. Mehran Kamrava, "Visions of Persian Gulf security, in Visions of Gulf Security", The Project on Middle East Political Science (POMEPS), Institute for Middle East Studies at the George Washington University, March 25, 2014, p. 5, at http://pomeps.org/wp-content/uploads/2014/03/Visions_of_Gulf_Security.pdf.
12. Rajeev Agarwal, "Iran's Nuclear Programme: How Real is the Threat", in R. Sidda Goud and Manisha Mookherjee (eds.) *India and Iran in Contemporary Relations*, Allied Publishers Pvt. Ltd, New Delhi, 2014, p. 107.
13. The Hawar Islands dispute between Qatar and Bahrain was resolved in 2001 by the International Court of Justice (ICJ). Summary of the judgement is available at http://www.icj-cij.org/docket/index.php?sum=443&code=qb&p1=3&p2=3&case=87&k=61&p3=5. Al Buraimi Oasis was claimed by Saudi Arabia, Abu Dhabi as well as Oman. Under the Treaty of Jeddah of 1974, Saudi Arabia recognised claims of Abu Dhabi and Oman to the oasis. In return, Abu Dhabi agreed to grant Saudi Arabia a land corridor to the Gulf at Khawr al Udayd and the oil from a disputed oil field. For details see "The UAE and Oman: Opportunities and Challenges in the Twenty-first Century", The Free Library, available at http://www.thefreelibrary.com/The+UAE+and+Oman%3A+opportunities+and+challenges+in+the+twenty-first...-a091660183.
14. Sam Sasan Shoamanesh, "A New Security Order for the Middle East", *Global Brief*, October 4, 2012, at http://globalbrief.ca/blog/2012/10/04/a-new-security-order-for-the-middle-east/
15. Robert E. Hunter, "Building Security in the Persian Gulf", National Security Research Division, RAND, 2010, at http://www.rand.org/content/dam/rand/pubs/monographs/2010/RAND_MG944.pdf.
16. Ibid.
17. Rajeev Agarwal and Prasanta Kumar Pradhan, "US Pivot to the Asia-Pacific: Impact and

Implications for West Asia" in S.D. Muni and Vivek Chadha (eds.) *Asian Strategic Review 2014: US Pivot and Asian Security*, Pentagon Press and IDSA, New Delhi, 2014, pp. 85-104.

18. Kayhan Barzegar and Mohammad Reza Agharebparast, n. 2, pp. 7-28.
19. Andrew Rathmell, Theodore Karasik, and David Gompert, "A New Persian Gulf Security System", n. 4.
20. Rouzbeh Parsi, "The elusive project of common security in the Persian Gulf, Visions of Gulf Security", The Project on Middle East Political Science (POMEPS), Institute for Middle East Studies, George Washington University, March 24, 2014, p. 14, at http://pomeps.org/2014/03/24/the-elusive-project-of-common-security-in-the-persian-gulf/.
21. Robert E. Hunter, n. 15, p. 93.
22. Richard L. Russel, "The Persian Gulf's Collective Security Mirage", *Middle East Policy*, 12 (4) December 2005, pp. 77-88.
23. "Saudi Arabia calls for 'strong and solid' Gulf union", *Al Arabiya News*, at http://english.alarabiya.net/articles/2012/12/24/256782.html.
24. "Oman opposes Gulf union", *Arab News*, December 8, 2013, at http://www.arabnews.com/news/488956.
25. "Gulf union is inevitable: Saudi Prince Turki Al Faisal", *Gulf News*, December 8, 2013, at http://gulfnews.com/news/gulf/oman/gulf-union-is-inevitable-saudi-prince turki-al-faisal-1.1264725.
26. "UAE, Saudi Arabia and Bahrain recall their ambassadors from Qatar", *Gulf News*, March 5, 2014, at http://gulfnews.com/news/gulf/uae/government/uae-saudi-arabia-and-bahrain-recall-their-ambassadors-from-qatar-1.1299586.
27. "Whither GCC-US relations?", *Arab News*, March 29, 2013, at http://www.arabnews.com/news/446395.
28. "US looks to allies to secure Arabian Gulf", *The National*, April 24, 2013, at http://www.thenational.ae/news/uae-news/us-looks-to-allies-to-secure-arabian-gulf.

# PART III

## External Interventions in West Asia

# 10

# A Love-Hate Relationship: External Interventions and the Middle East

*P. R. Kumaraswamy*

The Middle East has been struggling to identify, mitigate and resolve most of its core problems without external influence, interference and intervention since the demise of the Ottoman Empire a century ago. It does hold outside powers, especially the US, responsible, to a great extent, for the intensification and non-resolution of most of its problems. Issues such as democratisation, minority rights, extremism, hegemonic ambitions of regional powers, inter-state tensions, sectarianism as well as the Arab-Israeli conflict have been intrinsically linked to the active involvement of external powers. The US, though, not alone in having an interest and involvement in the region, is more prominent and widely commented upon. The perceived decline of its influence, especially in the Middle East, has not diminished it as the only power that has the political will and military capability to influence and affect regional developments. The periodic criticism of the US and growing anti-American sentiments have also not resulted in other countries or groups of countries stepping up to the plate to shoulder the myriad problems facing the region.

In order to understand this love-hate relationship between the Middle East and external powers, it is essential to identify the external powers, their interests and involvement. A proper understanding is vital for any Indian desire to be pro-active in the Middle East.

## Defining External Powers

During the Cold War, the USSR and its allies in the Third World called for the 'removal' of extra-regional powers. The same demand is now made by countries, which seek regional domination and hegemony. Seen in the context of the Middle East, it is not easy to define 'external powers'. Former colonial powers who played a decisive role in defining and shaping the post-Ottoman Middle East, namely Britain and France, are obvious candidates but their regional influence is residual, sporadic and confined to pockets. France enjoys some say in events in Lebanon and the North African states of Tunisia, Algeria and Morocco while a limited British role is noticeable in Oman, the UAE and, to a lesser extent, Bahrain where it has to compete with the more powerful and resourceful United States. The election of Vladimir Putin marked Moscow's re-entry into the Middle East, most palpably in Syria. It is trying to re-establish a foothold in its erstwhile allies such as Iraq and Yemen while Egypt, under Abdel Fattah El Sisi, appears equally attractive.

There are also new players like China. After staying aloof towards much of the Middle East for decades, it has off late been viewing regional tensions as an opportunity to establish its presence and have a say. Taking cue from the actions of Washington and Moscow, in 2002 Beijing named its first Envoy to the Middle East, in a bid to engage with key regional powers. At another level, the European Union has been seeking to resolve some thorny issues. And if the North Atlantic Treaty Organisation (NATO) was instrumental in enforcing the UN-mandated no-fly zone towards engineering a regime change in Libya, the nuclear dialogue with Iran is spearheaded by Britain, France and Germany, within the P5+1 format.[1] There are still some within the region who view Israel as an external player due to its non-Arab and non-Islamic character. Ideologies in some countries, including India, continue to see Zionism as an extension of colonialism and imperialism.

However, a general consensus exists regarding the US. It is seen by most countries and observers as 'external' to the Middle East. This perception prevails despite its prolonged engagement with the region and its strong military presence in the Persian Gulf. The Fifth Fleet is headquartered in Manama and the US has naval facilities, bases, weapon storage facilities and other forms of military assets in all the Gulf Cooperation Council (GCC) countries including Saudi Arabia.[2] The American presence in the wider Middle East includes a decade-long presence in Iraq and Afghanistan, special arrangements with Kazakhstan, special political relations with Middle Eastern monarchies and military bases in Turkey. In 2001 the US forged military-security cooperation with Yemen to fight Al Qaeda. The US has also concluded free trade agreements (FTA) with Bahrain, Israel, Jordan,

Morocco and Oman and has a long-term strategic partnership with Israel as well as with Egypt and Jordan. In spite of these linkages and engagements, the US is often depicted as an 'external power'.

The definition of 'external powers' gets complicated if one looks at specific contexts. The most notable example is of the popular protests that took place in Tunisia in December 2010—protests that soon engulfed other Arab countries and came to be called the Arab Spring. The Arab yearning for change and good governance offered immense opportunities to Iran and Turkey to intervene in Arab affairs. These two non-Arab states were quick to present themselves as a possible model for the Arab Spring. In their estimation, Islam offered a solution to beleaguered Arab countries whose secular rulers or monarchs could not provide an alternative that was acceptable to the wider public. After the fall of Egyptian President Hosni Mubarak on February 11, 2011, Supreme Leader Ayatollah Khamenei termed developments in the Arab world as an 'Islamic awakening'. In the following month during a speech on Nowroz, a festival marking the Persian New Year, he declared that the Islamic Republic "supports all popular movements which are under the slogan of Islam and (are seeking) freedom."[3] In a similar vein, the then Turkish Prime Minister, and later President, Recep Tayyip Erdogan advocated that his Islamist Justice and Development Party (AKP) presented a perfect model to the Arab unrest and a solution to the Islam-democracy dilemma. In September 2011 while touring Egypt, Libya and Tunisia, the countries most affected by the Arab Spring he stated: "Tunisia will prove to the world that Islam and democracy can co-exist. Turkey with its predominantly Muslim population has achieved it."[4]

Subsequent events proved Khamenei and Erdogan incorrect and overambitious. Both Iran and Turkey are external to the Arab world and their historical differences and conflicts with the Arabs could not be glossed over. Emulating Iran and Turkey as possible political models would not be easy for the Arabs even in their desperate and hopeless moments. When it comes to the Islamic Republic, the Arabs would have to look at the Shia dimension. In their enthusiasm to project their success, the Iranian leaders had overlooked not only the Arab-Persian schism but also Shia-Sunni differences that are intensifying.

If one expands the definition of 'external powers' to include Arab actors, then the picture gets more intriguing. The role of the GCC countries, especially Qatar and UAE, was critical for the UNSC Resolution 1973 that paved way for a regime change in Libya.[5] But Doha and Riyadh found themselves in opposite camps in the post-Mubarak Egyptian transition that contributed to the July 2013 military coup led by the then army chief and later President Abdel Fattah El Sisi.[6] Popular protests transformed the Kingdom of Bahrain into an intense political tussle between Saudi Arabia and Iran, with the former rallying behind the beleaguered Al Khalifa while the latter backed the Shia-dominated opposition. The active intervention of external powers and their military support to various groups contributed to the intensification of the Syrian crisis. The willingness of Qatar, Saudi Arabia and Turkey to actively support the Syrian opposition was a contributing factor to the Syrian civil war. At the same time, President Bashar Al Assad's continued hold on power was primarily due to the political and military support he managed to secure from Moscow. The exercise of veto by Russia and China prevented the UNSC from taking any effective measures to bring about a political solution to the Syrian crisis.[7] Indeed, in Bahrain and Syria, external powers have supported the regimes and the opposition and, in the process, prolonged the crises and human suffering.

The external flavour is also palpable in the ongoing Israeli-Palestinian conflict. For long, diplomatic moves aimed at resolving the conflict have been dominated by the US. Despite the occasional role played by countries like Norway (Oslo Process) and Egypt (temporary lull during Al Aqsa Intifada), since the 1950s the US has been the most dominant player in Arab-Israeli peace-making efforts. While every instance of its involvement may not have always yielded success, all successfully concluded peace agreements have had a strong American hand.[8] This was facilitated partly by the marginalisation of the USSR during the Cold War era, and by breaking of relations with Israel in the wake of the June 1967 war, Moscow formally disengaged from the Arab-Israeli conflict. This changed in October 1991 on the eve of the Madrid conference when Moscow restored its diplomatic relations with Israel. The American role was so predominant that even the UN was prepared to play second fiddle, agreeing to be a part of the US-dominated Middle East Quartet set up in 2002.

Following their peace agreements with Israel, Egypt and Jordan have also played significant roles in minimising Israeli-Palestinian tensions. Under Mubarak, Egypt has been a major point of contact for Israel vis-à-vis Palestinian groups, especially Hamas.[9] As mentioned earlier, the 2014 Gaza crisis witnessed the emergence of Qatar as a new player in the Israeli-Palestinian conflict.

Hence, at least in the Middle East, the term "external power" cannot be defined solely by geographical proximity as it is a political construct, one that is context specific. It can be interpreted differently by different players. The Bahraini rulers view Iranian support for the opposition as external intervention but not the UAE's involvement as they benefit from the politico-military support offered by Riyadh. Assad and his supporters do not view Russia as 'external' and also do not hesitate to vilify the role played by Turkey and Gulf states in the Syrian crisis.

## Key Contributions

Human relations are neither simple nor easy. Harmony and acrimony are an integral part of routine interactions. If harmony is the dominant mood, relations endure, flourish and strengthen, and individuals become dependable to one another. If acrimony is dominant, tension and animosity set in, conflicts emerge and eventually individuals part ways. The same holds true for engagements between societies, states and regions. Engagements between the Middle East and various external powers have followed a complex trajectory; some of them have been fulfilling and have contributed to progress while others have ended in misery, conflict and divisions.

The post-Ottoman Middle East is largely an imperial construct. Territorial and boundary-related fracas that turned into ethnic conflicts were the result of colonial cartography. Some of these states lacked historical roots or geographic logic. Some ethnic groups (Kurds) were dispersed into different states (Iran, Iraq, Syria and Turkey) or different groups were placed under one political arrangement (Lebanon) thereby sowing the seeds of tension and conflict. The disintegration of the four-century-old Ottoman Empire as well as the emergence of distinct ethno-nationalisms (Jewish and Kurdish) were partly consequences of the imperial intervention in the Middle East. The fragility of the nation-building process was exposed by the inability of all the post-Ottoman states, including Turkey, to evolve an inclusive national identity.[10]

If these were not enough, during the Cold War the region faced another problem: near virtual division as client states of either of the super powers. The monarchies sided with the US, republican regimes embraced the USSR and the region became the battleground for great power rivalry. Not to be left behind, under Mao Tse-tung, China sought influence by providing political and minimal arms support to various radical regimes and groups.[11] Wilting under American pressure, Israel was forced to abandon its much nuanced policy of non-identification during the Korean War and became a staunch American ally. Thus, the region's problems were intensified and complicated by the Euro-centric Cold War.

At the same time, devoid of blinkers and ideological bias, one must recognise the positive contributions of the external interventions. Outside powers, especially the former colonial and imperial powers immensely contributed to the political, economic and even social advancement of the Middle East. It is essential to remember that until the discovery of oil and large-scale commercial production, Al Saud relied upon the annual subsidy of £5,000 provided by Britain to run the fledging state. The modernisation of the region, especially in the realm of administration, education, military and above all economic development was largely due to constant external interference intervention. One could broadly identify two key issues with regard to which external powers played a significant and positive role in the Middle East.

One, the most significant impact of external powers has been in the political realm: on the emergence of territorial nationalism. For centuries, the region functioned under the universalising concept of community of believers or *ummah* that does not recognise differentiated territorial borders or units. Arab differences with the Turks and Persians existed at the ethnic level and were managed through co-option and coercion. With the exception of Egypt, Syria, and Turkey and to a lesser extent Saudi Arabia, most states of modern Middle East owe their conception, design and, in some cases, even materialisation to the West. The emergence of a common territorial identity beyond the overarching *ummah* was undoubtedly due to the influence of European intervention and the idea of nationalism. The prevalence of the loosely-defined and, to some extent, short-lived pan-Arabism was different from ongoing European moves towards a common identity; for the latter was the culmination of distinct territorial nationalism of various European countries. However, in the case of the former, it was a substitute for the lack of well-defined territory-based nationalism of individual Arab countries, which did not survive and hence paved the way for territorial nationalisms of the pre-EU Europe.

Two, external powers were largely instrumental in bringing about the recognition and, in some cases, the emergence of the ethnic, religious and national minorities in the Middle East. The emergence of Jewish nationalism and the formation of Israel was the most visible manifestation of this external intervention. But there were other lesser appreciated gains for the non-Muslim minorities. It was only due to European pressures and intervention that the Ottoman Empire came up with the *millet* system that provided limited communal autonomy to Jews and Christians.[12] The abolition of the millennium-old *dhimmi* arrangement by Sultan Abdulmecid in 1856 was the result of imperial pressures and Egypt did the same in 1857. Pressure exerted by external powers on behalf of the minorities did not end with the disintegration of the Ottoman Empire or the formation of modern states. Gradual improvements in the conditions of Kurds in Turkey[13], Copts in Egypt[14] and the Shias in Saudi Arabia[15] are largely because of external pressures and interventions. The same can be said about international support for the political rights of the Palestinians. And until the oil crisis of 1973, the Palestinian issue primarily remained a 'refugee' question.[16]

If one expands the 'external powers' to include regional powers that are playing an active role in various conflicts, the list grows. Since the end of the Second World War regional powers have been playing positive and negative roles in various regional developments. The Arab support was pivotal for international recognition of Palestinian rights and at various times Egypt, Syria, Saudi Arabia and Jordan were instrumental in the wider recognition of the Palestinian cause. At the same time, these countries also did not hesitate in exploiting the Palestine question to further their own individual national interests or to contribute to internal schisms by supporting rival Palestinian factions. External intervention also contributed to the civil wars in Yemen (1962-70), Lebanon (1975-89) and the ongoing violence in Bahrain, Syria and Yemen in the wake of the Arab Spring.

The 2014 Gaza crisis, more commonly designated as Operation Protective Edge by Israel, saw the emergence of Qatar as a new player in the Arab-Israeli conflict. After deposing his father in a bloodless coup, Emir Hamad bin Khalifa Al Thani used Qatar's financial clout (brought about by its oil and gas exports) to seek a larger diplomatic role in various conflicts in the region.[17] His primary efforts were to engage with rival factions in conflicts towards bringing about a political settlement and accommodation. Some of his efforts have been temporarily successful. Qatari efforts in Lebanon, Sudan and Palestine were seen as supplanting the unsuccessful Saudi initiatives.[18] These moves are signs of a Qatari desire to play an active role, independent of Riyadh. As part of its diplomatic outreach, Qatar has been maintaining political and diplomatic contact with Israel since the days of the Oslo accords.[19] The Israeli mission in Doha was officially closed in 2000 in the wake of the Al Aqsa Intifada and the prevailing Arab political boycott policy but political engagements were maintained. Indeed, Doha had hosted the external leadership of Hamas since November 1999 for over a decade after King Abdullah-II of Jordan declared the Palestinian group to be a 'foreign' organisation and closed down its offices. The Palestinian refusal to rally behind Assad following the outbreak of the Syrian uprising increased Hamas's dependence upon Doha for political and financial support.

The Gaza crisis placed Qatar in a situation where its narrow national interest overrode the larger Palestinian problem. By all accounts, Doha wanted a greater say in the Israeli-Palestinian conflict and egged on the Hamas leadership to reject and delay various peace initiatives put forth by Egypt since the conflict began in early July 2014. The terms and conditions of the cease-fire which came into being on August 26 were no different from the one President Sisi offered within the first week of hostilities. There was no progress on the principal Hamas demand of an end to the siege of Gaza. For long Egypt had been the sole Arab power that had a significant role in managing and minimising periodic upsurges of Israeli-Palestinian violence but the 2014 Gaza crisis saw the emergence of Doha as a new player. If Egyptian importance is driven also by its geographic proximity to Israel and Palestine, the Qatari importance lies in its newly acquired financial and hence diplomatic clout, especially vis-à-vis Hamas.

Thus, external powers, both the erstwhile colonial powers as well as powerful regional powers have made positive and negative contributions to the Middle East and in the process, have helped resolve some issues but created new ones or complicated earlier ones. However, the continuous presence of external powers in the Middle East nearly a century after the demise of the Ottoman Empire raises a fundamental question: how and why were they allowed to perpetuate their influence despite significant opposition in the region to external interference and influence? Or how did the external powers become an integral part of the political landscape of the Middle East?

## A Part of the Middle East Landscape

External powers have become an integral part of the political landscape primarily because most of the problems and challenges facing the Middle East were either too big for the countries of the region to handle on their own or were intensified or created by them. It is possible to identify four principal reasons that have contributed to external interventions.

One, most post-Ottoman states are small and suffer from acute insecurities and challenges. As a result of colonial legacies and cartography, these new states feel threatened by their neighbours and, in a number of cases, the immediate neighbours are their immediate threats. While border disputes are common the world over, a number of Middle Eastern countries are *not* recognised by their neighbours. Unlike the Africa Union, there is no regional arrangement which accepts the sovereign existence of the post-Ottoman Empire. The Arab League provides for a border dispute settlement mechanism but it does not demand an unequivocal recognition of independence of member states. Indeed, Arab countries can and have become members of the League even while questioning the very existence of others. The Arab-Islamic non-recognition of Israel as a sovereign country is smaller than the inter-Arab non-recognition. As and when political conditions demand, various Arab countries have questioned and even denied the existence of their neighbours. Such claims relied on history or historic injustices and the existence of small states has to be ensured by external interventions, often accompanied by military intervention.

The non-realisation of the Palestinian state as mandated by the UN partition plan was primarily due to the territorial ambitions of King Abdullah of Jordan and his annexation of the West Bank following the Arab-Israeli war of 1948. On the eve of the British withdrawal from the east of Suez Canal, the Shah of Iran claimed Bahrain and these claims have resurfaced in recent years. Various Iranian leaders identified with the Islamic republic have been reiterating these historic claims.[20] Interestingly, these noises come against the backdrop of continued

Iranian occupation of the three Emirati islands that were occupied by Iran in 1971.[21] In September 1970 the survival of the Hashemite Kingdom was threatened not only by the Palestinian *fedayeen* inside the country but also by the Syrian military. One cannot ignore the Turkish occupation of Northern Cyprus since 1974 and or the Moroccan control of West Sahara since 1976.[22]

President Saddam Hussain's reiteration of Kuwait being the 19th province of Iraq led to UN-sanctioned Gulf War and Operation Desert Storm in 1990-91.[23] For long Syria was reluctant to recognise Lebanon as a sovereign entity. Reiterating its opposition to the colonial origin of the Maronite-dominated state, Syrian leaders treated Lebanon as a part of the historic Bilad Al Sham. Indeed, since the outbreak of the civil war, Damascus has had a massive military presence in Lebanon and even the Taif Accord of 1989, which ended the sectarian violence, was unable to induce Syria's withdrawal. The Syrian envoy in Beirut was called 'governor' not ambassador. It was only due to persistent international pressures, incidentally led by the former colonial power France, that diplomatic relations were established in August 2008, more than six decades after Lebanon became independent.[24]

Their non-recognition or qualified recognition by their immediate neighbours forced smaller countries to seek external support and security guarantees to ensure their existence. And so it has been external powers, most often the US, that have ensured the existence of smaller Arab states. Hence, one cannot discuss external interventions without addressing the root cause of the immediate threats facing the smaller countries.

Two, security threats also emanate from periodic interventions by bigger neighbours, regional powers or hegemons. During the heyday of his popularity, President Gamal Abdul Nasser viewed Arab monarchs as stooges of western imperialism and sought to revolutionise the Arab world by supporting and propping up various anti-regime elements. This strategy contributed to military coups in Iraq (1958), Yemen (1962) and Libya (1969), the Ba'athist takeover of Syria in 1963 and political instability in Jordan. His desire to overthrow the Saudi monarchy led to a prolonged civil war in Yemen (1962-70). For their part, the monarchies responded by accusing Nasser of proclaiming to 'liberate' Palestine while seeking Egyptian security through the UN peacekeeping forces deployed along its border with Israel border. This verbal dual eventually led to the June war that proved disastrous for the Arabs. Likewise, at one time or another some countries provided political, financial or military support to various dissenting groups or allowed their territories to be used against their political adversaries. The support of the oil-rich Arab countries prolonged the Iran-Iraq war (1980-88) and is now repeated in Syria, where opposition groups receive political, financial and military support from the GCC countries and Turkey. The Russian support, thus, is the key to the survival of the Assad regime in Damascus. Above all, a few states had territorial designs and sought to covet parts of their neighbours. These include Egypt vis-à-vis Sudan and Libya vis-à-vis Chad.

Three, the asymmetry of the Israeli-Palestinian conflict necessitates external intervention. The ability of the Palestinians to reach a fair and honourable settlement rests squarely on them receiving or getting external support. Regional powers proved to be ineffective and have worked at cross purposes, thus making external intervention inevitable. While the Oslo model was primarily aimed at limiting the role of external players, the assassination of Prime Minister Yitzhak Rabin and subsequent stalling of the Oslo process exposed the flipside of the asymmetry. Lacking corresponding political, diplomatic, economic or strategic leverages, the Palestinians were left with violence as their only means to communicate not only their frustrations but also their demands vis-à-vis Israel. For a host of reasons, the Israeli and the Palestinian leaderships are unable to cross the Rubicon and reach an agreement. However, at the same time, they are unable to prevent the periodic cycle of violence and bloodshed. The odds of rekindling the Oslo spirit looks slim if not impossible and, at least in the short and medium terms, external intervention appears inevitable if one were to resolve the Israeli-Palestinian conflict.

Four, it is essential to recognise that opposition to external interventions come from countries that are regional hegemons or perceived to have hegemonic designs. Tehran's insistence on calling the water body between the Arabian Peninsula and Iran as Persian Gulf, is rooted in history. It is also the term recognised by the United Nations.[25] At the same time, this demand is accompanied by actions and statements that indicate that Iran is seeking to "Persianise" the Gulf as the nomenclature does not mean Iranian ownership. In recent years, Iranian leaders have been expressing their opposition to external intervention, especially in the Persian Gulf region.[26] In their view, outside 'meddling' contributes to regional instability and prolongs the non-resolution of various conflicts. This approach is pronounced in the Iranian opposition to American military presence in the region.[27]

In recent years, Iran is blamed for some Arab countries seeking external help in mitigating perceived threats from Tehran. Bahrain, for example, sees Iran as part of the problem and this assessment led to Manama being tied too closely with Saudi Arabia. The nuclear controversy heightened the security concerns of Iran's Arab neighbours and the eagerness with which P5+1 concluded the November 2013 Geneva interim agreement without accommodating Arab concerns which exasperated their concerns.[28] While the US has larger non-proliferation concerns and other interests, a nuclear Iran poses severe security and even existential threats to its Arab neighbours.[29]

If Arab concerns over the Iranian nuclear program, ongoing popular protests in various countries, civil wars in Syria and Yemen and the prolonged, violent Arab-Israeli conflict are insufficient, the region has been confronted by a new menace in the form of the Islamic State of Iraq and Syria (ISIS) or Islamic Caliphate.

## A New Actor Called Islamic Caliphate

Though similar moves are declared in different parts of the world including Somalia (Al-Shabab, 2006), Nigeria (Boko Haram, 2002) and Mali (Ansar Dine, 2012), the Middle East remains the heartland of the Islamic Caliphate.[30] The ongoing Syrian crisis and Shia-Sunni violence in Iraq have proved conducive for the emergence of this new form of militant 'jihad'. The Sunni-led violence was rekindled by their marginalisation in the Alawi-dominated Syria and in the post-Saddam political set-up in Iraq. The ISIS emerged as a magnet for other militant groups such as Al Shabab in Somalia and Boko Haram in Nigeria that are disappointed with existing regimes in their respective countries. The widespread anti-Americanism in the region is an added incentive.

In examining the ISIS threat, two things are noteworthy. The brutality and intensity of religious violence in the Middle East has grown over time. The Arab defeat in the June war is widely recognised as the trigger of religious conservatism in the Middle East and this has gradually transformed into extremism, first as extremist ideas, and then as physical violence. The Soviet invasion of Afghanistan in December 1979 offered the first opportunity for the religious elements to join a *jihad* against the "infidel" communists. Since the birth of the *Mujahideen* in Afghanistan, religious extremism has become more intense, violent and brutal. It first manifested as Taliban and the destruction of the 6$^{th}$ century Bamiyan Buddha statues in March 2001 and was followed by the Al Qaeda and the September 11 terror attacks that shook not just the US but also the international community.

Countries which directly or indirectly contributed to the emergence of the Frankenstein monster called religious extremism and Mujahideen, Taliban and Al Qaeda, have not hesitated to repeat their mistakes when popular protests broke out in Syria in March 2011. Saudi Arabia, Qatar and, to a lesser extent, the UAE joined hands with an amorphous anti-Assad coalition and provided political, financial and military support.[31] The emergence of Al Nusra in Syria and its brutal attack on civilian populations did not inhibit the oil-rich Arab countries from supporting the Salafi group. The irony is exemplified by the Al Saud. At one level, the monarchy has been fighting religious extremism and terrorism within the country in the wake of the Khobar bombing of June 1996. Following the ouster of President Hosni Mubarak, Riyadh identified the Muslim Brotherhood in Egypt as a terrorist organisation[32] and was quick to back the Sisi-led coup against President Mohammed Morsi in July 2013. Simultaneously, Riyadh has been at the forefront when it comes to providing financial and military support to various anti-Assad forces in Syria. Likewise, Qatar was instrumental in the suspension of Syrian membership from the Arab League in November 2011 and this was followed by the Syrian National Council taking the Syrian seat in the League.[33] Open support of the Gulf States to anti-Assad forces eventually culminated in the surfacing of the ISIS. In short, from the ideological conservatism of the late 1960s, religious extremism in the Middle East graduated into Mujahideen, Taliban, Al Qaeda, Salafi, Jihadist and culminated as ISIS.

Secondly, the origin of this process is equally interesting. Many observers both within the region and elsewhere have blamed the West, especially the US for supporting various extremist groups in the past due to narrow political considerations. Since the time of President Ronald Reagan various American leaders have hailed religious extremists in the Middle East as 'democrats' 'freedom fighters', 'liberators' and viewed them as engines of social change and democratisation in the Middle East. History has proved such naivety horribly wrong. The ill-fated US-led invasion of Iraq and the resultant sectarian violence led to Sunni anger and violence in Iraq. If one excludes the Hezbollah in Lebanon, much of the extremist violence in the Middle East for over three decades was perpetuated by Sunni groups such as Hamas, Islamic Jihad, Al Qaeda, Muslim Brotherhood and now ISIS. The emergence of various Salafi groups supported or sponsored by the Gulf Arab States was another contributing factor. Moreover, in line with conspiracy theories, some scholars have blamed Israel for the ISIS phenomenon.[34]

Important as they are, the root cause of ISIS to be found elsewhere is religious extremism: a narrow, extremist, xenophobic and intolerant interpretation of Islam which is responsible for the birth of ISIS. The fighters seeking to re-establish the Caliphate explain and justify their actions and brutalities in the name of Islam. Like its extremist predecessors, the ISIS sees itself as the new jihadi force working for the total rejection and annihilation of the other—both religious and political opponents—a mission it sees as both legitimate and Islam-ordained. Subjugation and enslavement of women, especially non-Muslim women, forced conversion of children and orphans and the brutal killing of non-Muslim minorities and of Muslims whose faith and adherence it does not approve off, have become the hallmarks of the ISIS campaign.[35] As with suicide terrorism, ISIS has managed to justify all its brutality in the name of Islam. If these were not sufficient, volunteers from a number of non-Arab countries, especially from the West have joined the ISIS and until mid-2014 there were as many as 2,500 Western nationals, mostly of Islamic faith, who were fighting with the ISIS.[36]

The campaign of hatred has attracted supporters and volunteers from a number of countries in the Middle East and beyond. Even those who live in and are exposed to liberal democratic values, freedom and political space are attracted to xenophobic ideas. Some of those who beheaded Western hostages ironically came from the West which indicates that a liberal environment is not an impediment to an extremist worldview. Volunteers from Australia, Britain, Canada, France and other Western countries are fighting on the side of ISIS. The desire of Muslim girls from the West to marry ISIS fighters has added romance and glamour to the ISIS campaign.[37]

Hence, if one takes the problem of ISIS to its roots, the Wahhabi interpretation of Islam has to bear a major responsibility. Its conservative worldview excludes even Shias from the purview of the faithful and over the years various senior Ulemas have vilified and denied the Islamic credentials of the Shias.[38] Social reforms initiated by King Abdullah during his reign marked some improvements and reduced Saudi intolerance towards the other, both Muslims and non-Muslims alike. The extremist interpretation of Islam, however, is not the monopoly of Wahhabis' but can be traced to thinkers like Sayyid Qutb who professed similar views towards non-Muslims.[39]

As discussed earlier, even in the best of times the Middle East has been unable to handle most of its problems and it will not be able to fight against extremism on its own. It needs external understanding, support and cooperation. The response of the international community has to be two-pronged. The urgent approach is the military response aimed at diminishing the fighting capabilities of the ISIS, reducing areas under its control and alleviating the existential problems faced by minority populations such as Kurds, Yezidis, women and children. The unanimous UNSC Resolution 2170 adopted on August 15, 2014 enabled the US to forge a coalition of the willing to launch a military offensive against ISIS. Political differences over Syria partly inhibited Russia and China from joining the military offensive. They argued that external intervention in Syria would lead to disastrous consequences and contribute to the strengthening of Al Qaeda-linked fighters in Syria who already received support from Arab Gulf countries.

However, a long-term response against ISIS would have to be political and cultural. Extremist violence is not the monopoly of Islam and similar trends can be noticed in groups that claim to practice various other religions including Christianity, Judaism, Hinduism, Buddhism and Sikhism. It is essential to remember that the most brutal killings in the 20th century were perpetuated not by religious extremism but by secular and non-religious fundamentalists. More people were killed in Hitler's Holocaust, Stalinist putsch, Mao's Cultural Revolution and Pol Pot brutality than in any other religious extremist violence. Any meaningful response has to be directed against extremism, both religious and secular.

On its own the Middle East cannot manage, let alone lead, the military-cum-political confrontation with ISIS. Even in the best of times, the region has not managed most of its challenges without external help or intervention and it would require external understanding, support and cooperation to fight ISIS. This in practice would mean a greater role for the US in the region's affairs and despite the love-hate relationship between the two, the Middle East would continue to need the involvement of the US in confronting ISIS.

However, continued American activism in the Middle East will not be without its share of problems. There is general agreement that the economic power of the US is on decline and hence it's political influence. This is more apparent in the Middle East where the US has not been able to project an effective policy and its political choices on issues such as the Arab Spring, the Iranian nuclear controversy, the Syrian crisis or the Arab-Israeli conflict have raised more questions than answers. None of the Middle East countries are even relatively satisfied with President Barack Obama and the Obama-Netanyahu personal tension has precluded any progress on the Israeli-Palestinian front. Even after its withdrawal the US has been counting the economic and strategic costs of its ill-fated invasion of Iraq and Afghanistan. Both the Arab protesters and besieged rulers are unhappy with Washington's approach towards the Arab Spring. There are voices growing louder within the US, calling for lesser involvement in, if not disengagement from, the Middle East. Prolonged anti-Americanism has dampened Washington's desire to play a dominant role. The emergence of Shale gas as a possible alternative energy source has markedly diminished the importance of the Persian Gulf in American energy security calculations. The pivot to Asia, as outlined by President Obama in 2009, the Asia-Pacific region appears more attractive and less troublesome than the Middle East.[40]

At the same time, despite criticisms there are no alternatives on the horizon. Individually or collectively, countries that do not favour or are critical of American preponderance in the Middle East, are unable to provide a viable leadership, strategy or alternative. As the world recognised following the ISIS crisis, countries of the Middle East continue to look to the US for leadership and resources to confront the menace. Beyond criticisms and disapprovals, Russia and China are not in a position to shoulder a leadership role. Thus, as the Middle East quagmire continues, the US is less influential and less effective but would not be able to relinquish its primacy. In other words, the Middle East is confronted with a stark reality: anti-Americanism without an alternative option to resolve its problems.

## Conclusion

Seen from India, intervening in the Middle East presents mixed prospects. The mixture of fortunes and curses should be a reminder for India if it wishes to seek any role in the Middle East. While the proponents of such a role might consider the region to be an extended Indian neighbourhood, New Delhi should be more receptive to local perceptions and apprehensions vis-à-vis external players. At one level, an active role in the region would demand India taking political sides in various conflicts that plague the Middle East. The Arab-Israeli conflict is just one of the many issues it would have to take sides on. At the same time, taking sides or favouring one of the parties would undermine its ability to influence the outcome, especially when a host of developments have widened the Arab-Persian and Shia-Sunni cleavages. Unless there are explicit and unequivocal requests from all the parties to a conflict, India should resist the temptation of presenting itself as a mediator or a go-between. Any unsolicited advice would be counter-productive, if not suicidal. The region is far too important to be ignored and as the Chinese proverb goes, India would be living through interesting times, if it wished to play a role in the ever-turbulent Middle East.

### NOTES

1. Britain, France and Germany were engaged in negotiations with Iran much before the US, Russia and China. See "Timeline on Iran's Nuclear Program", *The New York Times*, at http://www.nytimes.com/interactive/2014/11/20/world/middleeast/Iran-nuclear-timeline.html?_r=0#/#time243_7265.
2. Ben Piven, "Map: US Bases Encircle Iran", *Al Jazeera*, May 1, 2012, at http://www.aljazeera.com/indepth/interactive/2012/04/2012417131242767298.html.
3. Hanif Zarrabi-Kashani, "Iran and the Arab Spring: Then and Now", *Muftah*, March 7, 2014, at http://muftah.org/iran-arab-spring-now/#.VJZm0sAKA.
4. "Erdoðan offers 'Arab Spring' Neo-Laicism", *Hurriet Daily News*, September 15, 2011, at http://www.hurriyetdailynews.com/default.aspx?pageid=438&n=erdogan-offers-8216arab-spring8217-neo-laicism-2011-09-15.
5. Ben Barry, "Libya's Lessons", *Survival*, 53 (5), October-November 2011, pp. 5-14.
6. Abigail Hauslohner, "Rift Deepens Between Qatar and its Powerful Arab Neighbours", *The Washington Post*, March 8, 2014, at http://www.washingtonpost.com/world/middle_east/gulf-divisions-over-governance/2014/03/08/bee0a340-a6e6-11e3-b865-38b254d92063_story.html.
7. Neil Mac Farquhar and Anthony Shadid, "Russia and China Block U.N. Action on Crisis in Syria", *The New York Times*, February 4, 2012, at http://www.nytimes.com/2012/02/05/world/middleeast/syria-homs-death-toll-said-to-rise.html?pagewanted=all.
8. Laura Zittrain Eisenberg and Neil Kaplan, *Negotiating Arab-Israeli Peace: Patterns, Problems,*

*Possibilities*, Indiana University Press, Bloomington, 1998; and William B. Quandt, *Peace Process: American Diplomacy and the Arab-Israeli Conflict since 1967*, University of California Press, Berkeley and Los Angeles, 2005.

9. Khaled Elgindy, "Egypt, Israel, Palestine: Prospect for Peace after the Arab Spring", *The Cairo Review of Global Affairs*, June 2012, at http://www.aucegypt.edu/GAPP/CairoReview/Lists/Articles/Attachments/221/CR6-Elgindy.pdf.
10. P.R. Kumaraswamy, "Who am I? Identity crisis in the Middle East", *Middle East Review of International Affairs* (MERIA), 10 (1), March 2006, pp.66-76, at http://www.gloria-center.org/2006/03/kumaraswamy-2006-03-05/.
11. Yitzhak Shichor, *The Middle East in China's Foreign Policy, 1949-1977*, Cambridge University Press, Cambridge, 2008.
12. Benjamin Thomas White, "*The Emergence of Minorities in the Middle East: The Politics of Community in French Mandate Syria*", Edinburg University Press, Edinburg, 2011.
13. Ýnan Rüma and Dilaver Arýkan Açar, "External Pressure and Turkish Discourse on 'Kurdish/ Democratic Initiative", *The Turkish Yearbook of International Relations*, 40, 2009, at http:/ /dergiler.ankara.edu.tr/dergiler/44/1566/17005.pdf.
14. Patrick Elyas, *No Longer Dhimmis: How European Intervention in the Nineteenth and Early Twentieth Centuries Empowered Copts in Egypt*, Huntsman Program Honours Senior Thesis, University of Pennsylvania, 2012.
15. International Crisis Group, "The Shiite Question in Saudi Arabia", Middle East Report No. 45, September 19, 2005, at http://www.crisisgroup.org/~/media/files/middle%20east %20north%20africa/iran%20gulf/saudi%20arabia/the%20shiite%20question%20 in%20 saudi%20arabia.pdf.
16. UNSC Resolution 242 adopted unanimously on November 22, 1967 called for "a just settlement of the refugee problem".
17. Lina Khatib, "Qatar's Foreign Policy: The Limits of Pragmatism", *International Affairs*, 89 (2), 2013, pp. 417-431.
18. Ibid.
19. Uzi Rabi, "Qatar's Relations with Israel: Challenging Arab and Gulf Norms", *Middle East Journal*, 63 (3), 2009, pp. 443–59.
20. "Bahrain Rejects Iran's 'Motherhood' Claims", *Al Arabiya*, July 12, 2007, at http:// www.alarabiya.net/articles/2007/07/12/36493.html; and, "Bahrain Rejects Iran Comments on Sovereignty", *Today's Zaman*, February 23, 2009, at http://www.todayszaman.com/ world_bahrain-rejects-iran-comments-on-sovereignty_167742.html.
21. D. Zwaagstra, "Unresolved Territorial Disputes: The Tunbs and Abu Musa in the Gulf", *Peace Palace Library*, October 4, 2013, at http://www.peacepalacelibrary.nl/2013/10/ unresolved-territorial-disputes-the-tunbs-and-abu-musa-in-the-gulf/.
22. Yahia H. Zoubir and Karima Benabdallah-Gambier, "Western Sahara Deadlock", *Middle East Report*, 33, 2003, at http://www.merip.org/mer/mer227/western-saharan-deadlock; George Kaloudis, "Cyprus: The Enduring Conflict", *International Journal on World Peace*, 16 (1), March 1999, pp. 3-18.
23. For detail reading on Iraqi claims on Kuwait see, Majid Khadduri and Edmund Ghareeb, *War in the Gulf 1990-91: The Iraq-Kuwait Conflict and its Implications*, Oxford University Press, New York, 1997.
24. Ian Black, "Syria and Lebanon to Establish Diplomatic Relations", *The Guardian*, October 14, 2008, at http://www.theguardian.com/world/2008/oct/14/syria-lebanon.
25. United Nations Group of Experts on Geographical Names, "Historical, Geographical and Legal Validity of the Name: Persian Gulf", *Working Paper No. 61*, Twenty-third Session,

Vienna, March 28–April 4, 2006, https://unstats.un.org/unsd/geoinfo/UNGEGN/docs/23-gegn/wp/gegn23wp61.pdf.

26. Kayhan Barzegar, "Balance of Power in the Persian Gulf: An Iranian View", *Middle East Policy Council*, 17 (3), 2010, at http://www.mepc.org/journal/middle-east-policy-archives/balance-power-persian-gulf-iranian-view?print.
27. Ibid.
28. Damien McElroy, David Blair and Peter Foster, "Iran Nuclear Deal Changes Middle East Alliances as Saudi Arabia Rebels against US", *The Telegraph*, November 25, 2013, at http://www.telegraph.co.uk/news/worldnews/middleeast/iran/10474143/Iran-nuclear-deal-changes-Middle-East-alliances-as-Saudi-Arabia-rebels-against-US.html.
29. Ibid.
30. For further reading on radical Islamists in Africa see Hans Krech, "The Growing Influence of Al-Qaeda on the African Continent", *Africa Spectrum*, 46 (2), 2011, pp. 125-137; Philipp Sander, "Ansar Dine: Radical Islamists in Northern Mali", *DW*, December 18, 2014, at http://www.dw.de/ansar-dine-radical-islamists-in-northern-mali/a-18139091; and Abimbola Adesoji, "The Boko Haram Uprising and Islamic Revivalism in Nigeria", *Africa Spectrum*, 45 (2), 2010, pp. 95-108.
31. For details see Roula Khalaf and Abigail Fielding Smith, "Qatar Bankrolls Syrian Revolt with Cash and Arms", *Financial Times*, May 16 2013, at http://www.ft.com/intl/cms/s/0/86e3f28e-be3a-11e2-bb35-00144feab7de.html.
32. Mustapha Ajbaili, "Saudi: Muslim Brotherhood a Terrorist Group", *Al Arabiya*, March 7, 2014, at http://english.alarabiya.net/en/News/middle-east/2014/03/07/Saudi-Arabia-declares-Muslim-Brotherhood-terrorist-group.html.
33. "Opposition takes Syria Seat at Arab League Summit", *BBC News*, March 26, 2013, at http://www.bbc.com/news/world-middle-east-21936731.
34. "ISIS Leader Abu Bakr Al Baghdadi Trained by Israeli Mossad, NSA Documents Reveal", Global Research, July 16, 2014, at http://www.globalresearch.ca/isis-leader-abu-bakr-al-baghdadi-trained-by-israeli-mossad-nsa-documents-reveal/5391593.
35. Graeme Wood, "What ISIS Really Wants", *The Atlantic*, March 2015, at http://www.theatlantic.com/features/archive/2015/02/what-isis-really-wants/384980/?fb_ref=Default.
36. Richard Barrett, "Foreign Fighters in Syria", The Soufan Group Report, June 2014, New York, at http://soufangroup.com/wp-content/uploads/2014/06/TSG-Foreign-Fighters-in-Syria.pdf.
37. Jamie Dettmer, "The ISIS Online Campaign Luring Western Girls to Jihad", *The Daily Beast*, June 8, 2014, at http://www.thedailybeast.com/articles/2014/08/06/the-isis-online-campaign-luring-western-girls-to-jihad.html.
38. At times even moderate Sunni scholars such as Yusuf Al Qardawi have vilified the Shias, see Jeffrey Fleishman, "Egyptian Sheikh's Outburst against Shiites Roils Iran", *Los Angeles Times*, September 28, 2008, at http://articles.latimes.com/2008/sep/28/world/fg-islamic28. To understand the IS's views on Shias, see Graham E. Fuller, "Why Does ISIS Hate Shia?", *Lobelog*, December 17, 2014, at http://www.lobelog.com/why-does-isis-hate-shia/.
39. A.E. Stahl, "'Offensive Jihad' in Sayyid Qutb's Ideology", International Institute of Counter-Terrorism, *IDC Herzliya*, March 24, 2011, at http://www.ict.org.il/Article/1097/%E2%80%98Offensive%20Jihad'%20in%20Sayyid%20Qutb's%20Ideology.
40. Kurt Campbell and Brian Andrews, "Explaining the US 'Pivot' to Asia", *Chatham House*, August 2013, at http://www.chathamhouse.org/sites/files/chathamhouse/public/Research/Americas/0813pp_pivottoasia.pdf.

# 11

# External Intervention in West Asia: Regional and Global Implications

*Waiel Awwad*

The capture of Mosul city of Iraq in June 2014 and its surrounding areas has attracted the world's attention to the sudden rise of Islamic State of Iraq and the Levant (ISIL) also known as the Islamic State of Iraq and Syria (ISIS) or the Islamic State (IS). The group has grown rapidly and has extended its influence into large portions of Iraq and Syria. But its attacks on Erbil, the Kurdish dominated region of Iraq, showed the growing confidence of the organisation. US and its allies had to intervene to halt the ISIS advances and ensure the safety of almost 3,500 American marines stationed in the US consulate there and to protect US giant oil companies (Exxon Mobil and Chevron) in Iraqi Kurdistan region. The intervention also protected the minorities from being persecuted at the hands of the fanatic members of ISIS, who had carried out massive ethnic cleansing campaigns against Yazidis, Shia Turkmen, Chabaks, Christians and even Sunni Muslims. Hence, the emergence of ISIS was not a sudden phenomenon, but a well planned and executed project. In June 2014, it declared the establishment of a Caliphate in Iraq and Syria. Now its leader Abu Baqr Al Baghdadi, who claims to be the Caliph, is claiming to be the Amir of Muslims and calling upon Muslims all over the world to join hands with him and declare their loyalty to his leadership.

## Decoding ISIS

If the creation of Al Qaeda in Afghanistan by US-Saudi Arabia-Pakistan was to topple the Soviet Union as admitted by Hillary Clinton in her testimony[1], then the creation of ISIS is nothing but an old wine in a new bottle. The sudden success of ISIS in controlling large portions of Syria and Iraq in a short span of time with the help of local militant groups led many to believe that there are some powerful entities behind them. The success of this group was only in areas that were under the influence of other militant groups that were sheltered, armed and trained by the West and US. According to Edward Snowden, the ISIS was created by US (CIA), Britain (MI6) and Israel (Mossad). The release of the classified document from the American intelligence has clearly exposed the Caliph project 2020.[2]

The invasion of Afghanistan and subsequent occupation of Iraq in 2003 led to the creation of a vacuum where US ensured the ground was fertile for the growth of Islamic fundamentalism and radicalism. A Jordanian sectarian and highly violent militant named Abu Musab Al Zarqawi was appointed the leader of the Al Qaeda in Iraq (AQI). He was active in Al Anbar province, Fallujah and Al Ramadi. It was difficult for the US to bear the outcry and anger at home whenever a coffin of a US soldier was returned from the battlefield in Iraq and Afghanistan. The war was not an American one as per the US public opinion. This led to the change of the war doctrine in Pentagon and a plan for extending logistical support to local groups, and to incite sectarian violence in Iraq. The objective was that the US and its allies should achieve their goals without losing a soldier.

This ensured arms industry to flourish and anarchy spread to other countries of the region, which would ultimately lead to external intervention and changes in the regional balance. Its global impact will widen the division between the superpowers and UN Security Council members about their areas of influence. The US and the West incited wars in the region and intended to turn it into stateless, failed states and non-state actors. That is because such a situation will ultimately lead to external intervention because of the growth of sectarian fighting and an unstable new regional order. The current situation and turmoil in West Asia is nothing but a manifestation of Western policy and its intention of capturing the natural resources in the Arab world and ensuring the security of the Israeli state.

After the fall of the Ottoman Empire, the Arab world was divided into 19 small countries by Britain and France (Sykes-Picot Treaty) to retain the region under their influence. In the middle of the last century, Israel was created by US and the West to ensure that this oil rich region remains under their control. Post World War II, European countries weakened and there was a fear of spread of communism. Most of the Middle Eastern countries gained independence and it was a transformation of the Arab world from a turbulent period, similar to that of Europe in the 18th and 19th century. It was a transformation from feudal agricultural society to a modern industrial society, a struggle for realm of ideas. Leaders were installed, autocratic regimes encouraged, and opponents' supported secretly and then encouraged to take their resentment to the streets to allow the mobs to rule. These mobs comprised of the educated unemployed youth, low-wage workers, ill-treated victims, criminals and bystanders. The result is that the state collapsed and non-state actors prevailed. Such a situation leads to chaos and then invites the international community to help manage the mess, thereby legitimising military interventions.

European intervention in the Arab world was evident from encouraging coups against regimes opposed to their policies and replacing them with unpopular figures under the pretext of stopping the spread of communism and Soviet threats. Internal conflicts in the newly independent Arab countries were encouraged. The birth of a Pan Arab movement was challenged by UK, France and US, who encouraged and supported autocratic regimes, monarchies and even dictators. Heavy militarisation of the region was one of the top priorities of the West and US policies toward West Asia so that weapons were poured in to support their puppet regimes. The Eisenhower Doctrine stated that the United States is "prepared to use armed forces to assist" any Middle Eastern country "requesting assistance against armed aggression from any country controlled by international communism." This intended to keep others away from the region and to have exclusive influence over the Middle East and its oil fields by the United States, and that anyone who tried would be, by definition 'communist'.[3]

The birth of Israel led to conflict between Israel and the newly independent Arab countries. In 1917, Lord Arthur Balfour, the British Foreign Minister, issued a declaration (the Balfour Declaration) which announced the British Empire's support for the establishment of "a Jewish national home in Palestine." While European nations ensured the birth of Israel state, US protected it and ensured its expansion and annihilation of Palestine.

The political reforms in the Arab world were minimal and many political parties were barred, especially those with a pan Arab slogan and popular gatherings were allowed only in mosques. This hardened the stands of those movements in the Arab world for any reconciliation with the ruling elite and demanded calls for regime change. The youth in the Arab street got fed up with the regimes that did not carry much of reforms to meet the minimum requirements and they decided to take the law and order into their own hands to get rid of those regimes that suppressed them and denied them their basic rights.

External intervention in West Asia played a catastrophic role in creating chaos and encouraged dictatorship and sedition. The foreign intervention was evident from the military invasion of Afghanistan. The US invasion of Iraq led to more resentment in the Arab streets, which was aggravated by the global financial crisis and economic recession. US intention of occupying Iraq was never for weapons of mass destruction, but for the natural wealth of Iraq. Hence to speak of US pulling out after occupation, was a culmination of Pentagon policy of spreading anarchy, sectarianism and nourishing radicalism, which led to the birth of ISIS, a by-product of the Al Qaeda terrorist organisation.

The Arab Spring spread from Northern Africa to the Middle East. The ISIS in Iraq formed Al Nusra Front in Syria, which started the war there and recruited locals. The Turkish government opened its 900 km border with Syria for mercenaries to enter Syria freely from Libya, Tunisia, Saudi Arabia, Chechens, Caucasians, Afghanistan, Pakistan, Taliban, Uzbeks, Malaysians and Indonesians to name a few. The border crossing between Turkey and Syria was under the control of "foreign mercenaries in collaboration with of intelligence agencies" of US, UK, France, Turkey, Israel, Qatar and Saudi Arabia who ensured the flow of arms to reach anti-Syria militant groups under the pretext of supporting moderate rebels against Syrian government forces. Turkey with sole ambition of reviving the Ottoman Caliphate era supported the Muslim Brotherhood and later supplemented with Mujahideen to gain ground and topple secular regimes in the Arab world. They were sheltered, trained, armed and extended logistic support on its soil.

In Aaron Klien's report[4] "Blowback! US Trained Islamists Who Joined ISIS", secret Jordan base was a site of covert aid to insurgents targeting Assad. In February 2012, *WND News* was the first to report that US, Turkey and Jordan were running a training base for the Syrian rebels in the Jordanian town of Safawi in the country's Northern desert region. The source told *WND News* that at least one of the training camps of the ISIS is in the vicinity of Incirlik Air Base near Adana, Turkey, where American personnel and equipment are located.

The revolution erupted in the Arab world under the banner of Arab Spring which was indigenous as it appeared, and then radical Islamist forces, the only organised opposition, hijacked the aspiration of the people. This led to the promotion of tribal regional warfare (Libya and Yemen). The overseas terrorists were trained in bases in Turkey and were allowed to flow into Syria and Iraq remotely controlled by intelligent agencies similar to that in Afghanistan in the 1980s.

The US is responsible for the formation of ISIS, as most of the top leaders were born in US training camps of Al Qaeda in Afghanistan. The spread of ISIS was only possible with the US occupation of Iraq. In his article "How the American made ISIS", Tom Engelhardt[5] states that "when the US was done, when it had set off the process that led to insurgencies, civil wars, the growth of extremist militias, and the collapse of state structures, it had also guaranteed the rise of the ISIS—as well as of other extremist outfits ranging from the Pakistani Taliban, now challenging the state in certain areas of that country, to Ansar Al Sharia in Libya and Al Qaeda in the Arabian Peninsula in Yemen."

In 2007, Former NATO Director General Wesley Clark commented on the Neo-cons plans that NATO was planning to occupy 7 countries in 5 years including Libya, Yemen, Somalia, Sudan, Syria and Iran.[6] Even WikiLeaks revealed the US plan to a military coup in Tunisia and Egypt to gain logistic support to invade Libya. Before the inception of ISIS by the Western media (as far back as 2007), Pulitzer Prize-winning veteran journalist Seymour Hersh would portend the creation of such a terror group in the *New Yorker* titled, "The Redirection: Is the Administration's new policy benefitting our enemies in the war on terrorism?"[7] The drawing of new Middle East and North Africa is meant to divide the region into small countries on ethnic and religious basis. The Islamic parties gained power in most of the Arab states that went for election from Morocco, Tunisia, Libya and Egypt. Many have accused Qatar and Saudi Arabia of pumping billions of dollars to let the Islamist parties gain control.

The "Constructive Chaos" project in the Arab world started with Sudan dividing into two. Regimes were overthrown in Tunisia and Egypt, but eyes were on Libya, which was attacked by the NATO forces under 'humanitarian intervention' that compounded the problems and prompted other super powers to prevent similar action in other country like Syria. In fact, even Silvia Berlusconi, the former Prime Minister of Italy accused France's President Nicolas Sarkozy on the request of his friend Bernard Livy Henry[8], that Libya was peaceful and there was no revolt against the Libyan president.

## ISIS Expansion

There is no doubt that the sectarian policy followed by US after Iraq occupation was meant to institutionalise it and destroy decades of nation building. This included ethnic cleansing, marginalisation, tribal representatives and encouraged widespread corruption. Creating "Sunni suffering" like situations in Iraq—torture, sectarian killings, bomb blasts and ethnic cleansing—were sufficient to create anger against the government in the centre. This helped the rise of insurgent groups opposed to Nouri Al Maliki's government and made recruitment and support initially easy for ISIS to launch its attack on the Iraqi government forces.

The ISIS has benefitted a lot by selling stolen artifacts and oil from Iraq and Syria. As Dahr Jamail writes, "funded by Arabian Gulf petrodollars from Qatar and Saudi Arabia, among other places, and for a long while supported, at least implicitly, by the Obama administration, radical Islamist fighters in Syria opposing Bashar Al Assad have been expanding in strength, numbers, and lethality for the last 3 years. This winter, they and their branches in Iraq converged, first taking Fallujah, and then moving on to the spring and summer debacles across Sunni Iraq and the establishment of a "caliphate" in the territories they control in both countries... Today, Washington's policies continue in the same mindless way as more fuel is rushed to the bonfire that is incinerating Iraq."[9]

Clergies in Saudi Arabia, Qatar, Kuwait, UAE and other Salafi and Wahhabi centres kept on promoting Jihad and calling on the people to topple the 'infidel regime' in Syria. All criminals and life imprisoners from Saudi Arabia and some other countries were released under one condition, that is, to go and fight in Syria.

ISIS is well trained, well financed, militarily proficient and equipped with modern vehicles and weaponries. The formation of 'pseudo gang' was part of a successful project implemented to facilitate intervention. During the occupation of Iraq, US formed two camps: Camp Cropper and Camp Bucca (Al Qaeda School) in Umm Qasr between 2007 and 2009. Most of the released Guantanamo detainees found their way into Syria and Iraq to join ISIS and Jabhat Al Nusra Front.

With the spread of anarchy the European countries are trying to come back to the Arab world. For example, UK is trying to do so through Qatar and Iran, whereas France through Lebanon and lastly, Saudi Arabia and Israel through the minorities card. Now NATO countries are planning to expand their operation and form a special unit to intervene whenever required. The creation of ISIS was a pretext to destroy nations, topple unfavourable regimes to its policy and prepare the ground for military intervention like in Libya, Syria and Iraq.

## The Return to Cold War

The development in West Asia cannot be seen in isolation from what the global scenario and reshaping of the international new world order. When former Saudi Ambassador to US Prince Bandar Bin Sultan met with President Putin, he tried to buy his loyalty and disown Syria. Bandar threatened Putin with dire consequence if Putin refused. Now the Islamic State is issuing statements against Russia and have vowed to liberate Chechnya and other Muslim minorities' states.

Tartus Port of Syria is the only military base for Russia in the Mediterranean Sea; so disintegrating Syria and regime changes are of prime importance to US, NATO and Israel, which will ensure no Russian presence in the Mediterranean Sea and guarantee Israel's dominance in the region. Russia is still holding ground on Syria's front and this strengthens her belief that US and NATO are trying to isolate Moscow and what happens in Crimea and Ukraine is a culmination of this policy of US and the West against Russian federation. Firstly, it was the gas pipeline that triggered the war on Syria, where Qatar wanted to extend a pipeline to Turkey and Europe through Jordan and Syria. Secondly, large reservoir of gas was discovered in the Levant which is shared with Syria, Lebanon, Cyprus, Israel and Palestine.

A number of NATO members supported the terrorists in Libya. From the outset of NATO's 2011 "humanitarian intervention" on Libya, the Atlantic alliance was working in close liaison with the "pro-Al Qaeda brigades" led by former Libya Islamic Fighting Group (LIFG) leader Abdul Hakim Belhhadj. He received his military training in a CIA sponsored Guerrilla camp in Afghanistan. He constitutes a CIA "intelligence asset" operating in the Libyan war theater. A 2011 report suggested that he had some 1,000 men under his command.[10]

## The Folly of External Intervention

The external intervention in Middle East has been there for decades which is clear from many released documents like: Israel Strategy for the 19th century (Yenon Oded plan 1982), PNAC-Clean and Break Plan (Lin Perk document 1996) to ensure security of Israel and the Brzezinski project (Richard Pearl document: Israel strategy till 2000 where he called for USA to invade Iraq). Condoleezza Rice announced "The Middle East and North Africa New Order" after the Israel war on Lebanon in 2006.

The role of Israel in the ongoing intervention in Middle East was not only limited to Syria and Iraq but to Libya, Tunisia, Sudan and Egypt as well. It intervened repeatedly in the Syrian conflict and kept on attacking Syria's military installations under different pretexts. Israel's only objective is to tilt the balance of power in favour of the insurgent groups to topple the Syrian government. It believes that the insurgent groups extended logistic support to Hamas in Gaza and Hezbollah in Lebanon to foil the US-Israel emergence of a Greater Middle East.

The main objective of US in Syria is regime change and it has been planning to intervene in the Syrian affairs since a very long time. This was stated by Collin Powel to President Assad when he visited Syria after the 2003 US invasion of Iraq. Powel dictated to President Bashar Al Assad the US terms to avoid invasion of Syria. Both candidates in their debate to the US Presidency stated that regime change in Syria is one of the priorities of the US foreign policy that will help in protecting Israel.

The "pro-democracy uprising" was supported, and the "moderate rebels" trained and armed. US weapons found its way into the hands of Al Qaeda in Syria and Iraq. The pretext to intervene militarily under the banner of "humanitarian intervention" was foiled by Russia and China. Now it is inching closer after President Obama revealed his plan to counter its own cultivated ISIS groups. This may lead to imposing a 'No Fly Zone' in some part of Northern Syria. There is a devious strategy to divide Syria similar to their 'divide and conquer' policies in Iraq and Libya. NATO and US forces will continue their bombing campaign, military incursion and occupation in Syria. On the other hand Russia, Iran and other Syria's allies will support the Syrian government's efforts in fighting ISIS to foil the Western plot of intervention. The unlikely scenario is a tactical rapprochement between US and Russia to fight the global threat and the hysteria generated by the brutality of ISIS. There is no doubt that there is a plan to reshape the Arab world and divide it further under the pretext of humanitarian intervention. It will have a devastating effect regionally, where it is spreading to Jordan and Lebanon, but it has a global dimension of isolating Russia in the Mediterranean Sea and putting pressure on Iran as well. The outcome of the war on Syria and Iraq will shape the new regional and world order, whatever that might be.

## NOTES

1. See the link to the video, at https://www.youtube.com/watch?v=4nsQ5POIRUI.
2. "Mapping the Global Future", Report of the National Intelligence Council's 2020 Project, National Intelligence Council, Washington D.C., December 2004, at http://www.futurebrief.com/project2020.pdf.
3. William Blum, *Rogue State: A Guide to the World's Only Superpower*, Common Courage Press, Monroe, 2000, pp. 131-132.
4. Aaron Klein, "Blowback! U.S. trained Islamists who joined ISIS", *WND News*, June 17, 2014, at http://www.wnd.com/2014/06/officials-u-s-trained-isis-at-secret-base-in-jordan/.
5. Tom Engelhardt, "How America Made ISIS", *Huffington Post*, February 11, 2014, at http://www.huffingtonpost.com/tom-engelhardt/how-america-made-isis_b_5751876.html?ir=India&adsSiteOverride=in.
6. See the interview with General Wesley Clark, "We're going to take out 7 countries in 5 years: Iraq, Syria, Lebanon, Libya, Somalia, Sudan & Iran", *Global Research*, March 2, 2007, at http://www.globalresearch.ca/we-re-going-to-take-out-7-countries-in-5-years-iraq-syria-lebanon-libya-somalia-sudan-iran/5166.
7. Seymour M. Hersh, "The Redirection: Is the Administration's new policy benefitting our enemies in the war on terrorism?", *The New Yorker*, March 5, 2007, at http://www.newyorker.com/magazine/2007/03/05/the-redirection.
8. See the video link, at http://www.dailymotion.com/video/xhdrv8_l-appel-de-bhl-depuis-benghazi-libye-en-direct-sur-tf1-au_news#.UPOateTBjFk.
9. Dahr Jamail, "A Nation on the Brink: How US Policies Sealed Iraq's Fate", at http://americanvisionmagazine.blogspot.in/2014/07/a-nation-on-brink-how-us-policies.html.
10. "Libyan rebels at pains to distance themselves from extremists", *The Globe and Mail*, March 11, 2011, at http://www.theglobeandmail.com/news/world/libyan-rebels-at-pains-to-distance-themselves-from-extremists/article570971/.

# 12

# US and 'The Other Side of the World'

*Jon B. Alterman*

It was no coincidence that President Barack Obama became the first sitting US President to visit India twice while in office, nor is it a coincidence that his India visit in January 2015 came less than six months after Prime Minister Narendra Modi visited him in the White House. The warm embraces and broad smiles that the two leaders shared in Washington and New Delhi followed months of fraught relations between the two countries that left New Delhi without a US ambassador. While the two leaders appear to have a good personal chemistry, the growing intensity of relations between the two countries is about much more than personal chemistry. It represents the confluence of two major trends: India's greater global engagement, and greater US engagement across Asia.

A great deal of attention has been paid to the effects of a US "rebalance toward Asia" on East Asia. With longstanding and close relations between the United States and Japan, South Korea, and Taiwan, and with global attention being paid to a rising China, East Asia is an obvious focus. Much less attention has been paid to the effects of a rebalance on West Asia—understood in the United States as "The Middle East" and thus a part of the world where the US presence will be modified—and on the ties between East Asian energy-consuming nations and their West Asian energy-producing counterparts. This essay will attempt to address that lacuna, considering an under appreciated aspect of the US rebalance toward Asia: how that rebalance is managed and what it means in the maritime space between the Strait of Hormuz and the Straits of Malacca: what is clearly for the United States "the other side of the world."

The Obama administration's policy of focusing on Asia represents an historic shift for the United States, which has long seen its principal interests across the Atlantic. The ethnic roots of the US population are overwhelmingly trans-Atlantic, and the relative economic underdevelopment of Asia through the first half of the twentieth century made the Pacific a second-order issue for the United States. Even when the United States invested deeply in Asia—as it did in supporting economies (and anti-Communist governments) in Taiwan, South Korea, and elsewhere and fighting in Vietnam—doing so was largely in reference to the Soviet Union, and the US-Soviet struggle was principally the one focused on Europe.

Throughout, the US commitment to what many call the Indian Ocean Region, has been entirely discretionary. That the United States has an Atlantic and a Pacific shore, makes the security of these oceans an undisputed matter of US national security. The US role in what many call the Indian Ocean Region is less clear. The Indian Ocean does not lap at US shores, and the United States has only modest trade with most of the countries in the region. The major US trading partners in Asia—China, Japan, and South Korea—are Pacific countries, not Indian Ocean countries, and major US trading partners in Europe send goods across the North Atlantic. And yet, countries with which the United States has extensive trading relationships trade across the Indian Ocean. How the United States thinks about its Indian Ocean role—and more broadly, about the space between the Strait of Hormuz and the Straits of Malacca—will have profound implications for the US role in the world and the order that emerges, but primarily by affecting areas and issues that matter more for potential future US interests than the current ones.

## US Presence and Engagement in Asia

Discussion of US government efforts in Asia (or anywhere else) can focus on a few different things. A good deal of emphasis is placed on "presence," which refers to the US troops and material available in the event of warfare. The United States has invested in a considerable military infrastructure in Asia, focused on the East. The United States maintains major force deployments on the Korean Peninsula and Japan; has significant naval presence in both Hawaii and Guam; and maintains a significant naval presence in Singapore to help protect the Straits of Malacca. Further west, the United States maintains a Naval Air Station in Diego Garcia, and has land, sea and air forces deployed throughout the Persian Gulf. In addition, the United States has growing activities in Australia and several carrier strike groups operating at a time in Asia.

Despite the fact that the United States has spent decades fighting wars in the Middle East; Europe and East Asia have hosted most US troops (aside from the anomaly of the Iraq War, when troop levels in the Middle East exceeded 200,000). The presence in Asia to some extent is due to historic commitments to Japan and South Korea, partially due to the broad expanse of the Pacific itself, and in some way to a perceived need to deter China's regional ambitions. At of the end of 2014, there were more than 85,000 active US military personnel stationed in the Asia-Pacific region,[1] down from between 130,000 and 150,000 in the mid-twentieth century and as many as 769,000 at the height of the Vietnam War.[2] By comparison, far fewer than half as many US troops were in the Middle East as in East Asia, despite ongoing operations in Iraq and Syria.[3]

A more subtle measure of the US effort in Asia is to consider "engagement." Engagement includes the sorts of institutional relationships that the United States and its partners build through regional organisations and agreements. Engagement also encompasses the human relationships that the United States seeks to foster through trade, education, and governmental and non-governmental partnerships. Presence can be "surged," or expanded rapidly to respond to new threats or challenges. Engagement is harder to surge, and takes considerably greater and broader investment of time and resources. It is hard to measure engagement, and it is even harder to measure its benefits with any precision. Individual components are observable—for example, the fact that US exports to Asia doubled in the decade before 2013, and six of the country's top trading partners are in Asia[4]—but other parameters are more elusive. Soft power cannot be easily quantified (although researchers can try to approximate measurements of its effects by studying public opinion), nor a nation's abilities to use soft power can easily be judged.

Perhaps arising out of the fact that much of the US encounter with the world in the 18th and 19th centuries was through missionaries more than traders, the United States has favoured ideas and the institutions that foster them over the colonial logic of using troops to maintain economic hegemony. The North Atlantic Treaty Organisation (NATO), the United Nations, and a whole series of other organisations reflect a significant US effort to invest in the global commons precisely so that unilateral enforcement would be unnecessary.

The Indian Ocean region, however, has been relatively free of either US presence or US engagement. While there was some effort to enlist countries in anti-Soviet alliances in the 1950s, the United States has put greater effort into developing individual bilateral relationships with countries in the region (and to alleviating tensions on the India-Pakistan frontier) than into conceptualising the littoral or maritime space in this region into a single construct. Britain had lingering influence in the region through the Commonwealth, but in point of fact, the United States neither felt the stakes were sufficiently high to develop something similar, nor did states actively seek US involvement in the region.

Often left out of a discussion of a US rebalance toward Asia is a discussion of the space between two places the United States has clear investments, East Asia and West Asia. But as one discusses that space, what should be the baseline to judge US efforts? Is a "rebalance" about the US effort compared to its efforts elsewhere, or would it be more appropriate to compare it to levels elsewhere in Asia? It is simple to measure military commitments, but how does one account for softer measures, including the millions of non-resident Indians (NRIs) in the United States and their impact on the politics and economics in the United States and India? And how should a country such as the United States measure its level of engagement—in absolute terms (or compared to their own historical trends), or versus other actors in Asia?

## China's Role: For or Against the Status Quo?

If one takes the last point, the most important actor against which to measure any US action or "rebalance" is China and how Chinese actions affect dynamics in Asia and the Indian Ocean. It will be decades before China can confidently project power across the Asian maritime space, including in the Indian Ocean. Bluewater operations remain beyond the easy capability of the People's Liberation Army (PLA) Navy, and they would potentially antagonise India. China's instinct appears to be to tread cautiously, and to protect its interests in the Middle East through maintaining constructive relations with the countries of the region and with United States. In order to have a freer hand in Middle East operations, China would not only have to invest mightily in training and equipment, but it would also need to invest in having a strong relationship with India. Even if China were determined to pursue an ability to secure its communications with the Middle East, it would take decades to create a system which did not in large measure rely on the security guarantees of the United States.

China's Asian strategy is not all maritime, of course. Given the long term difficulties of securing maritime routes, and given US preeminence both in the Strait of Hormuz and the Straits of Malacca, China is developing alternative routes to the Middle East and beyond, into Europe. One of those routes is a Russian route, which is all but certain to circumvent areas of US hegemony. But Chinese-Russian relations historically have been fraught, and Russia is certain to extract a high price from China were it to become reliant on Russian passage. China might hope that Russia would become more reliant on China instead, but creating that reality would take years of careful diplomacy and thoughtful investment by China.

The second potential route is an overland route across Central Asia. Pakistan has already begun construction on the Hazara Motorway, extending the

Karakoram Highway (which runs from Kashgar in Xinjiang Province to Abbottabad) to link Islamabad to China. The construction is part of a series of agreements with China to build US$ 45.6 billion of infrastructure to improve economic relations between China and Pakistan.[5] Extending west from Pakistan would be the next step. Here China would be likely to face compliant partners, since in its bilateral relations with the host states it would clearly be the stronger party. Yet, a greater Chinese presence in Central Asia would probably antagonise Russia, which has traditionally been the dominant power in the region. In addition, the topography of much of Central Asia is challenging. Many overland routes to the west would likely be much more expensive for China than the current rates for sea shipment. Further, it is unclear what China would want to import from Europe, which could help fill railcars when they go eastward after travelling westward with manufactured goods. Securing a Central Asian alternative to a maritime route would be difficult and long-term proposition.

Still, China is investing heavily in building ties with Central Asian and West Asian states. The Shanghai Cooperation Organisation (SCO) is an inter-governmental group with a security focus that encompasses many of China's western neighbours. While the SCO is more than a decade old, two initiatives launched in the last year give a sense of China's new found westward focus. The Asian Infrastructure Investment Bank and the New Silk Road together represent almost US$ 100 billion in new Chinese commitments to Central Asia, and are a sign of China's plans to place enduring emphasis on the region.[6]

As China looks to develop its Asian commercial presence, it is unclear how a greater focus on Asia will affect either China's foreign policy or its global behaviour. Some argue that the norms of international business are fairly well established and meet the needs of Western corporations. One might ask if China is so locked into its present commercial relationships as to remove the option of creating different patterns of behaviour through new banks and funds, or though security ties with governments. After all, Chinese businesses operate increasingly like Western businesses. China has organised itself economically to take advantage of the current norms in global trade. The requirements of international capital, and the bureaucratic and institutional imperatives of large organisations lead some to question how much China could affect order in Asia.

But Chinese leadership in the global commons in general, and in the Indian Ocean in particular, might manifest in implementation rather than in design. For example, how do governments deal with pariah states? If there is broad agreement on sanctions, would China seek to capture the benefits of acting independently and reaching out to otherwise-isolated countries? The question is a relevant one in the trans-Asian context, where Western countries have often sought to isolate and sanction so-called rogue states, with Iran being the most prominent case. The difference of a China-led order is especially likely to be manifested in cases where Western states are acting because of concern over human rights violations and other concerns about domestic behaviour. China's strong historic preference is toward noninterference in the domestic affairs of other states, maintaining a strong bias toward order and stability, and remaining skeptical toward efforts to impose international sanctions.

## Variables that Influence Outcomes

A large part of determining what China is able or willing to do across Asia will depend on how the United States chooses to act toward China and its neighbours. China prefers to have bilateral relationships with its neighbours, where it is the stronger party. With a larger military, a larger economy, and a larger regional footprint than any of its neighbours, China has the advantage in any one-to-one relationship. China does less well, however, in a genuine multilateral arrangement, and also, when the United States plays an active role supporting China's neighbours and enlisting them in multilateral frameworks. In this regard, the Association of Southeast Asian Nations (ASEAN) unity in the face of Chinese efforts to exert control of the South China Sea is instructive.[7] To the extent that China creates confidence with its neighbours, the United States' role to balance against China becomes much less necessary. The intra-Asian rivalries are also boiling to some extent for which the Asian states will seek to bring in the United States to balance against China, not just in Southeast Asia, but in the Indian Ocean region, too. An assertive China, or even an aggressive China, creates the demand for an antidote, and that invites the United States in.

Another variable here is the role of India. Since any Chinese engagement in the Middle East maritime space necessarily passes by India, the nature of India's approach to the Indian Ocean region and to China, has a profound effect on what China can do in the Middle East. If India were to feel threatened by China, or were to feel hemmed in by China (it already has expressed concern over China's port-building activities in the Indian Ocean region), it could work with other neighbours of the middle Kingdom to constrain China's ability to reach westward. The close relations between India and China, or even security understandings between the two, would lay the groundwork for a very different kind of Chinese presence in the Middle East.

But stronger India-China cooperation is far from guaranteed. India's future trajectory with respect to both China and the United States will depend on how its "Look East" policy evolves—that is, how actively India seeks to involve itself in the politics and economics of Asia, and of Southeast Asia, in particular. India has been increasingly drawn into ASEAN in recent years as countries there seek to push back against increasing Chinese sea claims.[8] India has also expressed an interest, at times, in more closely regulating (and potentially even restricting) foreign vessels' access to areas of the Indian Ocean beyond its territorial waters. In the near term, some argue, while China and India are unlikely to engage in conflict in the Indian Ocean, they are likely to "bump into" one another on a more regular basis—getting into disputes or incidents which raise tensions between them and which would require careful political management. The kinds of crises that have become common in the South China Sea might start appearing in the Indian Ocean, too. One factor that could make such crises more common would be a reduced US presence in the Middle East.

## The United States in the Middle East—for Asia

Much of the foregoing is about the Asian effects of China reaching westward. Equally important is the question of what would happen if the United States put less investment into the other side of the world.

Many Middle Eastern governments like dealing with neighbours to the east because the relationships are more transactional and come with less lecturing about reforming law and governance. But Asia is more than a pressure valve for Middle Eastern states seeking an escape from Western sanctions and judgment. In a world with relatively flat demand growth for energy, producers looking for new markets find virtually all of them in Asia. That gives Asian consuming countries influence over Middle Eastern producers who must find markets for their goods. However, all the major Asian economies, including India, are reliant on Middle Eastern energy, and most of the energy arrives in Asia after travelling by sea through the Indian Ocean region. The Middle East is the source for more than half of China's oil imports (with oil making up 20 percent of its energy mix), more than 83 percent of Japan's oil imports (44 percent of its energy mix), 87 percent of South Korea's oil imports (41 percent of its energy mix), and 62 percent of India's oil imports (around a quarter of its energy mix, and an input to its refining industry).[9] Japan also relies on the region for a third of its LNG imports (22 percent of its energy mix), and South Korea relies on the region for 53 percent of its LNG (17 percent of its energy mix).[10] Other countries across East and Southeast Asia also get much of their oil and gas from the Middle East.

For these Asian states, relying on energy supplies by sea is a persistent vulnerability, and relying on a small number of producer states in a single part of the world makes Asian consumers especially susceptible to political events that are far beyond their ability to control. When it comes both to protecting the sea lanes and being reliant on political military influence to ensure the flow of energy,

Asian states are disproportionately reliant on the United States, regardless of whether they have positive relations with the United States or not. That is because the United States has such a large maritime presence in the region, as noted earlier.

In contrast, some argue that the US presence in the Middle East itself does not actually enhance security in the Middle East, and that any effect from a reduction of its role there would be small. They argue that there are enough incentives for good behaviour in the current environment to promote security cooperation among current powers. One needs to look only at the persistence of warfare in the Persian Gulf, despite the presence of tens of thousands of US troops, to wonder just how much security the United States provides. Not only has the United States initiated several engagements in the region, but US allies have been party to almost every armed conflict in the Middle East. For many in the United States, the prospect of a diminished security commitment to the Middle East is an attractive one. The rise of energy independence in the United States, combined with fatigue after more than a decade of warfare in the Middle East, makes the prospect of reduced US military commitment to the region attractive.

Others argue that the United States plays a vital regional role, and that a US withdrawal from the Middle East would create a vacuum. The argument here is that while conflict is high in absolute terms, it would be relatively much higher were the United States not played an active role in securing the region.

But what lesson would US allies draw from a diminished US presence in the Middle East? Some might argue that walking away from long-standing partners such as Saudi Arabia would be a cautionary tale that is read with alarm in South Korea and Japan. One could interpret a US reluctance to confront an aggressive Iran as a signal that the United States would be unlikely to confront an aggressive China, or an aggressive North Korea. The politics of Asia is complex, and there are certainly different views among different constituencies in the region. But given the volatility of security issues in the Middle East; the enduring US commitment to the Middle East; and the reliance of Asian energy consumers in the Middle East; it is hard to imagine that US security actions (or lack thereof) in the Middle East wouldn't have a profound impact on the expectations of Asian consumer countries for future US action.

For many, the clear preference is for an architecture to emerge that is jointly maintained by all the powers in Asia and the United States, and which creates enduring incentives for positive behaviour. There are not many good models of this. NATO, for example, has helped secure Europe, but it has aroused concerns that it has freed member states from making adequate contributions to their own security, and increased reliance on the US security umbrella.

## Uncertainties and Decisions

Policymakers have and will continue to disagree about how much emphasis the United States should put place on investing in security in the Middle East and securing the maritime commons in Asia. They also have and will continue to disagree about what China's expanding engagement in Asia and around the world means for global politics. In a world of constrained resources, the United States will have to make some very hard choices.

Among the hardest choices is judging the nature of future conflicts. While piracy is a nuisance, it requires a modest military footprint, and it is greatly affected by cooperative police action. Piracy requires an entirely different military presence and humanitarian assistance and disaster relief, and even more different presence than the possibility of deterring or even fighting a large state actor. If United States and its allies believed it was necessary to fight China in order to shape its behaviour in the Indian Ocean region that would have required a very different military presence than a set of cooperative arrangements intended to preserve the interests of all actors in the region. And yet, it may be precisely a large US-led military presence that persuades large states in the region that cooperation is the only way forward. Others see that the military presence has been doing little more than militarising the region, making the prospects of conflict more rather than less.

What is most clear in all of this is how much depends on decisions that have not yet been made. How India deals with its near abroad, and how India decides to deal with its overlapping security concerns with China, is one factor. How China decides to secure its energy routes to the Middle East is another. Perhaps most unclear is how the United States will see its global role in the decades to come. After many decades on a Cold War footing, the United States has not yet come to a strategic consensus on its role in the world, especially those parts of the world that do not border the United States.

The Indian Ocean region is truly "the other side of the world." While it has close allies bordering the ocean, the direct security implications of events in the region are not always clear to US decisionmakers. The extent of the US commitment to the Indian Ocean region, the extent to which that commitment is direct or indirect, principally military or principally economic and political, are among the key discretionary decisions that a future US president will make. Those decisions will have only indirect effects on core US national security decisions, but the implications of those decisions have profound effects not only on the security of the Indian Ocean region itself, but also on the US place in the world.

## NOTES

1. Defence Manpower Data Center, "Total Military Personnel and Dependent End Strength by Service, Regional Area, and Country", December 31, 2014, at https://www.dmdc.osd.mil/appj/dwp/rest/download?fileName=SIAD_309_ Report_P1412. xlsx&groupName=mil RegionCountry.
2. Tim Kane, "Global US Troop Deployment, 1950-2003", Heritage Foundation, October 27, 2004, at http://www.heritage.org/research/reports/2004/10/global-us-troop-deployment-1950-2003.
3. The International Institute for Strategic Studies (IISS), "North America", *The Military Balance*, 115(1), 2015, pp. 29-56.
4. Matthew P. Goodman, "US Economic Engagement in Asia and the Pacific", Statement before the US Senate Committee on Foreign Relations, Subcommittee on East Asian and Pacific Affairs, December 18, 2013, at http://csis.org/files/attachments/ts131218_goodman.pdf.
5. Gordon G. Chang, "China's Big Plans for Pakistan", *National Interest*, December 10, 2014, at http://nationalinterest.org/feature/chinas-big-plans-pakistan-11827.
6. Nyshka Chandran, "'New Silk Road' highlights China's two-speed reform", *CNBC*, November 17, 2014, at http://www.cnbc.com/id/102190017#.
7. Richard Javad Heydarian, "Face-Off: China vs. ASEAN in the South China Sea and Beyond", *The National Interest*, January 15, 2015, at http://nationalinterest.org/feature/face-china-vs-asean-the-south-china-sea-beyond-12000.
8. Ritika Katyal, "Why India's Blue Water Ambitions Matter", *Foreign Policy*, August 8, 2014, at http://foreignpolicy.com/2014/08/04/why-indias-blue-water-ambitions-matter/.
9. Compiled from US Energy Information Administration (EIA) data for 2012 and 2013.
10. Ibid.

# 13

# How to Deal with West Asia? Commonalities and Differences in the European and German Approaches

*Henner Fürtig*

After the Second World War, the entire political class of the young Federal Republic of Germany had internalised the behavioural concept of the so-called 'civil-power', which included some strict 'do's' and 'don'ts'. The main points were: 'never alone', 'never war, Auschwitz, genocide etc.', and 'strict preference of peaceful means' in the foreign policy. Whereas—for instance—the American constitution was written to protect the young nation from a largely hostile world, the German 'Grundgesetz' [Basic Law] of 1949 defined the Federal Republic as part of a larger system of collective security to which national sovereignty would be subordinated. As a matter of routine, every German government since 1949 underlined its commitment to multilateralism in the context of the EU and its predecessors, the NATO and the UN.

## The Watershed of 1990

Initially, the re-unification of Germany in 1990 did not alter the commitment to multilateralism but it led to a gradual revision of the 'strictly peaceful means'-doctrine. In 1993, the then Chancellor Helmut Kohl and his Foreign Minister Hans-Dietrich Genscher, were prepared for the first time since the re-unification to participate in military actions outside Germany. Of course, these actions were to be multilateral. Whereas Kohl had rejected Bush Senior's request for military assistance in Kuwait in 1991, and preferred to contribute financially ('check-book diplomacy'), he sent minor military contingents to Yugoslavia in 1993, and to Cambodia and Somalia in 1993 and 1994. After the Federal Constitutional Court's basic endorsement of military missions abroad in 1994, Germany participated substantially in the Kosovo war, a conflict for which not even a UN mandate existed. Nevertheless, the participation proceeded still within the behavioural concept: 'never Auschwitz' prevailing over 'strict preference of peaceful means'. Though retrospectively, it becomes clear that the Kosovo war went a long way in reducing reservations concerning military missions. In 2002, Germany's soldiers were sent to Afghanistan, and in 2006 Germany provided troops for the UN mission in Lebanon. In Afghanistan, the German units moved step-by-step from a strictly defensive role to a position that included responsibility for the security of the northern part of the country, in the end they assumed leadership for any hostilities outside the NATO zone. These developments meant the end of Germany's *Sonderweg*, literally special path, of obvious and demonstrated military restraint that had emerged after 1945 as a reflex against the cruelties of the Third Reich era.[1] An important side-effect of all these steps and developments was the gradual familiarisation of politicians and broader public alike to the fact that Germany had transformed itself from a 'consumer' to a 'producer' of international security.

Whereas the end of this special *Sonderweg* did not mean—as explained before—the revocation of the multilateralism concept, another remarkable act of emancipation happened in 2002. In a campaign speech on August 5, 2002, the then Chancellor Gerhard Schroeder informed the public of his Social Democratic Party's (SPD) decision not to participate under any circumstances, in a war to disarm Iraq or to topple Saddam Hussain's regime. The media were quick to call this new approach the 'German Way'. Commentators and political experts were sure that the 'German Way'-formula secured Schroeder's re-election in September 2002; Schroeder's decision to make the German (non)-participation in a probable Iraq War. The main pillar of his election campaign is still breath-taking when considering Germany's foreign policy after 1945 and its, at best, junior partnership to the US during these decades.

Attempts to explain this 'revolution' in German post-War foreign policy were manifold. Some sought an answer to this in the biographies of the chief political characters. Gerhard Schroeder, as well as his Foreign Minister Joschka Fischer, and other real or pseudo mouthpieces of the 'German Way' were prominent representatives of the 'Generation 1968', a generation that had challenged the existing political, social and economic system of the old Federal Republic more fundamentally than all its predecessors since 1945. Of course, the rejection of the old incrusted structures included the traditional foreign policy, but they had to wait until they possessed the necessary political means to realise a new political approach.[2] Others argued that the 'German Way' was more or less a personal crusade of Schroeder and his side-kick Muentefering, whereas the front man of the Greens and Foreign Minister Fischer tried to curb the Chancellor's zeal. As proof, they stated that Fischer avoided using the notion 'German Way' and that he had urged the Chancellor right from the outset to include France so as to avoid going it alone on foreign policy.[3]

In August 2002, Schroeder had ignored President Chirac, who seemed uncertain what to do. By opposing a war against Iraq at all odds, Schroeder had gone further than Chirac ever did. Yet, this alone does not make Fischer the sober-minded among the wanderers on the 'German Way'. As early as in January 2002—months before Schroeder's famous statements—Fischer had declared with regard to US policy on Iraq: "We won't be treated as a satellite".[4] One year later, in February 2003, it was Fischer who directly confronted US Secretary of Defence Donald Rumsfeld's pro-war arguments during the Munich Security Conference by stressing firmly: "Excuse me, but I'm not convinced". The German media was quick to translate this into a declaration of independence from the United States, and the culmination of 50 years of almost automatic compliance with American wishes.[5] Citing this episode opens the way for a broader, more in-depth explanation of the shift in German foreign policy. Schroeder's quest to win the elections of September 2002 by using the overall pacifist nature of German society and its latent anti-Americanism was usually used to explain the reasons for the 'German Way'. There is some relevance in all these explanations, but they fail to present a proper answer to questions concerning the timing of the change, its sudden emergence and its focus on the Iraqi issue. The most important driving force behind the change was neither anti-Americanism nor pacifism, but rather Germany's political emancipation.[6] It was a result of the re-unification and the disappearance of the threats posed by the East-West confrontation. After the Cold War, subordination under the American security apparatus no longer seemed necessary for German survival. If this is true, the question comes up why the 'German Way' had not been proclaimed a dozen years earlier, for example, on the occasion of the 1991 Second Gulf War? The answer is simple: Germany's political class and its population had to become accustomed to the new situation, and were primarily focussed at domestic issues (i.e.: the many problems of reunification).

From their role as a 'producer' of security in Kosovo, Afghanistan, the Horn of Africa, Kuwait and elsewhere, Schroeder and Fischer extracted the 'right' to be consulted by their partners before they undertook far-reaching political and military initiatives. They also affirmed the 'right' to hold a differing opinion. Equal partners do not expect blind allegiance but, on the contrary, appreciate an honest counter-argument that might prevent their being harmed. As a result, German legal reservations concerning a 'Preventive War', unilateral action, especially in the conflict-ridden Middle East, or their doubts as to whether the US administration had sufficiently considered all the probable after-effects of a 'military adventure' in Iraq were sold to the world at large by the Red-Green coalition as serious efforts to avert a friend from damage.[7] Schroeder was the first who conceptualised Germany's new self-confidence. He called Germany a self-assured country that would neither be available for 'adventures' nor for generous check-book diplomacy. On September 13, 2002, the Chancellor said in the Bundestag that, "fundamental questions concerning the German nation will be decided upon in Berlin and nowhere else."[8] Hence, Schroeder's real innovation was his violation of the 'never alone' maxim. This was indeed an extraordinary step for Germany, causing the previously mentioned irritations, even within the Green coalition camp.

Therefore, Schroeder and Fischer were frightened at their own courage once the elections were won. Under the imminent threat of being isolated in Europe and punished by the US, the SPD and the Greens sought shelter within the EU in general, and under a French-Russian umbrella, in particular. The oppositional CDU pursued a contrary strategy by demonstratively closing ranks with the US: of course after defeat in the elections. Angela Merkel's 'pilgrimage' to President Bush in the Fall of 2002 was widely interpreted in the German media and public as strong proof for the fact that the other half of the political class in Germany would prefer to continue with the traditional roles within the trans-Atlantic framework.

Although Schroeder personally lost the early elections in September 2005, the race was so close that it resulted in a 'Grand Coalition' of SPD and CDU/CSU. Angela Merkel became Chancellor, but within the government and other leading political institutions both camps acted conjointly, more or less. In the context of the German foreign policy this led to a 'natural' compromise: Germany neither continued the 'German Way', nor put all its eggs in the American basket. Instead, it praised the European 'Common Foreign and Security Policy' (CFSP).

## The Approach towards West Asia

Although Germany demonstrated major acts of its political emancipation in the post-Cold War era in the context of developments in West Asia (Iraq and Afghanistan), the region as such did not rank very high on the foreign policy agenda. German politicians were even reluctant to define political interests in this region. In fact, the notion "interests" as such is not often found in the German political vocabulary because it has that ring of hard-edged power politics that is still not popular in Germany. According to Steinberg, "that applies especially to relations with Israel, the Palestinian territories, and their neighbours, where the German side always prefers to the point to historical responsibility as the motivations for actions ... After 1990, we saw in Germany only short-lived discussions, generally triggered by particular events and mostly about particular countries rather than the region as a whole. The Israeli-Palestinian conflict and Iran occupied important positions in the German foreign policy discourse, but other countries and sub-regions (Iraq, the Gulf region, the Maghreb) and regional matters (migration, Islamism, energy) played a very subsidiary role in politics and public debate."[9]

Not surprisingly, this neglect was very well noticed in the region. Germany is seen there as a respected and valuable economic partner but there are questions about its interests and its corresponding policy priorities. While German policy when it comes to EU matters is well known in the region, German interests and policies regarding West Asia do not appear clear or conceptualised. This has led to the image of an indifferent actor. It is much easier for the Arabs to find out what French or British policy in the region is. The same cannot be said for Germany with the result that the Arab side perceives a big gap between the Anglo-French and the German approaches. While France and the UK have taken on a much more visible role supported by frequent visits and exchanges and shown an obvious willingness to support their economic advances into the region by political initiatives, Germany appears to have concluded that such an effort on its part is not necessary.[10]

Consistently, if political interests are not articulated, a specific political strategy for a region cannot be developed. And indeed, many observers trace this lack of a consistent German West Asia strategy back to a basic post-Cold War division of labour within the EU. According to this formula, Britain dealt with the 'classic' Middle East (Mashriq), France cared for North Africa (Maghreb) and Germany endeavoured to get Eastern Europe smoothly into the EU. Therefore, if Germany was enforced upon acting politically in West Asia, it always preferred action within the EU 'Common Foreign and Security Policy' (CFSP). Thus, in West Asia the traditional 'never alone' concept survived most obviously. This did not prevent Germany from intensifying its activities in the region in the early 2000s. Examples include the multilateral Barcelona Process that gave rise to the Union for the Mediterranean in July 2008 and the European Neighbourhood Policy established in 2004. Germany led nuclear talks with Iran as a member of the EU-3 and later the P5+1 group.

Even if Germany was somehow hiding behind the shield of the CFSP in West Asia for good parts of the post Cold War era, the European role as a whole in the region was limited all in all. It was Simon Serfaty who once sarcastically commented that, "every country in Europe wants to be 'the Arab's best friend' but none can guarantee the protection they need to seal that friendship: only the United States can."[11] Although the EU as a whole represents a larger economic player than the United States, it cannot back common foreign policy initiatives, even when these are forthcoming, with military force projection. Thus, being primarily a civilian and economic power, the EU lacks the preconditions of a leading international actor: at least in comparison to the US. Its ability to influence events in West Asia in a meaningful way is therefore limited, meaning that—individually and collectively—the member states of the EU cannot match the weight of the United States in the region. Consequently, European countries were perceived as junior partners of the US in West Asia, expected at best to support American activities. In essence, what Germany did in Iraq between 2003 and the US withdrawal in 2011 was designed in the first place to improve the damaged relations with the US, and Germany's more prominent role in the Syrian and the Iranian context has much to do with the lack of sufficient US influence there.

## New Constellations after the "Arab Spring"

The Arab Spring marked only the beginning of one of the most fundamental transitions in the modern West Asian history whose final results are hard to predict. For instance, whereas the Arab Spring raised hopes of a positive, more pro-democracy transition, the emergence of the Islamic State (IS) and its terror system shortly after the Arab revolts initiated the outbreak of a myriad of militant conflicts and civil wars that led to overwhelmingly gloomy prognoses of the imminent future of the region. At any rate, the region is only in the very early stages of a general transition process that will most probably last for decades. Still, while the structures in West Asia have been broken apart, there is nothing already able to replace what existed before. This means that the West will be confronted with a long drawn-out process of political contestation that is highly volatile and marked by varying degrees of violence. No West Asian or North African country can be considered immune to political change in the coming decades.

According to Sager, "with no models to be copied or imported that will return the region to immediate stability, foreign influence will become much more limited than before and will, in some cases, even become counter-productive. Where domestic processes are concerned, the battles have to be fought domestically. This implies that the new political order that will eventually emerge will look very different from country to country, from Syria to Yemen and from Oman to Morocco. Each country will experience a step-by-step process that will see reform steps being implemented slowly and to varying degrees of success. The whole exercise will be three steps forward, two steps back—meaning that overall movement will be forward, but incremental, drawn-out, and uneven. For any (well meaning) outside power, the key areas to focus on are institution-building, the implementation of an effective rule of law, and economic reforms."[12]

When Western influence will decrease over time in general, the role of the US will be affected in particular. American strategic interests focus primarily on the Persian Gulf, Israel and its immediate neighbours. The US will remain involved in both areas, which is supported by most regional players. For all their differences, the Arab Gulf states depend on American help in curbing Iranian ambitions and even Arab countries that accuse the United States of partisanship in the Middle East conflict, acknowledge that there will be no peaceful settlement of the Israeli-Palestinian conflict without US participation. But Washington's strategic interests in the Mediterranean are limited. Egypt and Israel are seen as strategic partners, but the interest in other states is not as obvious. Especially in the context of the war in Libya, Washington has made it clear that it would have liked to leave the solution entirely to the European allies.[13]

India, China and South Korea have rapidly increasing economic interests in West Asia and North Africa: Chinese trade increased ten-fold between 2000 and 2010, India's eightfold and South Korea's threefold. All three run trade deficits with the region and are, therefore, seeking to increase exports and win more contracts for major construction and infrastructure projects, but they will pay little attention to political processes in these countries.[14] Limitations also apply for other—even if European—individual players such as France or the UK. Therefore, the only candidate that is seen by many Arab politicians to shoulder greater responsibilities in West Asian affairs would be the European Union as the organisation to combine European resources and capabilities. This is definitely a surprise when compared with the limitations the Europeans had to live with in West Asia before the "Arab Spring". Yet, the more soft power attributes count in the assessment of a partner's strength, the more the EU's chances increase to outdo the predominant hard power capabilities of the US.

And indeed, circumstances—not at least as an immediate neighbour—leave Europe as the only significant international actor tied to West Asia and North Africa by both political and security relations as well as trade, economic and development interests. After the people in the region themselves, Europe has the strongest interest in the success of political changes. A particular role for Europe emerges when it comes to the consolidation of democratic initiatives, economic development and social stabilisation. Therefore, in the initial months after the Arab uprisings, the EU started many policy and aid initiatives to support the

Arab reformers. Germany, for instance, sent election observers to Egypt, Jordan, Libya and Algeria; several strategic "transformation partnerships" were launched. In 2012, the federal government allocated an additional amount of 100 million Euros for the transformation process in the Arab world. Sixty percent of the funds support the political and economic change, 40 percent are designed to support education and academic initiatives. Until 2017, funds for transformation partnerships are fed into the budget. Europe has lots of own experiences when it comes to democratic transformations and can, therefore, supply much assistance to similar transformation processes in other parts of the world. It can support the organisation of free elections and can help monitoring elections. It can also help to reform the security apparatus and the judiciary. In addition, Europe is an expert in rather unexciting but very important topics: general legal reforms; drafting a modern labour law and regulating relations between employers and trade unions (including rules for strikes and collective bargaining after the legalisation of free trade unions and industrial action); anti-trust legislation and rules for transparency and responsibility in business; and last but not least the establishment of effective social-insurance systems. Market-opening measures remain important, but should encourage job creation and must, if they are not to undermine the political process, go hand in hand with a credible social policy.[15]

The importance of the Arab States for the European economy will most probably grow, taking into account the demographic structure of these countries. The overwhelmingly young population in West Asia and North Africa struggles to overcome the political impotence and economic backwardness of its home countries. During the next decade, more than 20 percent of those countries' inhabitants would enter the labour market for the first time. This means an enormous challenge for every government/regime. But this generation will also be looking for education, housing, consumer goods and communication, i.e. new opportunities for manufacturers of consumer and capital goods as well as for companies in the housing, health, education, energy infrastructure and electricity generation will be generated. European companies in these growing markets should, therefore, be involved in the democratic transformation process—at least indirectly—for example, in advocating that the working conditions, workers' rights, environmental protection and transparency standards that apply in their home countries, will also be aspired to in the region. This begins with adequate training or promotion of training in state institutions and in local businesses. Most employers know that such investments will eventually pay off.

In this sense, the EU should present itself as an 'open Europe' and offer the transforming states new forms of partnership that are not only directed at governments but that also include the involved societies. Openness should relate to people as well as goods. Although the EU has concluded free-trade agreements with Tunisia, Egypt and other Mediterranean states, it still maintains protectionist rules that need to be revised or abolished. Agricultural imports from Egypt, for example, are restricted by seasonal quotas. If compared, greater openness to the people of these countries is even more important than openness concerning goods. Of the three 'M's that characterise European institutions—money, market and mobility—the latter is the most important in connection with Arab states in the transformation process. West Asia and North Africa as a whole are not poor, and a "Marshall Plan" of the sort often proposed in remembrance of the post-WW II efforts in Germany would be more likely to make these states dependent than to solve their core problems. The EU and the international financial institutions might be willing to lend financial support to help these countries overcome their economic difficulties, but they cannot offer more than Saudi Arabia or Qatar.[16]

Of course, this approach has more of a strategy than that it is been shaped by tactical considerations. As long as the transformation process stagnates or proceeds into the reverse direction as some observers state at the moment for the region in general, and for Egypt in particular, the European support or the supportive mood diminishes or comes to a temporary halt. When West Asian or North African matters came up in Europe in 2015, the people in the EU were, for example, more concerned with the rapidly increasing numbers of migrants than with the stagnant transformation process. Yet, in the long run, Europe can neither escape its geographic proximity to the region nor its political, security and, to a lesser extent, economic dependence.

And even in general terms, one should never forget that Europe has lots of own problems. The financial crisis-catchword Greece-high youth unemployment and social protests in some states; differences over the path to stronger economic and financial governance, atleast in the euro-zone and the successes of euro-sceptic populist parties may all help make European policymakers hesitant to declare the Union more open towards others. There is, nonetheless, a strong consensus that Europe needs to respond positively if the transformation process in West Asia and North Africa would re-emerge. This is not at all altruistic because successful transformations will reduce security risks that emanate from the region and enhance the chances of economic cooperation; failed transformations will increase the risks.

These explanations will be more convincing the more Europe is open and honest about its own interests. All states have economic, political and security interests that sometimes require cooperation with authoritarian regimes. Europe needs Egypt, whether under Mubarak or El Sisi, for the peace process, as a transit route and as an economic partner; it will continue to need Saudi Arabia for its resources, but also as an export market and for its regional influence. Similar considerations apply to other states in the region. There is nothing wrong about that, as even the demonstrators of the Arab Spring acknowledged; "it would enhance the credibility of the EU and its member states if such interests were clearly stated, rather than cloaked behind sugary declarations."[17]

Europe has a major interest in the political and social stability at its borders and regional stability is, therefore, a central concept in European politics. This is legitimate and understandable. But Arab autocrats misinterpret the concept and present themselves as guarantors of national and regional stability. They usually claim that their governments represent the only alternative to Europe's fear of instability, chaos, terrorism and the victory of radical Islamism. Alas, it turned out often enough that these regimes are rather stagnant than stable. Many European politicians bought this story and also confused stagnation with real, i.e. sustainable stability. Europe will by no means have to abandon the goal of stability, but it needs a dynamic understanding of stability in the sense that a balance should be achieved in which change and transformation are possible. Europe knows from its own experience that democratic political systems are the most stable ones.

Even if the Arab transformation process is interrupted at the moment, one may doubt whether European politicians and the public alike have at least in the initial phase of the Arab Spring understood that the Arab revolutionaries have given a political signal far and wide beyond the West Asia and North Africa, and have even done a great service for the European democracy. China's increasing power in the worldwide competition of political models has more and more forced Europe's democratic market-economy model on to the defensive. Many began to think that the Chinese authoritarian market-economy model based on harmony, growth and wise leadership (as opposed to individual freedom, human rights and democracy) is more promising. Even if the political transformation in the Arab world stagnates, the revolts have nevertheless shown that the great Chinese narrative, so popular among ruling elites in West Asia as well as in Central Asia and many African states, does not offer a real prospect for the younger generation. According to Perthes, "instead, this generation proved how vital the desire for democracy and liberty remains, even in states that have long sought to repress it. The European narrative, according to which a combination of individual liberty, democracy and social justice ultimately represents (for all its deficits and drawbacks) the best political model, thus received support from an unexpected quarter."[18]

Yet, on the other hand, this younger generation does very often expect a more supportive and robust behaviour of the EU in the international arena. Unfortunately, as far as joint action by the EU and shared positions among its members are concerned, the EU did not perform really convincing so far. This became especially obvious in the Libyan crisis. While France and the UK acted promptly and clearly supported the overthrow of the Gaddafi regime in Libya, Germany abstained in the UNSC vote on "Resolution 1973" concerning military action to protect the civilian population in Libya. By doing this, Germany sided with Russia and China and not with its supposedly closest allies in Europe. For many Arab states, Libya was a clear-cut case and it offered a real opportunity for a new relationship between Arab states and European countries as well as NATO to be significantly strengthened. The majority of Arab states would have liked to see Germany on board, yet the decision to not support the UN resolution removed the country from this equation. It was not only an opportunity clearly lost, but another disappointment for all those in West Asia who would prefer a German leadership role in the EU context when it comes to their region. Similar concerns came up concerning Germany's current position on Egypt and Syria. Although the entire West Asia is facing unprecedented turmoil, there is a feeling that the ultimate consequences of developments in these key countries are not well understood in German policy circles. Instead, Germany is once again seen as hiding under a European or Transatlantic cover that leaves the initiative on defining policy direction to others, primarily the US, UK, and France.[19]

Many Arabs complain that German policy in West Asia is not "aggressive" enough and therefore, remains at the margins of a meaningful policy input. This is all the more deplorable as there are so many opportunities to play a more important role. The most current example of this German indifference is its initial zigzag course in the Iraq issue. Since US President Barack Obama's decision to bomb IS extremists in Iraq, German public opinion has debated whether to get involved and if so, why. In its initial reaction to the crisis, the German government, sensing that its citizens would prefer to stay out of any new international entanglement, tried to suggest to its international partners, first and foremost the United States, that Berlin would be able to help civilians in the embattled country with humanitarian supplies, but not with any military aid.

This cautious and reluctant stance followed a well-established pattern by the Merkel government. It also reflects the fact that for a decade Iraq was perceived by most Germans as an American problem. After all, then Secretary of State Colin Powell had warned President George W. Bush that "if you break it you own it".[20] The overwhelming majority of Germans thought the United States had indeed broken Iraq, had been unable to fix it, and then had hastily abandoned the country. This interpretation was supported by the fact that even the Obama administration seemed to think that ownership of the Iraq problem squarely fell on its predecessor's shoulders and it was time to move on.

But international challenges rarely adapt to domestic electoral considerations and public opinions. Not surprisingly, more recent developments in northern Iraq have not only dragged the United States back into the country, but the outright threat of genocide and a surprising critical reaction in German media have also caused a sudden shift in the German government's response. Three members of Merkel's cabinet, namely Vice Chancellor Sigmar Gabriel, Foreign Minister Frank-Walter Steinmeier, and the Minister of Defence Ursula von der Leyen have all opened the door for a more robust German involvement, including the delivery of some urgently needed military equipment to the Kurds in the north of Iraq. Finally, the parliament agreed to support the anti-IS Kurdish Peshmerga also, militarily.

Thus, initially the government had misjudged public opinion and promptly tried to correct the mistake later on. Is this the U-turn in German foreign policy that so many ask from Germany? Is Germany really more willing to abandon the role of the reluctant hegemon in Europe and play a more active role? It depends. Germany's critics underestimate Berlin's already well-established leadership role when they demand more. Conversely, the latest developments should not be interpreted as a dramatic departure from Germany's traditional foreign policy stance. But Germans are slowly realising that hiding from international challenges, albeit tempting, is not an option. Some might continue to dream of neutrality. But the vast majority will adapt to a new role in Europe and, possibly, in the world. Merkel's predecessor, Gerhard Schroeder, tried to force this process. Merkel has the enviable advantage that she only needs to gently nudge her people in the right direction. The process is not bump free, but it is taking place.[21]

## Prospects

Just to repeat, the EU, including Germany, should play a more important role in West Asia. Yet, Europe should also be aware, that it is only one player in a multi-facetted international orchestra. As regional powers' reactions to the Ukraine crisis demonstrate for example, world politics is no longer defined solely by what happens in Europe, even when a major conflict has its roots there. The international system has become so multi-polar that non-European states can now choose to follow their own interests rather than feel obliged to side with the East or the West.

Few world leaders doubt that Russia's use of force to challenge Ukraine's territorial integrity, change its borders, and annex Crimea violated international law. China's abstention in the subsequent United Nations Security Council vote clearly signalled its leaders' displeasure with Russia's policy. But nearly one-third of the UN's members sent an equally emphatic message by abstaining or not participating in a General Assembly vote condemning Russia's actions. Even Western-friendly governments—including Brazil, India, South Africa, and Israel—were not prepared to take sides. The Indian journalist Indrani Bagchi referred to the abstentions as a new form of non-alignment. The implicit message from the new non-aligned is straightforward: Why should we care about a territorial conflict in Europe when you Europeans fail to act decisively on Palestine, Kashmir, or territorial disputes in the East and South China Seas? Instead, many of these countries are calling on the West to de-escalate the crisis. That is good advice—and no different from what Europeans tell others in similar situations.

On the other hand, if Europe will be unable to resolve the Ukraine crisis with diplomacy, its global influence, and that of Russia, will surely fade. Russia has reminded the world that it is possible to bully one's neighbours and steal their territory using brute force; but, in a globalised, multi-polar system, this alone will not be enough to rally other countries to its cause. And the EU, as a highly sophisticated paper tiger, would be no more attractive.[22]

EU member states are not interested in a re-emergence of ethnic nationalism and power politics on their continent. The crisis between Russia and the Ukraine can, therefore, both become a challenge and an opportunity. If Europe wants to remain a visible pole in a multi-polar international system, it must prove that it can really pursue a common foreign and security policy, particularly in times of crisis and conflict and is able to formulate a long-term strategy that takes the growing international role and standing of emerging powers into account.

## NOTES

1. Andreas Rinke, 'The End of Germany's Sonderweg,' *Reuters*, October 8, 2012.
2. Gregor Schoellgen, 'Deutsche Aussenpolitik in der Ära Schroeder', *Aus Politik und Zeitgeschichte* 32 /33, 2005, pp. 3-15.
3. Felix Neugart, 'The EU and the Challenge of Iraq', in Christian Koch (ed.), *Unfulfilled Potential; Exploring the GCC-EU Relationship*, Gulf Research Center (GRC), Dubai, 2005.
4. Michaela C. Hertkorn, "Why German-US Relations Still Matter to the Transatlantic Alliance. One Year after the War in Iraq", Institute for Foreign and Security Policy, Duesseldorf, 2004.
5. Richard Bernstein, "The German Question", *The New York Times*, May 2, 2004, at http:/ /www.nytimes.com/2004/05/02/magazine/the-german-question.html?_r=0.
6. Tuomas Forsberg, "German Foreign Policy and the War on Iraq: Anti-Americanism, Pacifism or Emancipation?", *Security Dialogue*, 36, 2005, pp. 213-231.
7. Rainer Winkler, *Die Irak-Krise im Bundestagswahlkampf 2002*, Institute for Foreign and Security Policy, Duesseldorf, 2003.
8. Schoellgen, n. 2.

9. Guido Steinberg, "German Middle East and North Africa Policy", SWP, Berlin, 2009, at http://www.swp-berlin.org/en/publications/swp-research-papers/swp-research-paper-detail/article/deutsche_nah_mittelost_und_nordafrikapolitik.html.
10. Abdulaziz Sager, "Time for a more activist Middle East policy", Review 2014-Aussenpolitik weiter denken, Berlin, 2014, at http://www.aussenpolitik-weiter-denken.de/en/external-view/article/time-for-a-more-activist-middle-east-policy.html.
11. Simon Serfaty, *Memories of Europe's Future: Farewell to Yesteryear*, CSIS, Washington D.C., 1999.
12. Sager, n. 10.
13. Volker Perthes, 'Europe and the Arab Spring,' *Survival* 53 (6), 2011, p. 74.
14. Ibid.
15. Ibid., p. 76.
16. Ibid., pp. 76-78.
17. Ibid., p. 81.
18. Ibid., pp. 82-83.
19. Sager, n.10, p. 3.
20. David Samuels, "A Conversation with Colin Powell", *The Atlantic*, April 2007.
21. Alexander Privitera, "Germany's Future Iraq Involvement: U-Turn or Continuity?" AICGS, Washington D.C., 2014, pp. 1-3.
22. Volker Perthes, "Europe in a Multipolar World", *Project Syndicate*, June 9, 2014, pp. 1-2.

# PART IV

# Regional Instability and Energy Security

# 14

# Changing Text of Energy Geopolitics and West Asia

*Girijesh Pant*

Energy geopolitics has been a critical factor in scripting the West Asian text since the discovery of black gold in the region. Among the important markers in this trajectory have been US President Roosevelt meeting King of Saudi Arabia in 1945, signing of oil-security deal, Central Intelligence Agency (CIA) overthrow of Iranian Prime Minister Mohammad Mosadiq in 1952, Organisation of the Petroleum Exporting Countries (OPEC) formation in 1960, the Organisation of Arab Petroleum Exporting Countries (OAPEC) oil embargo in 1967, quadruple rise of oil prices in 1972-73, President Jimmy Carter's threat doctrine in 1980, the twin tower attack of 2001, US energy independence—shale revolution, oil is gradually but perceptibly moving away from the centrality of Western/USA energy strategic calculus in the region. Europe is cutting down its hydrocarbon consumption by enhancing efficiency level and moving to renewable, USA is emerging as net exporter of hydrocarbon, and the sustainability thrust for renewable is changing the global energy mix. Consequently, OPEC is not controlling the commanding height. With changes in the global energy text, the geopolitics of the oil suppliers from West Asia is reflecting corresponding shift. The 'Look East' policy is the new construct of oil suppliers. Moreover, the producers are finding presence of new set of players with varied leverage in energy market sometimes at their cost. Surely, hydrocarbon will remain the critical, possibly, the major component of global energy mix and hence will continue to enjoy strategic salience but in the context where the consumers are geographically located on eastern part of the globe. Despite the fact that the regional security architecture and political leverage continue to be with the West, a new set of parameters are playing out in re-defining the interface between energy and the geopolitics of the region. A new marker of regional energy geopolitics could be noticed since 2011 when following the Arab uprising, the region experienced regime changes and instabilities with new geography and polity in making. The paper argues that the post 2011 developments in the region are suggesting that the geopolitics of energy in the region is likely to be defined by the region itself. This would mean that energy geopolitics will be boxed in the region. This could turn out to be a major departure.

## Strategic Shift in Energy Market: Erosion of West Asian Leverage

The power projection capacity of oil producers from West Asia as principal player in global oil regime is peaking out much before their oil endowment. This has been demonstrated by the fact that the supply disruption from the region was offset by American oil thus displaying immunity of global oil market to the temper of the region. The oil prices declined by nearly 60 percent during June 2014 to January 2015. Recognising their declining leverage in market, the oil producers especially from the Gulf decided not to cut oil supply despite falling prices. Their strategy is to regain their say in oil price determination by putting the high cost producers in disadvantage position. Saudi Minister of Petroleum and Mineral Resources has expressed disapproval with loud and clear terms that high cost producers cannot be allowed to reap the advantage of oil prices at the cost of low cost producers. OPEC positioning of no supply cut imposed by the Gulf producers may not yield advantage to all its members, as the time frame of price recovery prolongs, the increasing fiscal burden will impact upon the legitimacy of the member governments. Not all oil exporters have deep pocket. Apparently drawing from past, the hope of recovery is based on the reading that the price behaviour is of cyclical nature hence it will bounce back. So, the members should have endurance. It is not a story of volatility but of steady decline. However, this is a simplistic assessment of the structural changes that the energy market is witnessing. The prices will indeed recover but the magnitude will not be of the scale to place OPEC members into the kind of fiscal comfort they have had enjoyed.

Some of the salient tendencies impacting on the changing power equation in oil market include the declining volume of OPEC crude amounting to 29.4 mbpd in 2015, a decline of 300,000 bpd from 2014. The non-OPEC supply estimated to grow by 1.3 mbpd in 2015 to average 57 mbpd, lower than the 2014 but estimated increase of 1.5 mbpd. It would mean the group's crude market share would fall to less than a third of the market at 32 percent, down from 35 percent in 2014. A recap of seventies may not be out of place, when OPEC was producing 51 percent of global oil. The most critical factor defining the strategic shift is the declining American dependence on the regional supplies. It is a fundamental change of the premise. Though the OPEC oil supply has been on rise since 2008 when it accounted for 6 mbpd, it did not reflect in the geopolitics because the framework of strategic engagement between the Gulf producers and their consumers get impacted by it. It was American positioning as oil consumer and producer that has altered the matrix. The assumption that flooring of oil prices will subvert American oil revolution has so far not worked and the assessment from the market is that it is not likely to be worked out. At best, its impact may sober down. It is not the question of American endurance alone but of OPEC members as well. It is significant to note that between 2008 and 2014, American oil imports have declined by 50 percent though it was by only 40 percent from the Gulf countries. Importantly from Saudi Arabia, the leading strategic partner, the decline has been of only 13 percent.[1] However the heavier nature of the Gulf oil and the changing configuration of refineries in USA could further restrict the volume of imports from the region. The important point is that there is oil in the market which under the given context could be replaced. This can play as a loss of leverage for the Gulf or for that matter Saudi Arabia's status as a swing producer.

From the geopolitical perspective it will be interesting to notice that rising global power China is emerging as leading energy importer from the region. Though in the larger context, emerging Asia is the future oil market for Gulf and West Asia, it is the strategic-security dimension of the energy engagement that places China on pre-eminence. The shift in oil trade, according to International Energy Agency (IEA) will mean, oil exports from the West Asia to Asia will increase by 1.2 mbpd between 2012 and 2018, including 0.4 mbpd to China. Exports to the US and Organisation for Economic Cooperation and Development (OECD) Europe will shrink by 1 mbpd and 0.3 mbpd, respectively. Asian imports from 2013-2019 will be 16 percent making it 22 mbpd accounting to 65 percent of the international crude market—as North America swings to net oil exporter. The vulnerability of Gulf oil exporters could be appreciated by the fact that many of them offered discounted price to Asian consumers. Saudi Arabia offered highest discount to Asian customers in the last ten years.[2] What is more alarming is that the discounted oil supply is perceived as beginning of price war among oil producers. According to Jacob Grahnlot, "a price war between producers has raged since Saudi Arabia and its Gulf OPEC allies last November chose to keep their taps open in a bid for market share over price, sending oil prices down more than a third to under US$ 50 a barrel in just two months.

Since then, Gulf producers—including Saudi Arabia and the United Arab Emirates—have steadily increased shipments to Asia, helped by low production costs that allow aggressive discounts, at the expense of West African and Latin American supplies."[3] While Asia is going to be the major energy market for the Gulf and the West Asian countries, the nature and dynamics of their engagement is not as comprehensive as it had been with the West or USA. It is largely energy transactional engagement. The issue that needs to be addressed is whether, in the context of complex nature of regional security, this one-dimensional engagement will be sustainable or not. So far this could work because the West has been undertaking the wider regional responsibilities. Now the limitation of the American power in the region and their re-assessment of scale of security engagement in view of their 'energy independence' is creating a situation where either the region plays out a responsible security dynamics or leading energy consumers from Asia, including China, recalibrate their energy vision with reference to larger premise of rising Asia. The larger frame is a necessity because China despite its robust economy has yet to acquire the power to underwrite the security needs of West Asia on its own. Yet it goes to the credit of China that it is exploring new terms of its Asian energy engagement.

## Reconnecting Asia: The Chinese Script of Energy Geopolitics

The massive US$ 16.3 billion proposal from China to promote Silk route by land and sea and commitment of 40 billion to Silk route fund is going to be the key word of new text of energy geopolitics in the region. It aims to overcome geographical barriers by creating infrastructure and connectivity altering the reference of time and space of transactions among the countries of the region. Its stated objective is to provide investment and financing support to carry out infrastructure, resources, industrial cooperation, financial cooperation and other projects related to connectivity for countries along the "One Belt and One Road". Indeed it is driven by economic imperatives of globalising China but its strategic connotation cannot be ignored. China is the emerging global power contesting the dynamics of global order defined by the power of USA. As it steps out in volume and reach as a global player, it needs a space for its growing requirements be it economic or strategic. It would like to construct a world order to its advantage as the US has done since the end of World War II. However, distinction needs to be made that US had the military backup to advance its economic cause and the global power differential was highly skewed to contain American "imperial march", while China does not enjoy the military power to impose its preferences. Further, it also does not have the advantage of the power asymmetry as well. More important is that the Chinese global drive emanate from its globalising profile. It is even argued that it reflects the Grand Strategy of China. Surely its geographical dimensions are huge. As per the Chinese sources, "the land-based Silk Road starts from the ancient capital city of Xi'an, stretching west through Lanzhou and Urumqi before running southwest across Central Asia, the Middle East and Europe. The sea-based Maritime Silk Road goes through Guangdong and the southernmost Chinese province of Hainan, an island, en route to the Malacca Strait and Indian Ocean. It traverses the Horn of Africa before entering the Red Sea and Mediterranean. The two roads are supposed to meet in Venice."[4] Crafting these land and maritime routes to Chinese advantage is not going to be feasible by financial resources alone. A full display of negotiations with high diplomatic skills to build confidence and develop the stakes of countries located on the route is going to be a challenge for China because the baggage of history is bound to evoke apprehension along with the appreciation simultaneously.

It needs no elaboration that the idea of reviving the Silk Road as a means of Chinese global engagement has not come from thin air. It cannot be the romance with the past, it is the intent of their thinking of future road map. The 'new normal drive' of Chinese economy would be reshaping its foreign economic engagement more by contributing to overseas manufacturing hubs by sourcing innovative clusters at home. Apparently, China finds that there are humps and road blocks. These humps are its neighbours with whom major-minor issues are irritants but the major challenge is to steer through the trappings of American Asian pivot. It will be relevant to juxtapose the Chinese formulations to the Trans Pacific Partnership (TPP). According to the Office of the United States Trade Representatives, TPP aims to open opportunity for America through trade with Asia Pacific.[5]

US President Barack Obama's trade agenda is dedicated to expand economic opportunity for American workers, farmers, ranchers, and businesses. That's why US is negotiating the TPP, a 21st century trade agreement that will boost US economic growth, support American jobs, and grow 'Made-in-America' exports to some of the most dynamic and fastest growing countries in the world. At the cornerstone of the Obama Administration's economic policy in the Asia Pacific, the TPP reflects the United States' economic priorities and values. The TPP not only seeks to provide new and meaningful market access for American goods and services exports, but also set high-standard rules for trade, and address vital 21st century issues within the global economy.

The humongous profile of TPP could be gauged by the fact that it supposedly accounts for 40 percent of the world's gross domestic product (GDP) and 26 percent of the world's trade. That makes it roughly the same size as the Trans-Atlantic Trade and Investment Partnership.[6] China is not its member. In fact, initially China perceived it as a part of US strategy to contain it. Of late, the leadership in China has expressed the desire to look at it with open mind. Though essentially project of larger free trade block, TPP disturbs China for its counterbalancing connotation by US engagement with its neighbours who have been needling Chinese global rise. China realises that peace with neighbours is essential for its global rise. China will certainly face constraints in tweeting its problems with the neighbours due to American presence.

The Silk route initiative is to soften the neighbours by its promises of developing trade logistics and its infrastructure which the countries in the region are looking for. It is argued that "China cannot win the battle for regional sentiment so long as the debate is about security and sovereignty, on which Beijing's hard position leaves little room for compromise. Many see negotiations on the Regional Comprehensive Economic Partnership (RCEP) with the ASEAN plus Six grouping as China's counterweight to the TPP in pushing the regional agenda towards more mutually beneficial concerns. Yet both of these endeavours are potentially pale in comparison with President Xi Jinping's fanciful idea of reviving the "maritime silk route" during his visit to Malaysia and Indonesia. This notion builds on the East Asia region's proven strengths in sharing production and deepening financial links while seeking to make greater use of the overseas Chinese communities in forging relationships to reduce tensions."[7]

The strength of the Chinese proposal lies in the possibilities of creating regional capacities to facilitate trade as a consequence of regional production network and supply chain. This merits attention because, "a sharp decline in transport costs along the contemporary maritime silk route allowed all countries in the region, regardless of their size and technological sophistication, to benefit from specialisation and economies of scale by producing components rather than complete products. This is the major reason why East Asia has performed so well relative to the rest of the world. With rising labour costs in China, many ASEAN economies now stand to gain from future outsourcing of production. This combines with the trade deficits that China runs with most of its Asian neighbours—in contrast to its persistent surpluses with the West—to make it easier for China to be seen as an opportunity rather than a threat."[8] Clearly Silk route, as a geoeconomic construct, is emanating out of the imperatives of globalisation processes. However, the geopolitical and geostrategic implications of this geoeconomic construct cannot be ignored.

The strategic gains that China will make from these projects are obvious. It will get legitimacy to its reach and presence in the region. It is no surprise that the Chinese government is projecting them as win-win proposition. It is aware of the project being read as another Marshall Plan or an architecture of Chinese hegemony. No wonder they emphasise that "China proposed to build the

Maritime Silk Road of the 21st century with the aim of realising harmonious co-existence, mutual benefit and common development with relevant countries by carrying out practical cooperation in various fields, such as maritime connectivity, marine economy, technically-advanced environmental protection, disaster prevention and reduction as well as social and cultural exchanges in the spirit of peace, friendship, cooperation and development." China does have resources, the wherewithal to push the mega projects, what it faces as crucial challenge is to have the leading powers in the region on board and not to antagonise its relation with the USA. In Chinese understanding, vision and strategy confrontation is not the option in short run. Their declaration to craft an alternative paradigm of international relation underlines this point, time and again. The Chinese Foreign Minister presiding over the Security Council meeting held on February 25, 2015 observed that, "the old mindset of confrontation should be discarded and consultation and cooperation among the parties should be encouraged if we are to address the major issues affecting world and regional peace and development."[9] The strength of Chinese proposal lies at its being seen as alternative to American Asian pivot.

## 'Subversive' Sub-Text

Couched in collaborative and co-operative mode, Chinese script has very distinct strategic message which could possibly restrict its pace or might even distort its meaning. The maritime expanse of Chinese strategy, often described as pearl of string, is creating more apprehension than confidence of its intents. It is argued that this will provide infrastructure and logistic support to People's Liberation Army Navy (PLAN) to have access to Indian Ocean. According to one assessment, "the PLAN's current capabilities, China's logistics capacity would only be dependable during peacetime; they would not survive in a contested environment, particularly if the US decided to close off key chokepoints like the Malacca and Sunda Straits."[10] The maritime implications of Chinese energy policy has been seen with reservation in India too. It is perceived as an excursion in its area of influence. So it has responded by a counter initiative called 'Project Mausam'. The project focus on "maritime routes and cultural landscapes across the Indian Ocean, the natural wind phenomenon, especially monsoon winds used by Indian sailors in ancient times for maritime trade, that has shaped interactions between countries and communities connected by the Indian Ocean."[11] Reportedly, the Indian Prime Minister's visit to Indian Ocean nations—Mauritius, Seychelles and Sri Lanka was aimed at giving a fillip to 'Project Mausam'.[12] It is observed that Prime Minister Narendra Modi has flagged a maritime security and defence cooperation plan prior to his visit to these countries. The plan is driven by defence support—like "giving patrol vessels, capacity building, expanding the trilateral

(India-Maldives-Sri Lanka) friendship exercise to include Seychelles and Mauritius and other measures to firm up maritime security cooperation."[13] There is an underlying perception that the China's military influence is growing in Seychelles, Mauritius, Sri Lanka and Maldives. China sees Seychelles as a potential resupply port for its navy ships and one of its submarines.[14] India is also talking of reviving old spice route which once linked Southern India with Europe. However India would not like to project Chinese moves detrimental to its interest. This is evident by the fact that India, as a leading energy consumer, would like to draw maximum gains from such cooperative initiatives coming from China. India and China are exploring the potential of regional cooperation. BCIM (Bangladesh-China-India-Myanmar) corridor is an example linking Kunming to Kolkata, Mandalay (Myanmar), Dhaka and Chittagong. It is intended to advance multi-modal connectivity, harnessing economic complementarities, promote investment and trade and facilitate people-to-people contacts.

## Energy Geopolitics Boxed in Regional Anarchy

If the present wave of regional geopolitics is characterised by "failed states, humiliated people, crippled economies, extreme inequality and poverty, devastated environment, plundered resources, conflicted geographies, foreign intrusions, and violent radicalism"[15], then it is argued here that the terms of regional global oil engagement will be defined by the power dynamics of the region itself. This is a reversal from the context when global energy geopolitics was shaping the regional power dynamics. This is not to argue that the regional oil will be losing global salience but to underline the surfacing of contradictions created by the distortion caused by oil in making of its political geography and the degeneration contributed by the power of the rent, undermining the role of institution and putting region on the brink of implosion. The principle argument made here is that any logical conclusion emanating from implosion namely regional order or anarchy will redefine the role of oil correspondingly but with reference to regional parameter. Region's demands will have more bearing on regional supply. The comfort of oil supply may turn into short term affair. Surely, except in worst case disruption scenario, oil supply from the region will be available for oil consuming nations, specially Asia, but it will not be enjoying the strategic premium of the kind it availed with the Western energy dependence on the region. Further, the region may not be positioning itself as a strategic supplier of energy despite exporting energy. The point made is that oil will be treated less as strategic commodity and would be moving on commercial platform. Saudi Arabia's decision to restructure Saudi Arabian Oil Company (ARAMCO) may be seen as a pointer to this direction.

The geopolitics of regional oil will be shaped by two distinct trends: one, the survival imperatives of the individual countries; and second, the intra-regional power rivalry mainly between Saudi Arabia and Iran, though Iraqi oil could equally be influential. Saudi Arabian oil policy clearly shows its own concerns be it for market share or subversion of US oil power or undermining the prospects of Iranian and Russian oil dividend. The following snippets further illustrates individual interest over the collective:[16]

I. Iraq's State Oil Marketing Organisation has been discounting prices for Basra Light to its main competitor in Asia, Arab Light, in order to win greater market share. These discounts were between US$ 0.40 and US$ 1.10 per barrel.

II. Iran, hard hit by sanctions, has offered cheaper oil on delivered basis using subsidised shipping or even free shipping as in the case of India as a pricing weapon.

III. Iraq, Iran and Kuwait have all offered term oil supplies on extended credit terms, up to 90 days in order to secure large contracts from countries such as India.

IV. UAE's Abu Dhabi National Oil Company (ADNOC) has recently offered first oil cargos without destination restrictions hoping to make them more attractive to customers by making crude optimisation and trading easier.

V. Saudi ARAMCO has increased both length and volumes of the leased storage facility in Okinawa, Japan so that they can offer short hauled crude oil to their North Asian customers.

VI. Abu Dhabi has signed a similar contract to lease storage in Yosu, South Korea. Many similar deals are in the pipeline.

## Conclusion

The emerging power rivalry in the region emanating from new dynamics of competition for regional hegemony by evoking Islamist identity politics could be a game changer. Unlike the past when oil price decline was addressed by collective political interest defined around fiscal anxiety, presently the region is witnessing ruthless struggle overtly or covertly triggered by Islamist identity as defining principle of the region. The competition is not confined between Saudi Arabia and Iran, many other formations of extremist profile like the Islamic State, Al Qaeda or the Muslim Brotherhood are in the play. There are multiple scripts on 'authentic Islamist Governance'. All will be using their oil power to consolidate their politics. The way Islamic State traded oil illustrates the point. The huge burden of military expenditure, financing of strategic partners both state and non-state players, public expenditure to negotiate with domestic discontent or the huge destruction of oil assets to inflict injury to regional enemy are the regional factors that are going to define the oil supply from the region. A plausible scenario could not be ruled out when countries of the region may rise 'above the region' thereby redefining the regional geopolitics on the strength of their energy power—Qatar did it.[17] Ironically as the regional rivalries are playing out, it is increasingly going to be difficult for extra regional players to engage substantially to revert to a globally defined regional geopolitical construct. However, it may be relevant here to mention that energy being boxed in the regional quagmire, is not good news for the emerging market of Asia which will be looking for energy flows from the region. The consequences of changing text of the regional energy geopolitics was the matter of deliberation in the last meeting of the Energy Ministers from Asia-Pacific held in Beijing in 2014 where a need for collective Asia-Pacific Economic Cooperation (APEC) framework was considered as defining text of West Asian energy geopolitics.

## NOTES

1. Herman Franseen Iddle, "Obama and Declining US Dependence on Imported Oil and Gas", *Middle East Institute*, November 25, 2015, at http://www.mei.edu/content/article/obama-and-declining-us-dependence-imported-oil-and-gas.
2. "Saudi Slashes January Oil Prices for Asia, US", *Gulf Business*, December 7, 2015, at http://gulfbusiness.com/2014/12/saudi-slashes-january-oil-prices-asia-u-s/#.VUdyw46qqko.
3. Jacob Grahnlot, "In oil price war, Gulf producers grab market share in Asia", *Reuters*, February 6, 2015, at http://www.reuters.com/article/2015/02/06/us-asia-gulf-crude-idUSKBN0LA0J720150206.
4. "China Said to Plan $16.3 Billion Fund for 'New Silk Road'", *Bloomberg*, November 4, 2014, at http://www.bloomberg.com/news/articles/2014-11-04/china-said-to-plan-16-3-billion-fund-to-revive-silk-road.
5. "Unlocking Opportunity for Americans through trade with the Asia Pacific", Office of the US trade Representative, at https://ustr.gov/tpp.
6. Lydia Dipillis, "Everything you need to know about the Trans Pacific Partnership", *The Washington Post*, December 11, 2015, at http://www.washingtonpost.com/blogs/wonkblog/wp/2013/12/11/everything-you-need-to-know-about-the-trans-pacific-partnership/.
7. Yukon Huang, "Courting Asia: China's Maritime Silk Route vs America's Pivot", *The Diplomat*, April 25, 2014, at http://thediplomat.com/2014/04/courting-asia-chinas-maritime-silk-route-vs-americas-pivot/.
8. Ibid.
9. "China highlights 4 'dos,' 'don'ts' in developing international relations", *CCTV*, February 24, 2015, at http://english.cntv.cn/2015/02/24/ARTI1424745180020616.shtml.
10. William Yale, "China's Maritime Silk Road Gamble", *The Diplomat*, April 22, 2015, at http://thediplomat.com/2015/04/chinas-maritime-silk-road-gamble/.
11. Sachin Prashar, "Narendra Modi's 'Mausam' manoeuvre to check China's maritime might", *The Times of India*, September 16, 2014, at http://timesofindia.indiatimes.com/india/Narendra-Modis-Mausam-manoeuvre-to-check-Chinas-maritime-might/articleshow/42562085.cms.

12. "China says 'Mausam' can be linked to 'One Belt One Road", *Deccan Herald*, March 15, 2015, at http://www.deccanherald.com/content/463755/china-says-mausam-can-linked.html.
13. Jayanth Jacob, "PM to flag off maritime security plan for Indian Ocean Region", *Hindustan Times*, March 9, 2015, at http://www.hindustantimes.com/india-news/china-on-mind-pm-to-flag-off-maritime-security-plan-for-indian-ocean-region/article1-1324215.aspx.
14. Ibid.
15. Hooshang Ahmadi, "Dark New Geopolitics of the Middle East", *The Cairo Review of Global Affairs*, July 5, 2015, at http://www.aucegypt.edu/gapp/cairoreview/Pages/articleDetails.aspx?aid=852.
16. Adi Imsirovic, "Asian Oil Market sin Transition", *Journal of Energy Security*, April 24, 2014, at http://www.ensec.org/index.php?option=com_content&id=520:asian-oil-markets-in-transition&catid=143:issue-content&Itemid=435.
17. Jim Krane and Steven Wright, "Qatar 'Rises Above' its Region: Geopolitics and the Rejection of the GCC Gas Market", London School of Economics, March 2014, at http://eprints.lse.ac.uk/55336/1/__lse.ac.uk_storage_LIBRARY_Secondary_libfile_shared_ repository_Content_Kuwait%20Programme_Krane_2014.pdf.

# 15

# Safeguarding the SLOCs from West Asia as an Energy Security Policy: A Japanese Perspective

*Toshitaka Takeuchi*

For the purpose of this paper, energy security is defined as it has been adopted by the United Nations Development Programme (UNDP) in 2004.[1] According to UNDP, energy security is the availability of energy at all times in various forms, in sufficient quantities and at affordable prices, without unacceptable or irreversible impact on the economy. One difference from the original UNDP definition is that this paper omits the environmental aspect because of the focus on the transportation side of energy security, without any disregard to the importance of environmental protection. Safeguarding Sea Lines of Communication (SLOCs) is a crucial aspect of energy security. Asian, especially East Asian efforts are important in this regard since keeping SLOCs safe is a matter of multilateral concerns and interests.

## Demand Side

It is a well-known fact that today's world is dependent on fossil fuels, especially oil. The world produces approximately 40 percent of its energy from fossil fuel sources. Oil is mostly used in the transportation sector, amounting to 95 percent of that sector's energy needs. Our world is such that we cannot live normal lives without gasoline. The production and reserves of oil and gas are quite concentrated geographically. The Middle East produces about 40 percent of the world's oil and 20 percent of world's gas, while holding an even larger share of world oil and gas reserves.[2] Because of this, it is easy to understand that oil rich countries in the Middle East can and do have inordinate influence on world economy. This influence is exemplified in the 1973 oil embargo, which precipitated the world-wide stagflation (simultaneous inflation and recession). During that crisis, Japan experienced its first period of negative economic growth since World War II.

It is also easy to see that political and societal instability in the Middle East will surely have a large impact on world economy. For example, the Iranian Islamic revolution in 1979 precipitated a world-wide economic recession. The regime change that happened in Iran after the revolution altered the political picture in the Middle East drastically, which of course affected world politics in a significant way.

These kinds of impact will become more pronounced in the future. Global energy consumption in 2030 is anticipated to rise to 1.4 times its present level, with half of that increase caused by Asia. China and India are now going through rapid economic growth with attendant need for more energy resources such as oil. The oil consumption of China and India with their combined population of more than 2.4 billion, one third of the world total, is expected to grow quite rapidly along with their economies. China's gross domestic product (GDP) is expected to increase at about 7.5 percent while India's is expected to increase 5.5 percent per year. As a result, "by 2030 Asia will import 80 percent of its total oil needs and 80 percent of this total will come from the Persian Gulf."[3] This increase in demand might intensify the already competitive nature for energy resources among East Asian nations. Nonetheless, it also gives the region a big incentive for cooperative behaviour.

## Supply Side

The supply side of this issue does not look promising because of the instability in the Middle East which has been politically volatile since the Arab Spring that started in 2010. For instance, Syria is in a bitter protracted internal conflict, which can be termed a civil war. Libya and Iraq are also witnessing severe internal conflicts. Egypt may appear to be stabilised, but there may be a big amount of magma waiting to erupt from underneath that fragile surface. The shale oil revolution currently taking place in the US may be a silver lining in this bleak supply picture in the future. US oil production has increased from 5 million barrels a day in 2008 to 8 million barrels a day in 2014. One consequence of this increase is that US imports of oil are down to 8 million from 10 million in 2007. According to International Energy Agency (IEA), the US is expected to be the biggest oil producer in the world in 2015.[4]

The US has prohibited crude oil exports, with some exceptions such as

Canada, since just after the oil crisis in 1975. However, it has loosened some of those restrictions in order to export light oil starting in June 2014.[5] Thus, if and when the US starts exporting shale oil, crude oil supply situation of the world might change drastically. However, the prospect is not necessarily so bright because US crude oil exports might make domestic gasoline prices rise; something which may hit the US consumers. The US also is now producing an abundant amount of shale gas.

## Transportation (Safeguarding SLOCs) Side

When we speak of energy security, we tend to focus only on supply and demand because these are the fundamentals of the matter. However, there is one more essential aspect to energy security that should not be underestimated. It is the transportation and delivery side, for which safeguarding the SLOCs is crucial. If the transport and delivery of goods are disturbed or disrupted, no matter how much oil is produced in, say, the Middle East, it is obvious that consumers cannot get access to it. This aspect is especially crucial for East Asian countries such as Japan, China and South Korea because almost all of their imported oil has to go through the Persian Gulf, the Indian Ocean and the Malacca Strait. Therefore, security, safety and safeguarding the SLOCs should be included as one of the three pillars of energy security. This paper devotes most of its attention to the transportation portion of energy security.

Depending on one's perspective, the current energy resources transport situation is a dangerous powder keg waiting to be ignited. Alternatively, this is an area that has a good potential for cooperation among interested stakeholder countries. The former is based on a zero-sum view that safeguarding the SLOCs is a competition such that one country's benefit is another's loss. The latter is of the view that the SLOCs are global commons (international public goods) that all parties can benefit from without hurting anybody else's interest. As long as we hold the former view, one cannot deny a theoretical possibility that there might be a military confrontation over these SLOCs in the future. This possibility must be kept in mind at all times lest there be some unfortunate happenstance. We have to change our mind-set so that everyone shares the latter perspective.

## Japan's Energy Situation

### *Overview of Energy Generation*

Let us first take a look at Japan's energy security. An article claimed that "Japan is the most vulnerable of all Organisation for Economic Cooperation and Development (OECD) nations in terms of energy supply security."[6] This assertion may indeed be correct. It is a well-known fact that Japan is a resource poor country. Before the tsunami and nuclear accident on March 11, 2011, Japan relied on nuclear energy for 30 percent of its electricity generation. One goal of the national policy to improve energy security was to increase the share of the nuclear generation to up to 50 percent by 2030, according to the "New National Energy Strategy" of 2006.[7] However, none of that electricity is available now since none of Japan's 48 commercial reactors are in operation at present.

Japan has resorted to oil burning thermal electricity generation to partially make up for this energy shortfall. Because of that, more oil has to be imported, most of which comes from the Middle East. The share of the Japan's imported oil coming from the Middle East is a staggering 80 percent or more. In fact, imports of fossil fuels (mainly crude oil) jumped about 25 percent, totalling nearly a third of total import spending.[8] This increased quest for oil by Japan has also exacerbated the so-called Asian Premium, a higher oil price in Asia than elsewhere, because of purchasing competition among Asian nations such as Japan, China and India. Finally, Japan has been running a trade deficit since 2011, which has made even the current account in the red sometimes. People and industry are hard pressed by price hikes for electricity that was already much higher (two to three times) than neighbouring countries such as South Korea. Japan's electricity price is one of the highest in the world (see Fig. 1). Also, the "end-use retail prices have been among the highest in OECD countries."[9]

### *Possible Measures*

What can or should Japan do in order to alleviate this acute energy supply situation, especially its heavy dependence on the Middle East for oil? The answers are obvious and clear: namely, conserve to decrease the demand, supply more energy that is not thermal and diversify the sources of imports. First, in terms of conservation, Japan is already one of the most energy efficient countries in the world. So, there is only so much more efficiency that Japanese energy conservation can produce. Second, there are some promising alternatives to fossil fuels for energy production such as solar, wind and geothermal generation. At present, solar energy is the most practical and is currently being utilised for energy generation. However, the generation of solar energy is negligible amounting to less than 1 percent of Japan's total electricity production and the cost of production is way too high without government subsidies (See Fig. 2). In sum, alternative energy generation methods are for the future, not a present solution to make up for the 30 percent that was recently lost. Diversification is also easy to say, but difficult to do, because oil reserves are concentrated mainly in the Middle East. The only practical and feasible solution that one can think of now

**Figure 1: Average IEA Industrial Electricity Prices in 2013**

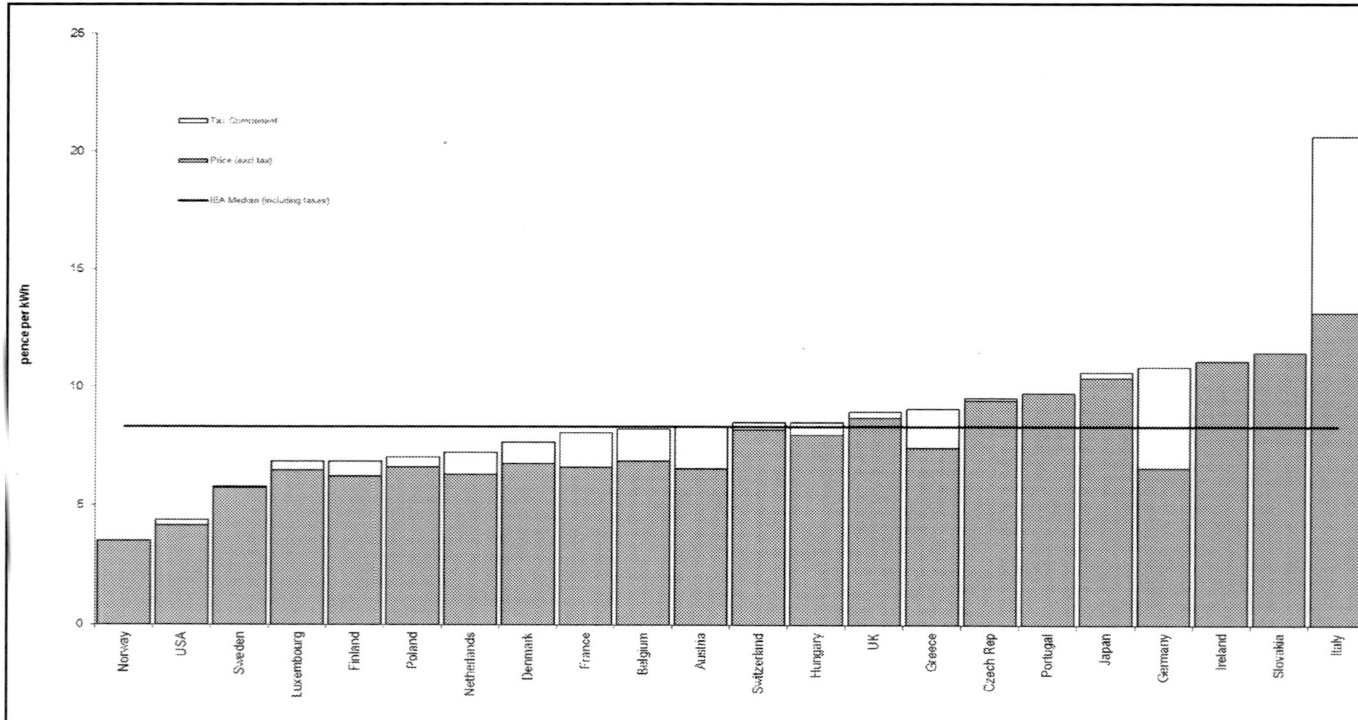


*Source:* Statistical data set; International industrial energy prices (last updated: September 25, 2014), Department of Energy & Climate Change, UK Government, at https://www.gov.uk/government/statistical-data-sets/international-industrial-energy-prices. (Accessed October 8, 2014).

is nuclear energy as long as Japan wants to lessen its heavy dependency on Middle East oil.

**Figure 2: Electricity Supply: Share of Renewables in Total Electricity Production in 2012**

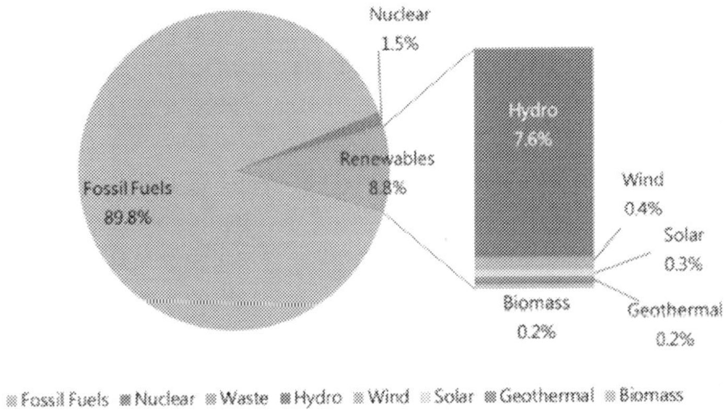


*Source:* Japan Renewable Energy Foundation, at http://jref.or.jp/en/energy/statistics2/energy_01.php#energy_0102 (Accessed October 8, 2014). (Please note that this is a figure for the year 2012. There has been no nuclear power generation since May 2012).

## *Nuclear Power Generation*

The current Shinzo Abe administration of the Liberal Democratic Party (LDP) that came to power after a landslide victory over the previous Democratic Party of Japan (DJP) administration in the December 2012 general elections is in favour of re-activating nuclear reactors. It has adopted a policy to make nuclear energy generation "an important base-load electricity source."[10] This is an about-face from the previous Yoshihiko Noda administration, whose policy was to phase out or eliminate nuclear power by the 2030s. However, in order to re-activate a nuclear reactor, there are regulatory hurdles to clear that are far more stringent than before the accident. This is a time-consuming process. There are also political hurdles because the memory of the meltdown disaster in Fukushima in 2011 is so fresh in people's minds.

Recently, two reactors at Satsuma-Sendai in Kagoshima Prefecture that is located in the southernmost part of the Kyushu island got a nod of approval from the Nuclear Regulation Authority indicating the reactors have met the current, far more stringent, safety regulations. However, there are other regulatory and procedural hurdles left to clear in addition to meeting these safety regulations. First, the public has a period of time in which to submit comments on the re-activation activities. After that, local and prefectural approval must be garnered prior to re-activation. The approvals would be in doubt if the public comments are overwhelmingly negative. This approval process for the two reactors in Satsuma-Sendai should not be rough sailing, however, because the Mayor of the Satsuma-Sendai city and the Kagoshima Governor are reportedly inclined to support re-activation.[11] Even if these two reactors are re-activated, the fact remains that almost all of Japan' reactors will be kept inactive for more years to come.

## Safeguarding the SLOCs: Japan's Participation

### *Japan's Constitutional Restraints*

Piracy has been a persistent problem in recent years. This issue has traditionally plagued the Malacca Strait, but nowadays it seems the Gulf of Aden has taken over as the main area where pirates operate. It is ironic, but this threat provides one hopeful sign in that even some countries who suffer from poor relations can cooperate and collaborate when they have common and mutual interest. This aspect will be discussed later, but let us first look into the constitutionality and legality of Japanese participation in anti-piracy operations.

Japan has recently begun participating in the anti-piracy operations in the Gulf of Aden. This participation was not an easy decision for Japan because of the self-imposed restrictions stemming from Article 9 of the Japanese Constitution. These restrictions directly relate to the current issue of re-interpreting the traditionally held view that the Constitution banned the "exercise" of the right of collective self-defence, details of which will be debated in successive sessions of Japan's Diet (Parliament). This re-interpretation issue has been debated hotly. The Abe administration made a cabinet decision that allows Japan to "exercise" the right of collective self-defence on July 1, 2014.

Article 9 reads as follows:

> *Para. 1*: Aspiring sincerely to an international peace based on justice and order, the Japanese people forever renounce war as a sovereign right of the nation and the threat or use of force as means of settling international disputes.
>
> *Para. 2*: In order to accomplish the aim of the preceding paragraph, land, sea, and air forces, as well as other war potential, will never be maintained. The right of belligerency of the state will not be recognised.

The erstwhile interpretation stipulated that Japan as a sovereign nation does have the right of collective self-defence as Article 51 of the UN Charter clearly states.[12] However, Japan could not "exercise" the right of collective defence because of Article 9 of the Japanese Constitution. Therefore, whenever Japan's Self Defence Force (SDF) was activated by the Minister of Defence issuing a self-defence order, it had "something to do with the defence of Japan", which is within the matter of constitutional individual self-defence. What "something to do with the defence of Japan" means has been also subject to interpretation. Its application used to be confined within Japanese territory. This was enlarged when a law enacted in 1999 included aspects which called "situations surrounding Japan". According to the Government, "surrounding Japan" is a situational rather than a geographical concept. Therefore, it will be judged on a case by case basis. It is usually assumed, unofficially of course, that "surrounding Japan" would cover the areas from north of the Philippines. It still has "something to do with the defence of Japan" although the area that it can be applied was enlarged.

### *Brief History on Interpretation*

There was much confusion as to how to interpret Article 9 even for the right of (individual) self-defence. Initially, in 1946 when Japan was still under Allied occupation, Prime Minister Yoshida denied even the right of (individual) self-defence, expressing confidence and trust in the UN's collective security system for the protection of the then feeble Japan. However, Yoshida himself in 1950 abruptly reversed his understanding and expressed that the denial of war potential and the right of belligerency did not mean that Japan abandoned its right of self-defence. The Government did not make its interpretation of collective self-defence clear back then because the concept was not yet clearly defined or widely accepted in the 1950s, according to the Government. The Govenment's understanding of collective self-defence had begun to be set after the signing of the revised security treaty with the US in 1960. At that time, the basic tenet of the erstwhile interepation can be said to be establised: namely, Japan as a sovereign nation does have the right of collective self-defence, but cannot "exercise" it due to the restrictions imposed by Article 9.

### *Reminder*

An important point to remember is that there may be a misunderstanding that Japan can now "fully" exercise the right of collective self-defence just because of the cabinet decision on July 1, 2014. This is not the case. A general direction to permit its exercise is decided and proclaimed by the Cabinet, but no law has been changed thus far. Every detail as to what kind of situations and cases to which this re-interpretation might apply must be decided by the Diet, which is the supreme organ of the state, according to the Constitution. Having mentioned this, however, one might hastily add that because Japan employs a majoritarian Cabinet system, it is almost certain that the Cabinet decision in principle will be accepted.

The decision itself is a compromise between the ruling parties, the LDP, which is a conservative party, and the (New) Komeito (Clean Government Party), which is backed by a lay Buddhist organisation and inclined to be liberal and "peace-minded". One big item that is left unclear because of differences of opinion between them is safeguarding the SLOCs in, say, the Indian Ocean. Abe seems in favour of it, but his coalition partner is against it. Therefore, it is not clear as of yet whether or not Japanese participation in SLOCs safeguarding operations in general will become possible. However, if they are made possible, Japan can fully and "jointly" participate in safeguarding the SLOCs in the Indian Ocean.

### *Anti-Piracy Operations*[13]

Japan dispatched two destroyers in March 2009, and two P-3C patrol aircrafts in June 2009 to participate in the anti-piracy operations in the Gulf of Aden. It has established a base outside Japan in Djibouti for the first time since World War II. The facility is not a military base as such, but instead contains living quarters for Japanese personnel who are participating in the anti-piracy activities. Japan's flotilla could only defend and safeguard Japan related ships (Japanese flagged ships and those operated by a Japanese company), however, before the enactment of the so-called anti-piracy law in June 2009. They were dispatched under the marine protection order which is considered to be within the realm of a police action. Since no SDF personnel can perform police duties, there are eight Coast Guard personnel on the SDF ships to perform these actions. The anti-piracy law was initially set to expire, but was extended until July 2015.

The law clearly states in Article 7 that it is primarily the duty of the Coast Guard to carry out anti-piracy activities. However, if and when there is a special need, the SDF can participate in those activities. Since anti-piracy is regarded as a police action, the SDF personnel are under strict regulations in terms of the use of firearms and physical force. Article 7 of the Police Personnel Law stipulates, in part, that SDF personnel can only use firearms, etc., that might hurt a person when in self-defence, in imminent danger, or if there is resistance to arrest in a case of offence. Violations of these restrictions will make SDF members subject to criminal prosecution so they must be extra cautious in those situations.

To repeat, this anti-piracy law made it clear that anti-piracy actions in the Gulf of Aden were police, not defence, actions. Therefore, they had nothing to do with the constitutional prohibition on the "exercise" of the right of collective action, in principle. However, since Japan's Coast Guard, the maritime police, has no practical ability to operate in far seas, it was determined that SDF ships had to be dispatched. The issue was that Article 82 of the SDF law stipulated, whenever the SDF was involved in an activity, including police actions, it had "something to do with the defence of Japan." This meant in effect Japan's SDF must stand by and watch idly when a non-Japanese ship was being sea-jacked, for example, unless it can be determined that the SDF ship itself would be harmed, which would be considered as an exercise of individual self-defence. This is a horrifying scene for Japan.

Because of this situation, Article 82 of the SDF law was amended without much controversy so that a SDF ship can police and safeguard non-Japanese vessels as part of an anti-piracy police action. So, Japan's SDF personnel dispatched to the Gulf can now protect non-Japanese ships including, for example, Chinese ships. China is also protecting Japanese ships in that area. So far, this law restricts the area of operation in the Gulf of Aden and cannot extend it to the Indian Ocean per se.

As of July 2014, Japan completed 545 protecting sorties for 641 Japanese and 2758 non-Japanese ships. This is an average of 6.2 sorties a day.[14] By a special measure law (a sun-set law only for a specific situation) passed in November 2013, in areas with high levels of piracy activity, it is now possible that private guards on board can carry small arms to protect Japanese ships. Japan has worked with the Headquarters of the Combined Maritime Forces (CMFHQ) in Bahrain, a coalition of nearly 30 nations, by sending 3 liaison offers. Japan does its own independent operations in the sense of the Japanese word of "shiki"[15] (of course, it coordinates its activities with other participating nations). Because of the fear that an operation might be regarded as an "exercise" of collective self-defence, despite the fact that their activities are usually considered to be police actions.

As far as China's participation in this anti-piracy operation is concerned, about half the ships the Chinese Navy has protected (escorted) between 2008 and 2012 were foreign flagged, including Japanese merchant ships. China has also conducted various naval activities with, for example, Russia, Pakistan and the US.[16] In terms of cooperation and collaboration among Japan, China and South Korea in this anti-piracy activity, it has a hopeful sign for the future. Japan and China (along with India) started Escort Convoy Coordination in early 2012, for which South Korea joined later in the same year. This Coordination mechanism is wide-ranging and includes not only deployment schedule coordination, but also landing aircraft on each other's vessels, holding joint drills, working together to organise visits of officers on the other countries' vessels, among other activities.[17] This is clearly a good example that cooperation and collaboration on-the-ground among not so friendly countries, to put it mildly, are indeed possible. And, hopefully, this kind of on-the-ground practical cooperation in safeguarding the SLOCs will become a reality.

## Safeguarding the SLOCs: The Indian Ocean and the Strait of Malacca

### *Indian Ocean*

It is easy to see that India and its navy in particular have a significant role to play in safeguarding the SLOCs in the Indian Ocean. Japan has a security agreement with India signed in 2008 for this effect. Furthermore, Japan and India's Coast Guards have been conducting 'joint exercises' since 2000. This is allowed because the Japanese Coast Guard is a maritime police force and not under the restraint of Article 9. This paper does not want to recommend a cluster of bilateral agreements between, for example, India and other seafaring stakeholder nations, however, because this approach might as well indicate a zero-sum kind of mind-set. That is, SLOCs are something that individual countries themselves must safeguard for their own sake, with bilateral cooperation.

Of course, each country has to take care of its own energy security. Nonetheless, there are more efficient ways to ensure the security of SLOCs. One possible way is to have a joint operation, and some kind of regime or set-up to talk about how to safeguard the SLOCs in the Indian Ocean. India's agreement in setting up a forum of some sort is crucial in this regard since India and especially Indian Navy would regard the Indian Ocean as their front yard. The SLOCs in Indian Ocean are not in any imminent and real danger at present and probably for a foreseeable future. Therefore, setting up a regular meeting of concerned stakeholder nations might suffice for the time being. India (including its Coast Guard) should take a leading role for the forum, the main purpose of which is to foster a perspective that SLOCs are global commons that should be secured "jointly" with multi-lateral cooperation and collaboration, not something that each country compete for against other nations. Of course, this forum would not be a panacea for the all the problems and there would still many issues for the international community to tackle.

### *ReCAAP*

There is a good precedence that should be considered when thinking of regional cooperation in the Indian Ocean; namely anti-piracy cooperation in the Strait of Malacca called Regional Cooperation Agreement on Combating Piracy and Armed Robbery against Ships in Asia (ReCAAP). Former Japanese Prime Minister Keizo Obuchi first broached this idea at the November 1999 ASEAN+1 Summit Meeting held in Manila.[18] The ReCAAP has 19 member countries including major East and South Asian countries such as India, China, South Korea, Japan, as well as some of the ASEAN countries. However, Malaysia and Indonesia, which have jurisdictions over some parts of the Strait, are not members. The fact that it has a permanent secretariat and a monitoring station called the Information Sharing Center (ISC) is significant because they indicate that it is not a mere forum for discussion. The ISC was established in Singapore in November 2006.

This is in contrast with the ASEAN Regional Forum (ARF). The ARF is without any doubt a very important, if not the most important, regional security forum. However, as the name itself suggests, the ARF is merely a forum and does not have a permanent secretariat. Thus, despite its importance, there are some detractors who suggest that it is a mere chattingspree. The ReCAAP is different and might evolve into a foundation for a future maritime security (not military, but maritime police function) organisation that has practical enforcement power. Therefore, one can say that the ReCAAP would be a good starting point, or seed for a possible and wider regional cooperation that might go beyond anti-piracy operations. One might add that there is an observation that "much of the credit for increasing Chinese acceptance of norms of maritime cooperative security is due to Japan's influence and the formation of ReCAAP."[19]

However, the ReCAAP has some weaknesses that may be slightly hard to overcome. First, as was mentioned above, Malaysia and Indonesia, two of the biggest stakeholders, are not members because of a perennial sovereignty issue. Without these two countries, the ReCAAP is much less effective. Another weakness is that the ReCAAP's ISC is a monitoring station and does not have any authority to conduct operations. One has to hope, though, that its potential for regional cooperation could be enhanced.

## Conclusion

This paper has emphasised the transportation aspect of energy security: namely, safeguarding the SLOCs and anti-piracy activities. It also explained in some detail about Japan's energy situation after the nuclear disaster on March 11, 2011 as well as its anti-piracy activities in the Gulf of Aden. Overall, the energy security picture in the world cannot be said to be good given instability in the Middle East in terms of oil supply and expected increase in demand for oil due to economic expansion in many countries, particularly China and India.

Even in the demand side where competitive nature among countries tends to be emphasised; there are many areas that countries in Asia can cooperate and collaborate for mutual benefits. Take, for example, Japan and China, whose relationship is and will remain mediocre, if not downright tense and chilly. They can and should cooperate with a goal of decreasing or eliminating the Asian Premium instead of outbidding each other. Japan is a leader in energy conservation technology. Therefore, Japan is in a position to help and cooperate with China in its efforts to conserve energy.

Domestically, Japan should consider using a common and standard electric frequency for the whole country, although this would be a very costly endeavour. At the very least, conversion of electricity between the west and east should be made easier. Although there may be strong political opposition, the Asian continent might be able to develop a common and connected power grid. EU members, for example, have connected their power grids and, thus, have created a much larger power market, within and through which they can share electricity in times of crisis or need. This has enabled them to tinker with and utilise alternative, renewable energy as well as increasing their energy security. Japan being an island nation cannot participate in this continental Asia-wide endeavour, but China and India certainly can.

It is the argument of this paper that there are areas in which Asian countries can and should cooperate for their own sake. Some kind of Asia-wide energy security forum can be contemplated by the Asian countries. In order to create this forum, however, major Asian powers have to change their current zero-sum kind of mind-set to a global (Asian) commons type of perspective. It is one thing to suggest this forum but quite another to implement it. Nevertheless, the change of perspective is needed in hearts and minds, not in material ways alone.

## NOTES

1. United Nations Development Programme (UNDP), *World Energy Assessment: Overview*, 2004, p.42, at http://www.undp.org/content/dam/aplaws/publication/en/publications/environment-energy/www-ee-library/sustainable-energy/world-energy-assessment-overview-2004-update/World%20Energy%20Assessment%20Overview-2004%20Update.pdf.
2. Gal Luft, "Dependence on Middle East energy and its impact on global security", Institute for the Analysis of Global Security, p. 1, at http://www.iags.org/luft_dependence_on_middle_east_energy.pdf.
3. Ibid.
4. *Yomiuri Shimbun* (Newspaper), August 17, 2014.
5. Ibid.
6. Scott Valentine *et al.*, "Empowered? Evaluating Japan's national energy strategy under the DPJ administration", *Energy Policy*, January 2011, p. 1865, at http://scottvalentine.net/yahoo_site_admin/assets/docs/val_sov_mats_dpj_japan_cc_strategy.142173430.pdf.
7. Ministry of Economy, Trade and Industry, Government of Japan, Press Release, "New National Energy Strategy of 2006", 2006, at http://www.meti.go.jp/english/information/downloadfiles/PressRelease/NewEnergyStrategy.pdf.
8. Vlado Vivoda, "Japan's energy security predicament post-Fukushima", *Energy Policy*, July 2012, p. 136, at http://www.sciencedirect.com/science/article/pii/S0301421512002492.
9. ICF International, "An international comparison of energy and climate change policies impacting energy intensive industries in selected countries" (Submitted to Department for Business Innovation & Skills of the UK Government), July 11, 2012, p.22 at https://www.gov.uk/government/uploads/system/uploads/attachment_data/file/31768/12-527-international-policies-impacting-energy-intensive-industries.pdf.

10. Japan's New Basic Energy Plan, *Yomiuri Shimbun*, February 26, 2014.
11. Nihon Keizai Shimbun (*Japan Economic Journal*) web version, August 1, 2014, at http://www.nikkei.com/article/DGXLASFB01006_R00C14A8EAF000/.
12. "Nothing in the present Charter shall impair the inherent right of individual or collective self-defence if an armed attack occurs against a Member of the United Nations,..."
13. Hiroshi Sakamoto *et al.*, "Enactment of Laws as Anti-piracy Measures in the Somalian Offshore and Gulf of Aden", *Legislation and Research (Rippo to Chousa)* (in Japanese), August 2009, pp.15-28, at http://www.sangiin.go.jp/japanese/annai/chousa/rippou_chousa/backnumber/2009pdf/20090801015.pdf.
14. Ministry of Foreign Affairs, Government of Japan, at http://www.mofa.go.jp/mofaj/gaiko/pirate/africa.html.
15. Japanese words of "shiki" and "sashizu" can both be translated as "command" in English. However, Japan distinguishes them clearly and carefully. "Shiki" includes the authority to manage personnel affairs, whereas "sashizu" means an operational command without any personnel management authority.
16. Andrew S. Ericksonand Austin M. Strange, "No Substitute for Experience: Chinese Antipiracy Operations in the Gulf of Aden", US Naval War College, 2013, pp.103-108, at www.usnwc.edu/Research—Gaming/China-Maritime-Studies-Institute.aspx.
17. Daewon Ohnand Mason Richey, "Cooperation on Counter-Piracy in the Gulf of Aden among China, Korea, and Japan: Implications for Trilateral Security Cooperation in Northeast Asia", *The Korean Journal of Defense Analysis*, 26 (1), March 2014, pp. 84-85 at http://papers.ssrn.com/sol3/papers.cfm?abstract_id=2404343.
18. Joshua Ho, "Combating piracy and armed robbery in Asia: The ReCAAP Information Sharing Centre (ISC)", *Marine Policy*, 33, 2009, pp. 432-434.
19. Gaye Christoffersen, "China and Maritime Cooperation: Piracy in the Gulf of Aden", Institute for Strategic, Political, Security and Economic Consultancy (ISPSW) Publications, Berlin, p.6, at http://www.globalinitiative.net/download/piracy/subsaharan africa/China%20and%20Maritime%20Cooperation%20-%20Piracy%20in%20the%20Gulf%20of%20Aden.pdf.

# 16

# The Impact of Regional Instability on Energy Security: A Perspective from South Korea

*Jeongmin Seo*

South Korea is the fifth top energy importer worldwide with 64 percent of its oil coming from Organisation of the Petroleum Exporting Countries (OPEC) members. Over the last 30 years, South Korea accounted for a rapid increase in energy use. This in turn led South Korea to be totally dependent on oil and gas imports. Due to the increase of energy consumption and dependence, external and internal factors have forced South Korea to change its energy strategy and targets.

Among the external factors, political change or instability in the Middle East has been the most important variable in South Korea's energy security. The Middle East turmoil raises questions about possible implications for South Korea-Middle East relations.[1] In particular, the recent upheavals in the Middle East highlight the economic problems of South Korea's relations with the region. The rise of oil prices and the concern over stable production and supply since the 2011 Arab Spring have led the government and business circle of South Korea to make a close look at what is going on and what will happen in the region. This is because any disruption in production and supply of energy may have disastrous impact on economy and security of South Korea which has faced continuous military threats from North Korea.

Nevertheless, South Korea's response to the current political transformation of the Middle East has not been assertive, but defensive or passive. This is based on perception and tacit recognition of the government and people that South Korea unlike the United States, Russia, and China has not had leverage in the Middle Eastern affairs. Thus, the strategies and policies of South Korea on energy security have been focused on the two 'reactionary' measures. First, South Korea has made great efforts in expanding the use of nuclear power and renewable energies in order to reduce its dependence on oil consumption. Second, the Korean government has tried to build a strategic partnership with relatively stable Gulf countries like UAE and Saudi Arabia to secure its energy supply. This paper analyses South Korea's Middle East policy through the years and sheds new light on the implications of the Middle East turmoil for South Korea-Middle East relations.

## South Korea's Energy Security

The Northeast Asian region including South Korea has shown the most dynamic economic growth of any region in the world for at least the next two decades. China's growth lies at the center of this expectation. At the same time, the economic growth of South Korea and the status of Japan as a global economic leader also account for the important economic status of the region.

However, the region faces the greatest energy imbalance in the world due to rapid increase in energy demand of China. Since the high economic growth inevitably results in a huge volume of energy consumption, energy security of Northeast Asia is vulnerable. Moreover, as energy imports are largely dependent

**Figure 1: Total Energy Consumption of South Korea, 2013**

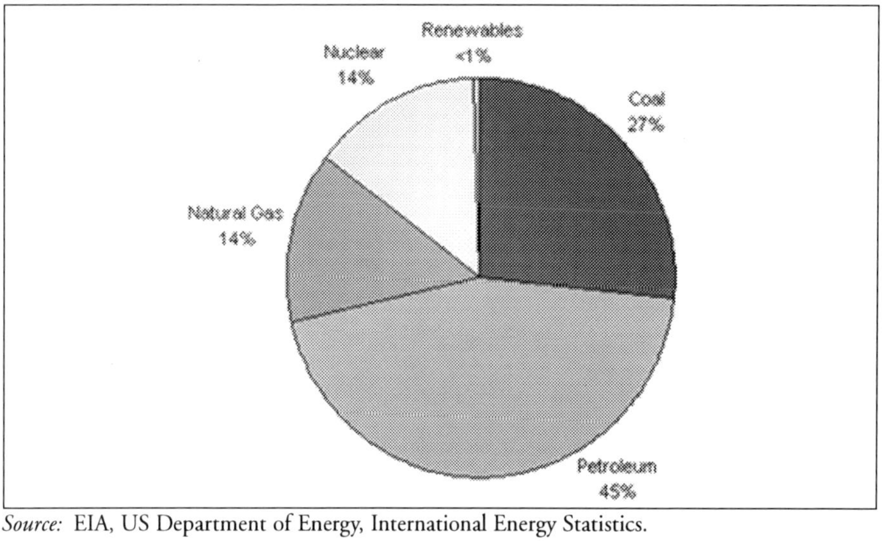


*Source:* EIA, US Department of Energy, International Energy Statistics.

on Middle East suppliers, any regional conflicts or marine transportation route crises could seriously impact the stability of energy supplies to Northeast Asia. Thus, the first and foremost challenge is to secure an adequate level of energy for supporting the economies.[2] It means that countries, especially heavy energy-consuming countries like China, Japan, and South Korea, are exposed to energy security.

South Korea, with its lack of domestic reserves, was the world's eighth largest energy consumer in 2013[3] and it is now one of the top energy importers in the world. The country is the fifth largest importer of crude oil and the second largest importer of both coal and liquefied natural gas (LNG). South Korea does not possess international oil or natural gas pipelines, thus, exclusively relying on tanker shipments. Therefore, the government makes efforts to guard the nation's energy security. In this respect, state-owned oil, gas, and electricity companies are aggressively seeking overseas exploration and production opportunities.

Although oil accounted for the largest portion (45 percent) of South Korea's primary energy consumption in 2013, its share has been declining since the mid-1990s when it reached a peak of 66 percent. South Korea is also highly dependent on the Middle East for its oil supply, with the Middle East accounting for nearly 75 percent of its total oil imports in 2013. Saudi Arabia was the leading supplier, and the source of more than a quarter of total oil imports.

**Figure 2: South Korea's Oil Imports by Major Sources, 2013**

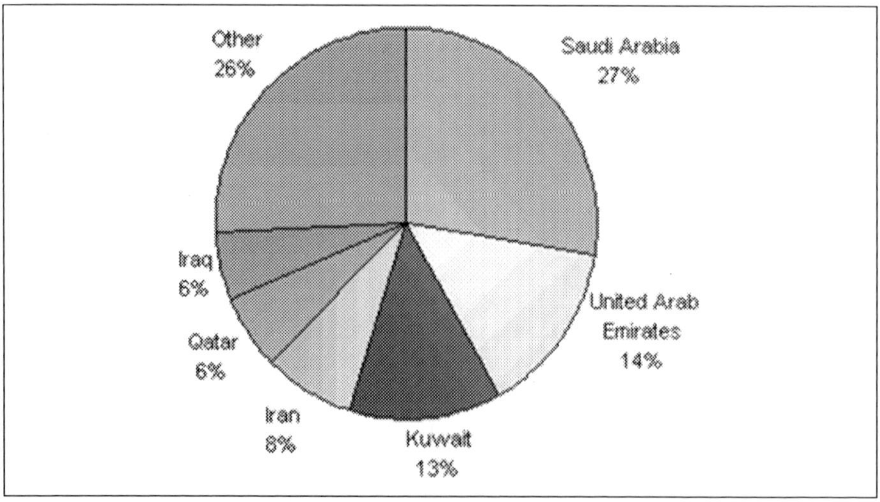


*Source:* EIA, US Department of Energy, International Energy Statistics.

South Korea relies on imports to satisfy nearly all of its natural gas consumption which has approximately doubled over the previous decade. South Korea does not have any international gas pipeline connections therefore it imports all gas via liquefied natural gas (LNG) tankers. As a result, although South Korea is not among the group of top gas-consuming nations, it is the second largest importer of LNG in the world after Japan. Although the associated 2008 KOGAS-Gazprom memorandum of understanding indicated that the gas could be imported either as LNG or via pipeline from Vladivostok while Russian and Korean leaders acknowledged that the pipeline construction option will most likely not be deemed economically feasible without the cooperation of North Korea.

Energy profile of South Korea can be characterised by high consumption structure, import dependency, and large stockpiling of reserves. South Korea's rapid industrialisation has increased gross domestic product (GDP) but with greater increase in energy consumption. Stuck by the financial crises of 1997, however, the government focused attention and efforts on energy efficiency. The devaluation of the country's currency, which led to a doubling of energy prices, highlighted the need for improved energy efficiency and domestic energy sources such as nuclear plant and renewable energy sources. In a nutshell, South Korea's Energy Strategy aims at the following:[4]

(i) Energy consumption per unit of GDP should be improved by 40 percent.
(ii) Dependence on oil as a percentage of the total energy supply should be reduced to 33 percent or less from the present level of 43.5 percent.
(iii) The percentage of new and renewable in the total energy mix should be reached to 11 percent from the present level of 2.4 percent.
(iv) The percentage of electricity generated by nuclear power in the total generated electricity should be increased to 40 percent or more from the present level of 25 percent.

South Korea's future energy vision includes establishing an energy system for sustainable development, fostering a competitive, market-oriented energy industry, promoting energy technology exports, and becoming the hub of an open Asian energy system. South Korea has also pursed cooperative energy security strategies. South Korea joined various international organisations including the International Energy Agency (IEA) and has coordinated with other industrial countries in the event of a supply disruption. As mentioned above, the more assertive approach to energy security is also evident in South Korea's leadership in forwarding proposals for a large regional gas pipeline to bring Russian gas to China and South Korea and, possibly, even Japan.

## The Middle East Instability and its Implications for South Korea

The Middle East turmoil has raised concerns among the government and people in South Korea that the situation may endanger South Korean military and business personnel working in the region. The recent instability in Syria and Iraq caused by the Syrian civil war and the emergence of Islamic State is regarded as a possible threat to the South Korean soldiers in southern Lebanon. Any more serious conflict in Lebanon that will endanger the South Korean forces, might lead Seoul to consider withdrawing its forces from the country.[5]

Nevertheless, economic interests are more important to the government and people in Korea. Safety of thousands of South Korean workers working around the Middle East and being involved in various projects for South Korean companies has become an important security concern to the government. South Korea's President Lee Myung-Bak, called an emergency meeting to deal with this potential threat to South Korean workers. President Lee said, "the government should use every possible means to protect our people and workers at companies operating there."[6] For example, in Libya, which is one of the Middle East turmoil hotspots, there are almost 1,400 South Korean workers and 24 South Korean construction companies operating there. According to the Korean Trade-Investment Promotion Agency, South Korean construction companies are completing projects in other countries in the Middle East, where the turmoil threatens the safety of the South Korean workers and the government should prepare a contingency plan if the crises in those countries escalate.[7]

The Middle East instability has also aroused deep concern about South Korea's economic relations with the region. The significance of the Middle East to South Korea does not end with oil. The new millennium began with improved trade volume between South Korea and the Middle Eastern states. For example, trade with Iran, Oman, Saudi Arabia, and UAE tripled, with Libya it doubled, and with Kuwait it increased five-fold in the 1990s. South Korean companies also depend on the region for business opportunities. In the first quarter of 2014, South Korean companies won construction contracts worth a total of US$17.6 billion for oil refineries, gas pipelines, degassing stations (facilities that separate oil from gas) and housing projects in the Middle East. The figure accounts for nearly 80 percent of the value of all overseas contracts that Korean companies won during the same time-frame.[8] The importance of the Middle East for South Korea's economy, mainly to the South Korean construction companies, can be seen in the overseas construction projects that these companies are involved in. However, the Middle East turmoil threatens South Korea's economic interests in the Middle East.[9] Some of South Korea's trade partners in the Middle East are currently preoccupied with the survival of their regimes. The Arab uprisings in

Egypt, Tunisia, Yemen, Libya and Syria, where the regimes in some of these states are trying to stabilise the new political order while in others the battles between the opposition and the current regimes continue to destabilise the nation, and limit their trade with the Republic of Korea.

For example, the volume of bilateral trade between South Korea and Egypt exceeded US$3 billion in 2010. The uprisings led to the fall of Mubarak's government and the rise of the Muslim Brotherhood and ultimately, the military coming back to power. The need to stabilise the social and political unrest in Egypt limits government spending until the current political and social unrest stabilises. This transition period might take years until the *coupd'état* government will be able to legitimise its governance and stabilise the current unrest in the country. This might lead to a decrease in the volume of trade between Egypt and South Korea, until Cairo strengthens the regime change.

In Libya, the removal of Muammar Gaddafi in October 2011 did not end the political conflicts among various forces. The unrest among the political forces seeking wealth and power has threatened US$ 10.2 billion of construction projects. Finally, South Korea's builders decided to withdraw most of their workers, as its government re-imposed a travel ban on civil war-torn Libya in August 2014. The nation's builders, which resumed construction from early 2014 after withdrawals due to a civil war three years ago, are concerned over possible disruption of construction projects in Libya.[10] Even if the civil war is resolved, it will take some time until dominant political power will be able to consolidate a new government and fully control Libya. Syria was also one of the major trader partners in the region with US$ 1.4 billion of trade in 2010. The civil war in Syria and the uncertain survival of Bashar Al Assad's regime have brought an end of the trade relation. The Syrian ruling elite are making their utmost efforts to survive.

The biggest concern for South Korea is the stability of the Gulf countries. The oil and gas exporting countries such as Saudi Arabia, UAE, Qatar, Oman, Kuwait, and Iran have been traditionally friendly and benevolent to Korean companies. These six countries are the main oil and gas exporters to South Korea. Political instability would influence the activities of the South Korean companies. However, many South Korean experts and government official believe that the United States would probably intervene if the security of these countries is challenged.[11]

Finally, Iran is a controversial case. Bilateral trade between South Korea and Iran in 2010 was US$ 11.5 billion.[12] However, the continuing international sanction in which Seoul was obliged to participate has jeopardised the bilateral economic relations.[13] As for restrictions on oil imports rendered by Iran sanctions, the Korean government first attempted to quickly make up for the petroleum, it no longer could import from the Persian Gulf country. The former president, Lee Myung-Bak, travelled to three members of the GCC—Saudi Arabia, Qatar, and the United Arab Emirates. Riyadh particularly promised to provide Seoul as much as oil it requested, bringing a relief to queasiness among South Korean officials about possible outcomes of oil shortage for the country. But the crux of the problem was not about replacing the oil loss supplied from Iran for many decades. When Tehran threatened, through its embassy in South Korea, that it would possibly ban in total the import of South Korean goods if Seoul went along with the decision not to buy Iranian crude, the South Korean government left with no other option but to capitalise more on back-door channels in order to finally get the name of the country exempted from the list of those nations which couldn't do oil business with Iran.

There are also some political considerations. South Korea strongly believes that Iran and North Korea have cooperated on missile technology, and suspected that they did so in pursuing their nuclear ambitions as well. But as tensions between the United States and Iran increase, Seoul is increasingly finding itself caught in the middle as its economic and national security interest come into conflict. Should it take part in sanctions that could harm South Korea's own economic interests, or back its closest ally in an effort to bring Iran back to the negotiation table over its suspected nuclear weapons program? This is where national security interests conflict with South Korea's economic interests. Like Iran, North Korea remains one of the world's pressing nuclear proliferation concerns. While South Korea has expressed support for US efforts to check Iran's nuclear ambitions, it has yet to announce if or how much it will reduce its imports from Iran. As Seoul weighs its options, it faces three considerations. First, because Iranian and North Korean nuclear proliferation are becoming linked in the United States and the international community, there is pressure for South Korea to take action against proliferation in general. Second, more specifically, as Seoul weighs options to reduce the potential economic impact on its economy, it must balance the efforts it makes and ensure that they do not inadvertently undermine US efforts to get other Asian nations to take part in the sanctions. Lastly, because the US Congress is taking a hard and bi-partisan line on sanctions, South Korea runs the risk of meeting requests of the US administration but not the expectations of the US Congress, potentially creating additional points of tension with the United States.

## South Korea's Policies on Energy Security

Oil remains the primary source of South Korea's energy needs, leaving the country exposed to the multitude risks associated with the commodity. South Korea's vulnerability is enhanced due to the volatile and often fragile nature of the region's geopolitics of its primary providers of oil, which has been historically limited to a group of six Middle Eastern countries in the Gulf. The lack of pipelines for delivery adds to the risk, leaving tanker shipments through the dangerous surrounding waterways such as the Strait of Hormuz as the only option. Iran and Iraq raise even greater risks because they are among the lowest levels of rule of law in the world. Given the exposure and dependency, achieving greater energy independence from oil remains a major policy goal with South Korea hoping to reduce its reliance upon oil as an energy source from 43.6 percent in 2006 to 34.2 percent by 2030.[14] This marks considerable progress relative to the mid-1990s when its reliance reached a peak of 66 percent. Becoming a proactive actor in the exploration and development of oil thus has emerged as an important objective.

## Diversification of Energy Supplies

South Korea imported an average of 2.14 mbpd of crude oil from the Middle East in 2013, roughly 86 percent of its total crude imports. In lowering this dependence, state owned and controlled enterprises maintained effective monopolies in the purchasing, importation or distribution of resources and have been the engine in implementing South Korea's overseas resource policy. The Korea National Oil Corporation (KNOC) and the Korea Gas Corporation (KOGAS) played the leading roles. In the oil sector, KNOC had 191 overseas projects in 25 countries in 2010, largely located in emerging states. The major countries include Russia, China, Vietnam, Malaysia, Indonesia, Kazakhstan, Uzbekistan, Iraq, Yemen, Canada, Peru and Nigeria. For gas, KNOC and KOGAS are participating together in exploration, production and development projects in 26 blocks in 16 countries. Through foreign direct investment, KNOC and KOGAS have been acquiring equity stakes in many of these ventures. Among the most aggressive moves as an investor to date, in 2010 KNOC gained control of UK oil company Dana Petroleum in a US$ 2.5 billion hostile takeover.

In addition to traditional public entities, Korea has also promoted larger private sector conglomerates to obtain resources through private international agreements. Private enterprises have taken the initiative to become key players in entering into international arrangements with foreign resource providers. They serve as key partners in coalitions or in a consortium with public enterprises such as KNOC and KOGAS. In an attempt to diversify their oil supplies of private companies, South Korean legislators have introduced new incentives for buyers to purchase crude oil from non-Middle East countries, lowering the minimum amount of non-Middle Eastern oil that can attract a reduction in shipping fees. The scheme allows South Korean buyers to receive up to 90 percent of the difference in freight costs between the Middle East and other longhaul destinations.[15]

Over the years, South Korea has also entered into a wide range of bilateral and multilateral agreements with resource providing countries. These agreements have taken the form of specific treaties concerning energy and minerals and more general bilateral investment treaties and free trade agreements as well as multilateral agreements. While not readily apparent, this network of international agreements have helped contribute to South Korea's public enterprises and private sector companies together pursuing an active "resource diplomacy" strategy. The agreements have provided the foundations for public and private entities to enter into transactional investment arrangements for overseas resources. Almost all of South Korea's resource providers are members in at least one of them. The aggressive resource strategy will, most possibly, continue into the future with international agreements playing a more visible role, particularly as disputes and the need for remedies arise. Several resource providing countries that lack these protections, however, pose considerable legal risks for South Korea's public enterprises and private companies.

Overall, through the government's vast financial support and proactive resource diplomacy, public owned and controlled enterprises have been able to pursue a new brand of resource strategy that allows them to play a more aggressive role. In close coordination with government policy makers, public enterprises have led efforts in exploring, producing, and developing overseas often through direct equity stakes that increasingly involve majority control. Furthermore, most of these overseas projects have been conducted in consortium with private sector companies. However, the majority of bilateral energy agreements signed by South Korea have been concentrated on non-Middle Eastern countries. For example, South Korea concluded five formal bilateral treaties with resource providers that specifically focused on energy and minerals between 1995 and 2006: they are Malaysia, Mongolia, Russia (2 treaties), and Australia.

## Nuclear Energy Diplomacy for Energy Security

South Korea's recent energy security policy has been based on this assumption that old notions of energy security and conventional methods to achieve them may no longer apply in today's growing global competition for energy. Although securing a stable and steady access to and supply of necessary raw materials particularly oil has long been a pillar of the country's foreign policy, the present South Korean administration has made energy security a primary national agenda in recent years and it has also drafted new action plans under the guise of energy diplomacy. The seriousness of this energy diplomacy was tested when the government used political persuasion to lock the nuclear energy deal with the United Arab Emirates. During the tough negotiation process, the South Korean president, Lee Myung-Bak, personally supervised the project and he even travelled all the way to Abu Dhabi to finally attend the signing ceremony of the deal he later called the "heaven-sent national fortune."[16]

In line with the county's new energy policy, the South Korean government has tried in recent years to cultivate a multilayered presence in the Middle East, a region with plenty of petroleum and gas resources. It has pursued a policy of changing the nature of some bilateral ties in the region from a short-term economic relationship to a sort of long-term strategic partnership. For instance, in the following months after signing the nuclear deal with the UAE, the South Korean government decided to dispatch a contingent of some 150 combat troops to the Arab country for a period of two years insisting that the mission will promote national interests and expand military and economic ties with the third largest oil exporter in the world. However, many observers, mainly the opposition party in the South Korean parliament, connect the mission to the country's nuclear deal with the UAE.[17]

Signing nuclear energy contracts with the Middle East countries could have significant implications for South Korea's foreign policy towards the region and separate bilateral ties. Engaging in such a sensitive business changes the nature of the East Asian nation's interactions with the region from a pure importer of hydrocarbon energies to an exporter of nuclear energy and the related technologies. Unlike many of South Korea's previous construction projects in the Middle East, nuclear energy projects are relatively a long-term contract. In the case of UAE's nuclear deal, the joint cooperation to operate and maintain the reactors will last for 60 years and such a time may provide enough opportunities to cement the foundation of a multifaceted relationship with a top oil exporter.

Going nuclear for the oil rich countries in the Middle East is obviously about strategic energy positioning as its application for electricity and other peaceful purposes will free more petroleum and gas to export particularly in a time when the demand for energy keeps soaring and the price even more. Helping nuclear energy projects in the Middle East by energy dependent countries such as South Korea is actually a wise long-term investment to assure the supply of enough energy resources from the region.

## Conclusion

As examined above, the relationship between Korea and the Gulf region has continuously strengthened and broadened since past several decades. This relationship has also evolved towards more positive direction in the new millennium when the Gulf countries are likely to balance their existing relationships with the Western powers and East Asia,[18] being enhanced by improving non-economic ties toward the military levels.[19] South Korea has gradually shifted its interests in the Gulf from the pure economic cooperation to more strategic areas like nuclear energy sector and military cooperation, ultimately to a comprehensive strategic partnership building. However, South Korea's response to the current political instability in the Middle East has been defensive and passive. This attitude has resulted in reactionary policies in the strategies and policies on energy security. South Korea has attempted to expand nuclear power and renewable energies in order to reduce its dependence on imported energy. The Korean government has also worked hard to consolidate the existing friendly relationship with the Gulf countries like UAE and Saudi Arabia to secure its energy supply.

According to Levkowitz, Seoul faces three policy options in dealing with the current Middle Eastern instability. He said that, "each policy will influence its relations with the states in the region and will bear costs and benefits for the short and long term: disengagement, sitting on the political fence or opportunity exploitation."[20] This paper agrees with the Levkowitz's third option, that is, sitting on the political fence. This is because the option is best suited to Seoul's traditional interests and behaviour in the Middle East. While maintaining its economic interaction with the Middle Eastern countries, South Korea is not likely to be politically identified with any particular side.

## NOTES

1. Louis Charbonneau, "North Korea, Iran trade missile technology: U.N.", *Reuters*, May 14, 2011, at http://www.reuters.com/article/2011/05/14/us-korea-north-iran-un-idUSTRE74D18Z20110514.
2. Doh Hyun-Jae, "Energy cooperation in Northeast Asia: Prospects and Challenges." *East Asian Review*, 15, 2003, pp. 85-110.
3. "Total Energy Consumption", Global Energy Statistical Yearbook 2014, Enerdata, at http://yearbook.enerdata.net/.
4. "The First National Energy Plan", Ministry of Knowledge Economy, Republic of Korea, 2008.
5. Alon Levkowitz, "Korea and the Middle East Turmoil: A Reassessment of South Korea-Middle East Relations", *The Korean Journal of Defense Analysis*, 24 (2), June 2012, p. 232.
6. "South Korea orders measures to cushion impact from Middle East unrest", *BBC Monitoring Asia Pacific*, February 24, 2011.
7. "South Korea considers contingency plans for Middle East crisis," *Yonhap News Agency*, February 28, 2011, at http://english.yonhapnews.co.kr/business/2011/02/27/34/0502000000AEN20110227001800320F.HTML.
8. Hyun-kyung Kang, "Is ISIS a Fire Seen Across River?", *The Korea Times*, September 14, 2014, at http://www.koreatimes.co.kr/www/news/nation/2014/09/116_164516.html.

9. "A New Boom of Plant Industries in the Middle East and Africa", *Hankook Ilbo*, July 14, 2014, at http://www.hankookilbo.com/v/58b4001f06ce4474b1cbc2dc9337ac56.
10. "S. Korean builders to pull out as government places travel ban on Libya", *MK News*, July 31, 2014, at http://news.mk.co.kr/newsRead.php?year=2014&no=1049529.
11. "South Korea mulling raising Russian oil imports amid Mideast unrest", *Asia Pulse News*, February 25, 2011.
12. Ministry of Foreign Affairs and Trade of Republic of Korea, at http://www.mofat.go.kr/english/regions/meafrica/20070824/1_1355.jsp?.
13. Choe Sang-Hun, "U.S. Presses South Korea to Reduce Oil Imports from Iran", *The New York Times*, January 12, 2012, http://www.nytimes.com/2012/01/18/world/asia/us-presses-south-korea-to-reduce-oil-imports-from-iran.html?_r=0.
14. "The First National Energy Master Plan 2008-2030", National Energy Commission, Ministry of Trade, Industry and Energy, Republic of Korea, at http://www.mke.go.kr/motie/in/pl/publication/b bs/bbsView.do?bbs_seq_n=573&bbs_cd_n=30.
15. "South Korean Imports from the Middle East Still High despite Incentives", *Global Oil Insight*, December 9, 2013, at http://www.cges.co.uk/news/1056-south-korean-imports-from-the-middle-east-still-high-despite-incentives.
16. Jaeyeon Woo, "U.A.E. Deal Caps Big Sales Push", *The Wall Street Journal*, December 29, 2009, at http://online.wsj.com/article/SB10001424052748704134104574623934045786504.html.
17. Sang-ho Song, "Cabinet approves UAE troop dispatch", *The Korea Herald*, November 9, 2010, at http://www.koreaherald.com/national/Detail.jsp?newsMLId=20101109000786.
18. D. Moran and J. Russell (eds.), *Energy Security and Global Politics: The Militarisation of Resource Management*, Routledge, London, 2008.
19. Christopher M. Davidson, "*The Persian Gulf and Pacific Asia: From Indifference to Interdependence*", Columbia University Press, New York, 2010.
20. Levkowitz, n.5, pp. 235-236.

# 17

# West Asian Turmoil and the Future of the Regional Gas Sector: Implications for India

*Shebonti Ray Dadwal*

The instability that emanated from the 'Arab Spring' brought to the fore concerns over energy supply disruptions from the West Asia and North African (WANA) region and energy security in general. However, despite a fall in oil exports from some countries—estimated at some 1600 million barrels over three years since end December 2010—particularly from Libya, and a concurrent spurt in prices, the price rise was short-lived as production from other countries as well as the US from its shale formations quickly filled the gap. However, in its 2011 World Economic Outlook, the International Energy Agency (IEA) has presented a bright future for the gas market based on rising demand in Asia, particularly China and India, increasing climate change concerns and the move away from "dirtier" fossil fuels like coal and oil, the versatility of gas as a fuel across sectors, and the increasing supplies from North America as a result of the shale revolution in the US.[1] All of this should have pointed to a promising picture for gas producers and exporters. With a reserve base of 52 percent of the world total, the WANA region is known more for its oil reserves. What has not been identified is that at 43-47 percent, the region also has the largest known conventional gas reserves.[2]

Moreover, four of the states—Qatar, Oman, UAE and Yemen, supply 40 percent of the world's liquefied natural gas (LNG) demand. Several decades ago, many of these countries relied on domestic supplies to meet their gas demand; several gas export projects were also constructed as domestic demand was low, thereby freeing up natural gas to be developed under export-oriented foreign

**Table 1: Proven Reserves of (Conventional) Natural Gas Reserves by Region (2014)**

| *Region* | *Proved reserves in tcf* | *In %* |
|---|---|---|
| West Asia | 2799.98 | 41 |
| Eurasia | 2164.80 | 32 |
| Africa | 545.69 | 8 |
| Australasia | 504.75 | 7 |
| North America | 412.39 | 6 |
| Central & South America | 270.85 | 4 |
| Europe | 146.94 | 2 |

*Source:* DOE, Energy Information Agency.

direct investment programmes. However, as populations in the region multiplied and demand for electricity, jobs and more industry intensified, many of these states found themselves increasingly suffering from supply deficits. Today, barring Qatar, Yemen and Egypt, all other Arab countries are net importers of gas. At the same time, their oil exports are not generating as much revenue due to an over-supplied oil market, leading to a sharp fall in the price of oil. Moreover, as most of these suppliers sell gas at oil-indexed prices, revenues from gas exports too have been affected.

**Table 2: LNG Exports by Country 2013 (in million tons per annum)**

| | |
|---|---|
| Qatar | 77.2 |
| Malaysia | 24.7 |
| Australia | 22.2 |
| Indonesia | 17.0 |
| Nigeria | 16.9 |
| Trinidad & Tobago | 14.6 |
| Algeria | 10.9 |
| Russia | 10.8 |
| Oman | 8.6 |
| Yemen | 7.2 |
| Brunei | 7.0 |
| UAE | 5.4 |
| Peru | 4.3 |
| Equatorial Guinea | 3.9 |
| Norway | 3.0 |
| Egypt | 2.8 |
| Angola | 0.3 |

*Sources:* IHS, US DoE, IGU.

With Europe yet to recover fully from the financial crisis, which in turn has led to a fall in the overall demand for energy, including gas, falling revenues and the spread of radical Islamic militancy on the one hand, and growing domestic discontent on the other, threatening to endanger seemingly well-entrenched regimes, the investment climate in the region is under stress. Moreover, with Iran poised to return to the international community following the signing of the nuclear deal between Tehran and the P5+1 nations and the impending lifting of the decades-long sanctions regime on Iran, the outlook for any recovery of oil and oil-indexed gas, prices are not very optimistic over the near and medium term. Moreover, the shale gas revolution that took place in the US from 2008 has seen the US transform itself from an energy-import dependent country to an energy exporter. This has allowed Washington to take foreign policy decisions that are no longer contingent on ensuring the free flow of energy resources from the West Asian region. How this will eventually impinge on the continuation of its security umbrella provided to the Arab regimes is a matter of conjecture; however, this has been the subject of much debate within the region.

The questions this paper seeks to address are how will the factors mentioned above affect the region's natural gas sector? Besides, as demand for gas increases the world over, particularly in developing Asia and in India, will exports from the region be endangered? Will the regimes succeed in retaining their hold as domestic unrest threatens to increase? What will the geopolitical fallout of falling energy prices be on the stability of the region and will the regional governments be able to deal with the coming changes in the energy sector? Furthermore, with the global gas market poised for a major transformation, what impact will this have on the region's gas sector, as well as client states?

## The WANA Gas Sector and Prospects for Regional Gas Trade

Ever since oil was discovered in the WANA region, it has seen more conflict and turmoil than in any other part of the world. The causes of the turmoil could be various, but it causes concerns as the region, with 865 billion barrels of proven crude oil reserves (around 52 percent of the world's total) was, and will remain the world's reservoir for conventional oil. What, however, is often overlooked is the impact of the turmoil both in terms of its export potential as well as on the region's gas sector.

Although in the early decades of oil production, natural gas was considered at best, a by-product of oil and was provided to domestic markets at low prices, from the 2000s, many of the countries in the region became net importers of gas, with a concurrent reduction in exports. Kuwait and Dubai began to import LNG in the late 2000s, while Abu Dhabi and Oman, while continuing to export LNG, also began importing significant quantities of gas from Qatar through the Dolphin pipeline. By the late 2000s, as more and more countries in the region began experiencing gas shortages, a sort of gas 'crisis' began emerging in the region as a whole.[3]

Some of the reasons for this rapid growth in gas demand included a spurt in population as well as a rapid economic expansion with a focus on constructing energy-intensive industries and an increase in the use of gas for power generation and water desalination, thereby injecting gas into oil reservoirs to enhance oil recovery. At the same time, the huge subsidies in gas pricing resulted in growth in consumption.[4]

Moreover, by the early 2000s, with the issue of climate change becoming an important factor in the energy policies of several countries, the demand for oil from many of the developed countries began tapering off, being replaced by gas, which is a cleaner fuel. By the mid-2000s, demand for gas was seen as the fastest growing of the fossil fuels in the Organisation for Economic Cooperation and Development (OECD) countries, with Japan being the largest consumer of gas among the Asian countries. As a result, the Gulf Cooperation Council (GCC) states who had been unwilling to pay Qatar its asking price for gas, led Doha to seek export markets beyond the region, where it secured much higher prices on long-term bilateral contracts, as well as selling its surplus cargoes on the spot market. As a result, there are only two regional gas trade projects of any significance in the region excluding the Dolphin pipeline network, which is controlled by Abu Dhabi state investment conglomerate Mubadala, with minority stakes held by Occidental and Total. The project began carrying gas from Qatar to UAE in 2007 and began delivering Qatari gas to Oman in 2008. Although the Dolphin Pipeline has a capacity to carry 33 bcm per year (3.2 bcf/day), its current operational capacity is limited to just 20 bcm/year. The pipeline could be filled to capacity if equipped with additional compression, but pricing disputes have undermined Qatari willingness to earmark additional gas for the pipeline.[5]

Another pipeline, known as the Arab Gas Pipeline, also exists, carrying gas from Egypt to Jordan, Syria, and Lebanon. However, with the growing demand for gas, Egypt's exports have been falling to the extent that Egypt has now signed a contract with Russia's Rosneft for 24 LNG cargoes for two years starting from the end of 2015. In the meantime, Egypt has signed deals with international oil companies (IOCs) like Eni and BP to develop gas resources and condensates. As an incentive, it has also raised the price of domestically produced gas in an effort to attract IOCs into its upstream sector.[6]

One of the fall-outs of this rise in gas demand is an increase in conflicting claims among the states over sovereignty over contiguous gas fields, some which have even led to disputes. For example, Saudi Arabia and Kuwait, who had agreed to jointly develop parts of the Dorra gas field in 2000, have seen projects being halted several times due to differences between the two sides. Recently, a dispute between the two countries flared up again over gas extracted from the jointly operated offshore Arash gas field, which is also shared with Iran and has recoverable reserves estimated at 13 tcf, saw work on the gas field being stopped. While Riyadh claims that any gas pumped from the field should go through its Khafji oilfield before being divided between the two sides, Kuwait argues that it should be able to take its share directly from the field.[7]

At the same time, although there has been a rapprochement between Saudi Arabia and Qatar, it is unlikely that Riyadh will import gas from Qatar due to regional political dynamics between these two countries. On the other hand, regional rivalry between Morocco and Algeria and the former's aversion to gas imports from Algeria scuttled the development of a pipeline to Spain till the late 1980s and early 1990s. Simultaneously, sanctions and/or threats of sanction have constrained the growth of the gas sector in some countries like Libya and Iraq.[8]

Second, despite the growing demand, the WANA countries have been tardy in reacting to the tectonic shifts that are taking place in the international gas market due to the emergence of North American shale resources as well as newcomers in the LNG market from Africa, Eastern Mediterranean and Australia. Although years of high prices have seen their sovereign wealth funds grow providing them with a financial cushion, unlike Saudi Arabia in the oil market, they have not tried to retain control over market share by showing flexibility in pricing formulae. Hence, while Saudi Arabia has resisted attempts by other Organisation of Petroleum Exporting Countries (OPEC) members in cutting production to shore up oil prices, the WANA gas-exporting states have, by and large, continued to adhere to oil-indexed gas prices and long term contracts, allowing new players to take away market share.

One of the reasons for this is, apart from few countries like Qatar, Algeria and Egypt, gas production remains secondary to oil. As a result, there is little production of non-associated gas in the region. In the case of Iran, the sanctions and lack of access to LNG technology has kept development of the gas sector from being fully exploited. Even now, with Iran being poised to return to the international energy market following the signing of the nuclear agreement with the P5+1, it will be a while, possibly even a decade, before it can take its place amongst the leading gas exporting countries, given the years of under-development of its gas sector. It has been estimated that Iran will require the country to need IOCs with requisite financial and technological expertise which will invest billions of dollars in upgrading and expanding its energy infrastructure.

Finally, the recent developments in the WANA region which began with the popularly termed "Arab Spring" and now with the spread of the Islamic State of Iraq and Syria (ISIS) in Syria, Iraq and to other parts of the region there are growing concerns that this will take a toll on the energy sector in the region, both in terms of production outages as well as prices. According to an October

2013 report by the World Bank titled *MENA: Investing in Turbulent Times*, the on-going political turmoil will impact on the region's economy and its attractiveness as an investment destination as a whole.[9]

Despite having extremely attractive reserves, both in terms of quantity as well as low production costs, high levels of investment both domestic and, along with technology are required if production has to be sustained, if not increased to match growing demand. Given the large financial commitments and long gestation period required for bringing resources to market, political stability is crucial for companies that want to secure benefits from their investment. Ironically, while earlier investment barriers were responsible, to a large extent, from keeping foreign direct investment (FDI) into the sector at bay, now the recent turmoil may turn out to be the disincentive that will prevent the requisite investment, both financial and technical, from being available. Far from improving, the security in the region appears to be worsening in many countries across the region, with militant groups becoming more active.

Of late, however, the Gulf states have been exhibiting a new willingness to invest in gas-specific exploration and production as well as to pay their gas-producing neighbours much higher prices for imports. According to the US Energy Information Administration (EIA), gas consumption in the WANA region's generating sector will grow by nearly 150 percent by 2035, replacing declining use of oil, thereby creating a possibility of an increase in regional gas trade. However, given the political and commercial hurdles that exist, many projects that have been under negotiations such as a pipeline from Qatar to Bahrain, and one from Iran to the UAE, Oman and Syria, with some agreements being signed in some cases, it is unlikely that any of them will be implemented in the near future.

## Potential Regional Gas Exporters: The Case of Iran and Israel

### *Iran*

Despite holding the largest gas reserves in the world, Iran accounts for less than 1 percent of global natural gas trade, and is, in fact, importing some gas from neighbouring Turkmenistan and Azerbaijan during seasonal demand hikes, although since 2012, it has reduced the volumes of imported gas from the former. Once the sanctions are lifted, Iran has the potential to become a major gas exporter, both to Asia as well as Europe. However, several challenges will have to be overcome before Iran can exploit its potential. These include the growth in domestic gas demand, with several factions within Iran opposing gas exports on the grounds that the country would require gas to meet growing consumption. In addition, there have also been disagreements in the past between Iran and potential gas importers over pricing. Finally, with Iran's oil reserves showing signs of depleting, Iran requires gas to augment oil recovery by reinjecting it into oil wells.

As a result, Iran exports small volumes to only three markets—Turkey, Armenia, and Azerbaijan, the latter as a swap deal. However, it is in the area of LNG that Iran has failed to succeed. Although Iran's aspirations to build a liquefaction plant goes back to the 1970s, it is yet to build one. Following the imposition of sanctions, companies with requisite liquefaction technology have exited the country, causing most of the work to be halted; on the other hand, the sanctions made it impossible to gain access to the finances and technology. As a result, Iran's LNG projects are years away from completion.

Nevertheless, the potential for increasing exports through pipelines have improved, with Iran seen as a viable source of piped gas to some of its neighboring countries. For instance, pipeline exports to Iraq are expected to begin soon following the completion of the pipeline from Iran's Ilam province to the Iran-Iraq border. Supplies of around 50 bcf per annum are expected to commence after the completion of the construction of the pipeline on the Iraqi side. Iran had also agreed to export some 350 bcf per year of gas to Oman in March 2014. However, the construction of the pipeline may be delayed because of pricing disagreements. Similarly, pricing differences have also seen the proposal of exports to the Sharjah mired in international arbitration. Finally, the Iran-Pakistan leg of the Iran to India gas pipeline (IPI) may see the light of day, with both countries stating their commitment to complete the project. The Iranian portion of the pipeline is believed to be complete, although construction on the Pakistani side has been delayed. If completed, the project could see the delivery of 274 bcf per year of gas over 25 years.[10] There is also a possibility of India (re)joining the project, although pricing and security issues with Pakistan may continue to prevent New Delhi from coming on board.

### *Israel*

A decade, since the discovery of the presence of hydrocarbon reserves off the coast of Israel in the eastern Mediterranean in the late 1990s and early 2000s, has drastically changed the politics of the region. Israel, which was dependent on oil and gas imports from its often hostile neighbours through the Arish-Ashkelon pipeline from Egypt and a small portion of LNG through a floating and regasification terminal, is now in a position to be free from this problem, and in fact has become an exporter. According to a 2010 report of the US Geological Survey (USGS), the Levant Basin has probability of undiscovered oil resources of 1.7 billion barrels and, more significantly, of undiscovered natural gas resources of 122 tcf. Israel's share of the reserves amount to about 31 tcf

(908 bcm) from Tamar, Leviathan and a number of small fields, while reserves in the Gaza Marine field, that is in the area off the Gaza strip, holds 1 tcf (30 bcm).[11] Although the discovery of gas has initiated various disputes, with Lebanon claiming that both the Tamar and the Leviathan gas fields fall within their Exclusive Economic Zones (EEZ), and a similar dispute between the Republic of Cyprus and Turkey, the Israeli government has taken a decision to export around 40 percent of its gas production, the market options being Turkey, Greece, Jordan, Egypt and South Korea, although the latter would entail the construction of a liquefaction plant which may be difficult due to environmental and security concerns. Another option could include building a terminal in Cyprus, given that Delek and Noble—the two main investors in the Tamar and Leviathan fields—have also gained rights to the Cyprus' Aphrodite gas field, estimated to hold 3.6-7 tcf. A third option would be to build an undersea pipeline to either Turkey or Greece, which would then link up to the European grid.[12] While this is a viable option, domestic opposition in Israel have held up any progress on this project. Interestingly, Israel had approached India to allow its oil companies to help in the exploration of its gas reserves, mainly to facilitate building closer economic ties with its neighbours, that is, Egypt, Jordan and Palestine, as well as Europe.

## Implications for India

### *Indian Gas/LNG Scenario*

The turmoil in the WANA region per se has not had any significant impact on India's gas (LNG) imports, although larger changes in the gas markets may have a fallout on India's relations with WANA gas suppliers. Though India is the 13th largest gas consumer of gas in the world, at 55 bcm (or 49 mmscmd), it is far behind other Asian gas consumers like Japan, South Korea or China.

Nevertheless, India's natural gas demand far exceeds domestic supply and this shortage is likely to continue as the share of natural gas in the Indian energy basket is expected to increase from the current 9 percent to 20 percent by 2025, which will see its rise upwards in the gas market hierarchy. Currently, the share of natural gas is subdued due to insufficient pipeline infrastructure and lack of a nationally integrated system. However, several companies are investing in pipeline projects, which if successful will increase the share—and demand—for gas in India.

As a result, imports are expected to increase over the next few years/decades. It is already the fourth largest LNG importer, and with the commissioning of the Kochi terminal, the re-gasification capacity has gone up to 22 mmtpa (79.2 mmscmd). By 2015-16, this is expected to go up to 25 mmtpa (90 mmscmd) and by 26-16 to 32.5 mmtpa (117 mmscmd). Apart from these terminals, regasification terminals of about 35.5-36.5 mmtpa are being planned on the eastern and western coasts of India by different entities.[13]

Therefore, India is certainly attracting the attention of global gas suppliers as a leading destination for supplies as against their earlier focus on the Western markets. With trans-border pipeline projects not showing much signs of success, and India's domestic output from its KG basin coming down, India's market for gas, particularly LNG, is perceived as bright. However, India's desirability as a gas market in the next few years will, to a large extent, depend on the overall energy reform process in the country, particularly in terms of the pricing mechanism, based on the economic feasibility for end use sectors. Currently, India procures around 80 percent of its gas (LNG) from Qatar, mainly based on term deals, and hence at a cost that is much higher than those that are available on the spot market or from hub-based—as against oil-indexed—markets. In fact, India has been negotiating with Qatar recently for reduced prices, or a cut in supplies, and has increased its offtake from the spot market. It has also contracted supplies from the US and Australia, although the cargoes will commence only from end 2015. With several suppliers from Australia, East Africa and Southeast Asia coming into the market, India is looking to expand its source base.

Secondly, given that large Asian LNG consumers like Japan and South Korea, whose demand for gas has grown, are also seeking better terms in LNG pricing, and forming a consumers' grouping is an option that could be looked at.

Thirdly, with the sanctions regime on Iran now poised to be lifted following the nuclear deal in July 2015, India could once again explore the option of importing gas through the pipeline from Iran, either as part of the IPI, notwithstanding the security concerns over transiting through Pakistan, or revive the sub-sea pipeline with Iran and Oman. Indian companies could also explore the option of taking equity stakes in LNG projects to enhance security of supply.

No doubt, India has the potential to become a leading gas market. However, until it introduces the much-needed reforms and regulatory mechanisms, it will not be able to leverage this potential.

## Conclusion

Due to the limited role of gas outside the region, the recent political turmoil in the region has not had a big impact on the gas market. Although there has been some impact on gas production in mainly North African gas exporters—Egypt, Libya, Algeria (and Yemen as well)—the largest and most important gas exporter, Qatar, has been protected, with little or no impact on its production or exports. The US is not as reliant on the region as it once was, as its shale gas revolution has made it relatively energy independent. Moreover, given that the main market for the North African exporters is Europe, the financial crisis there has seen lower demand since 2009; hence lower supplies have not had a major impact in the larger international market. On the other hand, the demand for gas has risen exponentially within the region, converting many of the gas producers into net importers. It is in this respect that the impact of the political turmoil arising out of the 'Arab Spring' incidents, may have longer term repercussions.

First, it will impact on the investment climate of the region, as security concerns would impinge on foreign investors' decisions. Secondly, the gas market is awash with new supplies from extra-regional and new producers from North America, the Eastern Mediterranean and East Africa. Already, the extra supplies have had an impact on prices, the consequence of which has been reflected on the surge in demand from the spot market as against the earlier preference for term deals. It has also set off a debate on the need for changes in the pricing mechanism in the Asian gas market, although given the current fall in oil prices, and its impact on oil-indexed gas, the advantages seen earlier with regard to hub-based pricing, may not last. Third, the eventual return of Iran to the gas market, albeit not for a decade, particularly in the LNG market, will have implications for both the WANA market as well as the larger international one. Finally, the advent of shale gas and the role reversal of the US as an exporter as against its earlier avatar as a major importer, will have implications far beyond the energy markets. Not only will American producers vie for an expanded share of the gas market, the US government may not be as invested in the region's security or in the endurance of the current regimes as it was prior to the shale revolution. This is a matter of concern in the Arab regimes in the Gulf region in particular, which in turn has seen them engaging with other power who are more invested in the region.

Under these changed circumstances, what should the regional countries do to ensure their markets and energy security? First, the government will have to adapt to the shifts in the market and the larger geopolitical changes that have taken place. Given the global ramifications of developments in the WANA energy landscape, what happens globally will impact the future of the region as well. Hence, long-pending reforms to allow more social inclusion and accountability to enhance the overall security environment should be implemented.

Second, the existing subsidy regimes should be revamped in order to reflect market forces. This will stem the rapid rise in wasteful consumption which in turn has severe implications for depleting reserves. Moreover, low energy prices provide an unattractive environment for potential investors in the region's energy market as well as for expanding regional trade. This is apparent in the case of

Qatar, which sought higher priced markets outside the region after its neighbouring countries refused to pay the asking price for its gas. Given the huge regional market, many of the region's energy security issues can be resolved if a vibrant regional energy market is developed.

Third, the diversification policy, in terms of moving away from hydrocarbon sector to other sectors, should be speeded up. In the case of the markets, they should allow more flexibility in their pricing mechanisms in order to gain more market share. With Asian markets now overtaking European and the US market, developing stronger linkages with Asian energy consumers that go beyond just trade-based relations is critical. Cross-investments in the downstream sectors of these states is also important, besides providing an assured market for the producers.

Despite the emergence of new producers coming into the gas market, the WANA region has an edge over its competitors not only with regard to reserves, but also with regard to production costs. For example, while it is estimated that the cost of producing and liquefying 1 mmBtu in Qatar is around US$ 2, for the US, East Africa or Australia, the cost would be between US$ 8-12/mmBtu.[14] This allows Qatar, as well as other WANA producers, to keep prices low, giving them an advantage over their competitors. But in order to fund social welfare schemes to stave off domestic political opposition, Qatari exports are priced much higher to earn larger revenues. By implementing the much-needed changes in the domestic energy sector and more realistic export pricing mechanisms, the WANA states could continue to retain their premier role in the energy market.

## NOTES

1. "Are we Entering a Golden Age of Gas?", Special Report: World Energy Outlook 2011, International Energy Agency, at http://www.worldenergyoutlook.org/media/weowebsite/2011/WEO2011_GoldenAgeofGasReport.pdf.
2. Laura El Katiri, Bassam Fattouh and Richard Mallinson, "The Arab Uprisings and MENA Political Instability: Implications for Oil and Gas Markets", Oxford Institute for Energy Studies Paper No. 8, March 2014, at http://www.oxfordenergy.org/wpcms/wp-content/uploads/2014/03/MEP-8.pdf.
3. Bassam Fattouh, "Current Developments in the Oil and Natural Gas Markets and their Implications for the Energy Sector in the Arab World", The Oxford Institute for Energy Studies, December 22, 2014, p. 78.
4. Ibid.
5. Jim Krane and Stephen Wright, "Qatar 'rises above' its region: Geopolitics and the rejection of the GCC gas market", Kuwait Programme on Development, Governance and Globalisation in the Gulf States, Number 35, London School of Economics and Political Science, March 2014, at http://eprints.lse.ac.uk/55336/1/__lse.ac.uk_storage_LIBRARY_Secondary_ libfile_shared_repository_Content_Kuwait%20Programme_Krane_2014.pdf.
6. "Egypt signs energy deals, MoUs worth over $ 40bn with investors at Sharm conference", *Ahram Online*, March 14, 2015, at http://english.ahram.org.eg/News/125244.aspx.

7. "Saudi Arabia, Kuwait Locked in a Dispute Over Gas Field", Natural Gas Asia, November 2, 2014, at http://www.naturalgasasia.com/saudi-arabia-kuwait-locked-in-a-dispute-over-gas-field-13935.
8. Fattouh, n. 3.
9. Faisal Hasan, "MENA Economy, Investments and the Specter of the Arab Spring", *Arab Business Review*, 2014, at http://www.arabbusinessreview.com/en/article/mena-economy-investments-and-specter-arab-spring.
10. "Iran", Energy Information Administration (EIA), US Department of Energy, June 19, 2015, at http://www.eia.gov/beta/international/analysis_includes/countries_long/Iran/iran.pdf.
11. "Assessment of Undiscovered Oil and Gas Resources of the Levant Basin Province, Eastern Mediterranean", USGA Fact Sheet 2010-2014, March 2010; and B. Shaffer, "Can New Energy Supplies Bring Peace?", The German Marshall Fund of the United States Eastern Mediterranean Energy Project Policy Brief, March 2014, at http://www.gmfus.org/ archives/can-new-energy-supplies-bring-peace/.
12. Jan-Justus Andreas, "Fact Sheet: Mediterranean Gas: A Third Corridor?", European Centre for Energy and Resource Security, Kings College, London, March 2014, at http://www.kcl.ac.uk/sspp/departments/warstudies/research/groups/eucers/fs-med-gas.doc.
13. "Natural gas scenario in India", Ministry of Petroleum & Natural Gas, Government of India, New Delhi, at http://petroleum.nic.in/docs/abtng.pdf.
14. Stanley Reed, "Liquefied Natural Gas Makes Qatar an Energy Giant", *CNBC*, August 6, 2015, at http://www.cnbc.com/2015/08/06/liquefied-natural-gas-makes-qatar-an-energy-giant.html.

# PART V

## India and West Asia

# 18

# India's Relationship with West Asia: Facing the Challenges of Arab Spring

*Prasanta Kumar Pradhan*

India's interaction with the West Asian region dates back to centuries when people from both the sides used to cross the Arabian Sea for trade and commerce. The frequency and intensity of interaction continued and movement of people from both sides led to spread of language and culture among each other. Such interactions of the past have laid the foundations for India's relationship with the region at present. Today India has serveral long term interests in the West Asian region spanning over political, economic, security and strategic issues. India considers the Gulf region as part of its 'extended neighbourhood' and its 'natural economic hinterland'. India is heavily reliant on the energy supply from West Asia importing around two thirds of its energy requirements from the region. Similarly India's bilateral trade with the region is over US$ 172 billion which makes it an important trade partner for India. Though economic relations remain the backbone of the relationship, both sides have been looking for new areas of cooperation and are trying to strengthen their political and strategic ties. Beyond trade and economy, India is engaging the Gulf countries in political and security arenas. The rise of terrorism and piracy has been a mutual concern for both India as well as the West Asian countries. As India has been affected by both terrorism and piracy, it is reaching out to the countries of the region for their cooperation in this regard. Besides, the seven million strong Indian expatriate workers living in the Gulf form a natural link with the region.

The recent phenomenon of 'Arab Spring' has led to instability in the region.

Longstanding authoritarian leaders in Tunisia, Egypt, Libya and Yemen were removed by the popular protests. At present Syria and Yemen are going through severe internal turmoil with an uncertain future. Internal conflicts among different groups have increased exponentially. Sectarian conflicts have further aggravated throughout the region. The rivalry between the two important regional players—Iran and Saudi Arabia—has further aggravated, leading to sectarian tension. Both the countries have been found engaging in proxy wars in different parts of the region such as in Iraq, Syria and Yemen. Capitalising upon the existing political instability in the region extremists and terrorists have been able to further spread their activities. The rise of the Islamic State of Iraq and Syria (ISIS) and its declaration of a caliphate by carving out space in Iraq and Syria is an alarming trend which has emerged in the region recently. Intervention by the extra-regional powers has further complicated the situation. US has remained the most important external player in the region. The Russian involvement in Syria since October 2015 has added a new dimension to the Syrian imbroglio with a US-Russia tension flaring up which will have implications for the whole region.

India is deeply concerned with the spurt in violence and deteriorating security situation in the region. Developments in the region has had its impact on India as well. The sudden surge in the oil prices deeply impacted India. The protests forced the Gulf regimes to adopt policy of nationalisation of their work forces in order to accommodate their own nationals in the job market and to reduce their unemployment. This has created apprehension among the Indian community in the Gulf. If implemented seriously, the programmes will definitely affect some of the Indians working in the region. The safety and security of the Indian citizens in the region amidst the protests is also a concern and India had to evacuate its national from countries like Libya, Egypt and Yemen. The protests and the subsequent protracted conflicts have thrown a challenge for India in the region. The challenge for India is to maintain the momentum in its ties with the countries of the region so that its stakes and interest are not adversely affected while the region reels under turmoil.

## Arab Spring: India's Concerns and Challenges

Arab Spring posed many challenges for India's interest in the region. Among many other issues, India was concerned over the safety of Indian expatriate workers living in the region, safety of oil supply lines, bilateral trade and commerce, increasing incidents of terrorism, possibility of pirates taking the opportunity etc. Thus far, India has treaded cautiously but effectively to protect its interests. But, at the same time, there have been calls from several quarters to strengthen India's security ties with the countries of the region so that India will be able to protect its interests with reasonable ease.

India has been affected by the rise in oil prices that followed the protests. India is a major importer of oil and dependent on Gulf oil and has been feeling the pressure on its economy. India imports around two thirds of its total oil imports from the Gulf region. The spread of protests from one country to another led to a temporary anxiety in the market regarding the unhindered production and supply of oil thus leading to rise in oil prices. For instance, oil prices went up from US$ 90 in December 2010 to over US$ 120 in May 2011. Such a steep rise in oil prices affects the growing Indian economy which is heavily dependent on the import of oil. This, however, had a minor impact on the Indian economy. In the event of intensified popular protests in countries like Saudi Arabia, Iraq, Kuwait and UAE, who are major oil suppliers to India, the impact would have been substantial. For a moment, the protests in smaller countries like Oman and Bahrain was looking frightening as they spread quickly and, if not controlled timely, could have potentially disturbed the production and the supply lines as well.

India is deeply concerned about the safety of its citizens living in the region in the event of the protests taking ugly turn in the Gulf Cooperation Council (GCC) countries. About seven million Indians are living and working in the Gulf region and in case of any emergency, it will be a formidable task for India to evacuate its citizens from the region. India has faced such situation in the past in 1991 when it had to evacuate Indian citizens from Kuwait when the later was invaded by Iraq. In recent years, India had to evacuate its citizens from Libya and Egypt in 2011 where the security situation deteriorated because of popular protests against the regimes. India began 'Operation Safe Homecoming' in February 2011 and evacuated around 16, 200 of its citizens from Libya by March 2011.[1] For this, India had to send special flights and ships to Libya to bring its citizens back safely. India also evacuated around 3600 of its citizens from Egypt as well. The situation in Yemen deteriorated with the Houthis capturing many parts of the country and the subsequent Saudi-led coalition attacks on the Houthis. As the security situation worsened, India undertook 'Operation Rahat' in April 2015 to evacuate its citizens from Yemen. India evacuated 4741 Indian nationals and another 1947 foreign nationals from different countries from Yemen.[2] But if some instability of that nature emerges in the GCC countries, where such large number of Indian live, it would be a daunting task for India to undertake such a large-scale operation.

The rise and spread of terrorism in West Asia as a result of the Arab Spring has been a big concern and challenge for India. The ISIS has emerged as the most fanatic terrorist group that has declared a caliphate in Iraq and Syria. The ISIS militants have captured and taken hostage some Indian nationals in Iraq. A group of 46 nurses taken hostage by the ISIS militants were released in July 2014 but there are still 42 Indian workers who are under the hostage of the ISIS whose fate remains unknown. In order to strengthen its diplomatic presence, Indian sent two more officials to Iraq in November 2014.[3] The ISIS leadership has also openly threatened to launch attacks on India. In June 2014, Abu Bakr Al Baghdadi stated that Muslim rights are seized in India and many other countries around the world, and appealed them to take up arms against the non-believers.[4] The reports of some Indian youths, though in a small number, being inspired by the ISIS and have joined the organisation is a concern for India.[5] India believes that the ISIS is not just a threat to West Asia but to the whole world. India has joined the call for international cooperation against the ISIS and its activities.

India has expressed its willingness to cooperate with the Gulf countries to work together to counter terrorism.[6] In this regard, India has signed agreements with a number of countries in the region to share intelligence regarding the movement and functioning of the terrorists. Recently, there have been a number of success stories of intelligence cooperation where some terrorists wanted in India have been deported following the request of government of India; for instance, Indian Mujahideen (IM) terrorist Fasih Mohammed, a key suspect in the 2010 Bangalore blast case was deported from Saudi Arabia in October 2012 and was arrested in New Delhi,[7] and another IM operative was deported from the UAE in May 2014.[8]

The protests have further widened the gulf between two important players in the region—Saudi Arabia and Iran. It has led to appearance of temporary uncertainties over the regional security of the Gulf region. Since the past, the relationship between both countries has been marked by regional competition and rivalry over political, ideological and strategic reasons. During the protests in the Arab streets Iran supported the protesters, attempted to internationalise the issue and proclaimed that the current uprisings are inspired by the Islamic Revolution of Iran of 1979. Iran's support for the protesters intended to overthrow the authoritarian Arab rulers thus changing the Arab world order. This very idea was against the Saudi interest in the region. Because of its economic and political clout, Saudi Arabia perceives itself as the custodian of the Arab affairs, and thus, wants Iran to stay away from the internal affairs of the Arab countries. Such kind of Saudi thinking aims at continuing its influence over the Arab politics and keeping Iran away from it.[9] Such a tense situation in the relationship between two important countries in the region poses several challenges for Indian foreign policy. India has important stakes and interests with both the countries and India does not seem interested in taking sides in this situation. As India continues to calibrate its policies carefully, the situation is certainly proving to be more testing. Similarly, the GCC as a whole is also at odds with Iran. Balancing interests between Iran and the GCC will remain a challenge for India. India's interests will be adversely affected if the GCC-Iran tensions reach a point where a choice has to be made between the two. India's policy of maintaining a fine balance between the GCC countries and Iran will have to continue for some time in the future as India keeps itself prepared to deal with a volatile Gulf region.

India faced diplomatic challenges at the high table as a non-permanent member of the United Nations Security Council (UNSC) during 2011-12 when issues of Syria and Libya came up for discussion and voting. India has adopted a calibrated approach keeping in mind India's principles and interests in the region. India opposed the imposition of a 'no fly zone' on Libya by the West. India abstained in the voting of UNSC resolution on 1973 on Libya in 2011 stating that is "little credible information on the situation on the ground in Libya"[10] to support measures under Chapter VII of the UN Charter which can include use of force. On Syria, India is of the view that any transformation in Syria should be led by the Syrians themselves and supported Kofi Annan's six point plan.[11] India was also against any kind of external intervention or aggression on Syria. Though India abstained on the UN resolution on Syria in October 2011, it later supported the UNSC resolution in April 2012.[12] The draft resolution could not be passed as it was vetoed by Russia and China. Though, India usually chooses to take a neutral position over the political developments in the region, sitting at the high table certainly brought some critical diplomatic challenges before it.

The protests have prompted the rulers to start the process of nationalisation of the workforce to deal with the problem of unemployment and discontent of the youth. As it has been witnessed during the protests throughout the region, a large number of youths participated in the protests expressing their dissatisfaction with the ruling regimes. They expressed their desires ranging from better employment opportunities to participating in the affairs of the state. To meet their demands, some GCC countries have started nationalising their workforces. To appease the youths, Saudi Arabia announced to create one million jobs in next couple of years. There are a large number of foreigners living and working in the region which makes the locals believe that the foreign workers are given priority in jobs and they remain unemployed. To address this concern of the educated youths, the governments have started programmes to employ locals. Saudi Arabia has taken the lead in this regard and has started a 'Nitaqat' programme. The programme makes it mandatory for the Saudi business establishments and companies to reserve 10 percent of the jobs for Saudi nationals. In 2012 there were 340,000 firms in Saudi Arabia that did not employ any Saudi nationals. The Nitaqat programme is intended to address the youth resentment in Saudi Arabia resulting from competition they face in the job market from expatriate workforce.[13] Nitaqat incentivises the establishments who adhere to the rule and deal strongly with the ones who do not follow it. Under Nitaqat law an expatriate worker should work only under his sponsor and the worker is not meant to perform any job other than the one mentioned on his job card. This has created some panic among the expatriate workers who run small scale shops and establishments under licenses in the names of Saudi nationals. Strict actions are now taken on such businesses by the Saudi authorities which affects some Indians in the Kingdom.[14] Other Gulf countries such as UAE, Kuwait, Oman and Bahrain have been seriously mulling over such plans for quite a long time. They have made such plans since 1980s and 1990s but those plans have not been implemented seriously. For instance, in 1990s the UAE government issued policies regarding quotas on expatriate labour and provide employment for their nationals. Later the government also indicated that all secretaries and personnel managers had to be UAE nationals.[15] UAE Ministry of Labour has issued decree for Emiratisation of managerial and secretarial positions in private companies and, since July 2006, work permits for expatriates for those positions are not issued. As per the decree, the expatriate workers holding secretarial posts would lose their jobs by default at termination of their fixed term contracts.[16] The Manpower and Government Restructuring Program of Kuwait recommended a quota-based policy suggesting 60 percent Kuwaitis in banks, 15 percent in real estate sector, two percent for manufacturing industries and so on.[17] Oman has also set quotas for different sectors to employ its own citizens than hiring expatriate workers. If implemented seriously, the programmes will definitely affect some of the Indians working in the region.

## Recent High Level Engagements

The turmoil in West Asia has not deterred India from engaging with the countries of the region. India has, through bilateral visits and exchanges, kept the momentum going. India possibly believes that it is necessary to continuously engage with the countries of the region to ward off any threats emanating from the continuing instability.

### *GCC*

The Gulf region has been of primary importance for India. India-GCC Political Dialogue has been continuing since it was initiated in 2003. In this regards eighth India-GCC Political Dialogue was held in New York on September 26, 2014, at the sidelines of the United Nations General Assembly meeting. India has been talking with the GCC since 2004 to sign a Free Trade Agreement (FTA) with the organisation. India has expressed its seriousness to sign the FTA and also operationalising the India-GCC Framework Agreement.[18]

There have been some high level exchange of visits from both the sides between India and the GCC states. In February 2014, Saudi Crown Prince Salman Bin Abdulaziz Al Saud (now the king) visited India and met with Prime Minister, President and the Vice-President. The previous Qatari Emir, Sheikh Hamad bin Khalifa Al Thani, visited India in 2012 when both countries signed MoUs/ agreements on cooperation in the field of oil and gas, education, legal affairs, banking, etc.[19] Besides, there have been several ministerial and officials visits exchanged between India and the GCC.

The recent visit of Prime Minister Narendra Modi to the UAE demonstrates the importance of the Gulf region for India. For India, the UAE's most critical importance lies in the field of trade and business. UAE is India's third largest trade partner (after China and the USA), with bilateral trade standing at over US$ 59 billion in 2014-15.[20] The India-UAE relationship has continued to grow with a number of crucial connections such as trade, energy, diaspora and culture. In the contemporary era, changing geopolitics and growing security challenges in the region have drawn the two countries even closer. However, what has not been satisfactory is the investment scenario. According to the Department of Industrial Policy & Promotion (DIPP), from April 2000 to June 2015, UAE investments in India totalled US$ 3.12 billion.[21] This is far below the UAE's investment potential considering its enormous Sovereign Wealth Fund (SWF) of about US$ 773 billion, which India intends to attract. The investment climate in India is known to be unappealing for foreign investors and would remain a major impediment for attracting greater investments from the UAE. With his visit and meetings with the UAE leadership, Prime Minister Modi has tried to instil confidence in their minds about the vast opportunity of investing in India.

In the joint statement issued during the Prime Minister's visit, both countries have agreed to strengthen bilateral defence cooperation including the ambition of joint manufacture of defence equipment in India. India and UAE had signed a defence cooperation agreement in 2003, with the aim of providing military training, arms import and export, peacekeeping operations, military medical services, security and defence policy and joint scientific research on defence, among other issues. Joint defence production would be a major boost to defence ties. Though regular defence cooperation in the form of training, joint exercises, goodwill visits, information sharing etc. continues, the issue of joint production of defence equipment remains a challenge as it requires both large sums of investment and technical know-how.

The depth of the India-UAE relationship can be measured from the fact that both countries have signed a number of agreements including on trade, labour, culture, security and so on in the past. The joint statement further reinforces the commitment from both sides on a wide range of bilateral issues. Modi's visit has tried to build upon the strong foundation laid by India in the last couple of decades. Both countries deciding to take the bilateral relationship to the level of a 'comprehensive strategic partnership' is also a big leap forward. Given their shared concern about a number of issues highlighted above, joint efforts in addressing these will be beneficial for both.

Modi's visit to UAE needs to be seen in the larger context of strengthening ties and further widening the scope of India's engagement with the Gulf region. In recent years, India has taken initiatives to engage with other countries of the region and has opened multiple fronts of engagement with them. The declaration of strategic partnerships with Saudi Arabia in 2010 and with Oman in 2008, and the agreement on defence and security cooperation with Qatar in 2008 are some of the high points in India's engagement with the region. In this context, Modi's visit to UAE, besides boosting bilateral relations with the UAE, would provide further impetus to India's engagement with the Gulf region.

### *Arab League*

Moving beyond the GCC, India is also engaging with the Arab League to connect with the wider Arab world. Secretary General of the Arab League, Nabil El Araby, visited India in December 2013. During the visit both the sides signed Memorandum of Cooperation and new Executive Programme for the years 2014-15 intended to 'imparting fresh momentum to the institutional links by providing for a structured engagement' with the Arab League.[22] The agreements also aim to enhance engagement between India and the Arab League on the issues relating to 'trade & investment, energy, small and medium enterprises, culture, capacity building, etc.'[23] Both the sides have also continued to engage with each other by holding India-Arab League Senior Officials Meeting in November 2014, second India-Arab Cultural Festival in Algiers in November, 2014 and the fourth India-Arab Business Partnership Conference in New Delhi in November, 2014. India's Minister for External Affairs Sushma Swaraj also met with Nabil El Araby during her visit to Cairo in 2015. Besides, President Pranab Mukherjee also visited Jordan and Palestine along with Israel in October 2015.

### *Egypt*

India has also been trying to engage with Egypt—another important country in the region. India and Egypt share civilisational ties with a long history of people-to-people contacts. Egypt under President Gamal Abdel Nasser and India under the leadership of its first Prime Minister Jawaharlal Nehru were the torchbearers of the Non-Aligned Movement (NAM). Their commitment to socialism also kept both the leaders and countries drawn towards each other. After the end of the Nehru-Nasser era, the relationship between the two countries lost much of its old sheen. Subsequent leadership in both the countries has acknowledged the importance of the other, but there has been a discernible absence of any meaningful efforts from both sides to further strengthen the relationship.

The popular protests against President Hosni Mubarak and his subsequent removal from power in 2011 drove Egypt in to deep political instability. Presidential elections held in 2012 saw the emergence of the Muslim Brotherhood coming to power and Mohammed Morsi becoming the President of Egypt. The electoral victory of Muslim Brotherhood became a watershed moment not only in the history of Egypt but the entire Arab world. It marked the emergence of political Islam in the mainstream of Arab politics. Despite Muslim Brotherhood being an Islamist party, it did not hesitate to engage with India. Morsi visited India in March 2013 and both countries signed agreements on information and communication technology, cyber security, cultural heritage, micro and small enterprises, vocational training etc. Morsi's rule ended abruptly due to intervention by the military and Abdel Fattah El Sisi became the new president of Egypt. Morsi's rule was short-lived, but his visit to India reflected his desire to rebuild ties with India.

Throughout the political turmoil in Egypt, India has consistently expressed solidarity with the people of Egypt appealing to the leadership to see the winds of change and address the aspirations of the youth. As Sisi continues to restore peace and order in his country, he has shown substantial interest in reviving India-Egypt relationship Nitin Gadkari, Minister of Shipping, Road Transport and Highways visited Egypt as the Prime Minister's representative to attend the opening ceremony of the New Suez Canal in August 2015. The visit of Minister for External Affairs Sushma Swaraj to Cairo in August 2015 was intended to bring both the countries closer by identifying mutual issues of concern and pledging to work together. Fighting terrorism has been identified as an important issue for both India and Egypt as they are concerned with the growing menace of the ISIS. As the ISIS continues to spread its activities throughout the region, both India and Egypt are trying their best to insulate themselves from the threat and cooperate in their fight against it. India and Egypt signed an agreement in 1995 to combat terrorism and organised and transnational crime. Though not much cooperation has happened on the ground, the resurgence of terrorism throughout the region provides an opportunity for both countries to cooperate.

Besides, economic engagement is another important issue which requires focused attention from the leadership of both the countries. Bilateral trade between India and Egypt has been negatively affected by the continuing violence and instability in Egypt. According to the Ministry of Commerce, Government of India, the total bilateral trade between the two countries was US$ 5.42 billion in 2011-12 which has come down to US$ 4.76 billion in 2014-15. Indian export to Egypt has increased only marginally from US$ 2.42 billion in 2011-12 to US$ 3 billion in 2014-15. Egypt's exports to India have been hit by the internal political and security situation. Egyptian export to India in 2011-12 was US$3 billion which has come down to US$ 1.74 billion in 2014-15.[24] Bilateral trade has never been an important element in the India-Egypt bilateral relationship. As Egypt is moving towards restoring peace and internal stability, it expects India to become a partner in its economic development. Sisi expects more Indian investment in Egypt which will boost their economy. India has around US$ 2.5 billion[25] investments in Egypt with around 46 Indian companies operating in the country. Both countries should explore the opportunities in trade and investment which can be a new instrument of cooperation in the coming days.

### *Iran*

India-Iran relationship has witnessed many ups and downs in the past. Iran has been defined as India's "proximate neighbourhood". Its geopolitical and strategic location, long coastline along the Gulf, and its influence over the Strait of Hormuz make it an important country in the region. For India, Iran is an important source of energy. Iran has the third-largest proven oil reserves and second largest proven gas reserves in the world. India's hopes rest on Iranian gas for its long-term energy security. Cooperation in sectors like investment in upstream and downstream activities in the oil sector, Liquefied natural gas (LNG)/natural gas tie-ups and secure modes of transport have been mooted by both countries. Iran is also an important trade partner for India. Total bilateral trade between the two countries stood at over US$ 13 billion in the year 2014-15.[26] Iran is the 19th largest trading partner of India.

Stronger relationship with Iran would provide India an access route to Central Asia and both would play an active role in Afghanistan as well. India has constructed the Zaranj-Delaram road in Afghanistan. As Central Asia is important and India needs a transit route to that region, the route via Iran would be economical and time saving. India is also helping Iran to develop the Chabahar Port, which would give India access to transport goods to Central Asian states. The two countries have signed an agreement to give Indian goods heading for Central Asia and Afghanistan preferential treatment and tariff reductions at Chabahar.[27] This will help India transport its goods, including humanitarian supplies, to Afghanistan and Central Asia. In May 2015, Nitin Gadkari, Minister for Shipping and Road Transport & Highways, visited Tehran and signed a Memorandum of Understanding (MoU) with Iran for the development of Chabahar Port. During his visit Gadkari also met President Rouhani and discussed other bilateral issues of mutual concern. President Rouhani expressed his optimism regarding Iranian ties with India and his willingness to join hands with India to fight terrorism and radicalism.[28] Underlining the importance of economic cooperation with India, President Rouhani stated that the economies of India and Iran 'complete each other.'[29]

Another potential area of cooperation between India and Iran is in maritime security. Indian interest in the Indian Ocean region and the proximate neighbourhood focuses on the need for regional peace and stability, mutually beneficial relations with littoral states, accessibility of oil and gas resources, the freedom of navigation through the Gulf and the Strait of Hormuz, and access to regional markets for Indian goods, technology, investment, labour and services.[30]

India-Iran relations were adversely affected because of the sanctions imposed on Iran by the US and West. Sanctions restricted the bilateral trade and payment through banks as they came under the sanctions. With the signing of the nuclear deal with the P5+1 countries and the possibility of all the sanctions on Iran being gradually removed, there is a new found hope and confidence between India and Iran to strengthen the relationship. Both the countries are looking forward to further enhance their relationship in several sectors. Since the signing of the deal with the P5+1, there have been several bilateral official and ministerial visits and meetings between India and Iran. Earlier, Prime Minister Modi met Iranian President Hassan Rouhani at Ufa, Russia, on the side-lines of the Brazil, Russia, India, China and South Africa (BRICS) and Shanghai Cooperation Organisation (SCO) Summit in July 2015. In August 2015, Iranian Foreign Minister Javad Zarif visited India and met with Prime Minister Modi along with other ministers to discuss about expanding the relationship between the two countries. Foreign Secretary S. Jaishankar and National Security Advisor Ajit Doval are senior officials to have visited Iran in 2015. The increase in bilateral visits reflects a growing understanding between the two countries of each other's importance and further strengthening the bilateral relationship.

## Conclusion

Arab Spring sprung up a number of challenges for India in West Asia. The challenges are political, economic and security in nature. Initially the steep rise in oil prices affected India which imports around two thirds of energy requirements from the region. But despite the turmoil the supply of oil was not disrupted which otherwise could have hurt India deeply. Similarly the trade flow has also not been severely affected with the region though India's trade with Egypt has been affected due to the prolonged conflict and instability in the country. In the political and strategic front, India has faced many complex challenges in the region. The further deterioration of the Saudi-Iran relationship and their involvement in the proxy wars in the region has complicated the geopolitical situation in the region. India has huge stakes and interests with both Saudi Arabia and Iran, and therefore, the deteriorating relationship between the two regional players is not in India's interest. India, thus, faces a long-term challenge of carefully calibrating its policies towards the two regional players. Similarly, India's non-permanent membership at the UN Security Council during 2011-2012 saw the crucial issues of intervention in Libya and Syria being discussed and voted upon. This was a test for India's approach and ability to handle the pressure sitting at the high table. The main challenge was to disagree with countries like US, Saudi Arabia and other GCC states over Libya and Syria who supported an armed intervention in these countries while India preferred talks and negotiations to resolve the conflict.

The ISIS has emerged as a security concern. India believes that ISIS is not only a threat for the West Asian region but also for the whole world. Though the ISIS has not been able to establish its presence in India, the involvement of some Indian youths who have been radicalised by the ISIS is a major concern for India. Throughout the period of turbulence, India has continued to engage with the countries of the region. By continuously engaging with the region India not only intends to ward off threats and challenges emanating from the region, but at the same time, it also aims to strengthen its bilateral relations with them. Despite the challenges, India has been successful, to a large extent, in maintaining momentum in its relationship with the West Asian countries despite the region going through a turbulent phase.

## NOTES

1. "Annual Report 2011-2012", Ministry of External Affairs, Government of India, New Delhi, p. xi.
2. Suo-Moto Statement by Minister of External Affairs and Overseas Indian Affairs in Rajya Sabha on "Recent Developments in the Republic of Yemen and Efforts Made for Safe Evacuation of Indian Nationals from There", Ministry of External Affairs, Government of India, April 27, 2015, at http://www.mea.gov.in/Speeches-Statements.htm?dtl/25129/SuoMoto+Statement+by+Mi nister+of+External+ Affairs+and+ Overseas+Indian+Affairs+in+Rajya+ Sabha+on+Recent+Developments+in+the+Republic+of+Yemen+and+Efforts+Made+for+ Safe+ Evacuation+ of+Indian+ Nationals+from+There.
3. "2 diplomats head to Iraq in bid to secure release of Indians", *The Times of India*, November 14, 2014, at http://timesofindia.indiatimes.com/india/2-diplomats-head-to-Iraq-in-bid-to-secure-release-of-Indians/articleshow/45142325.cms.
4. "India among jihad targets of ISIS", *The Hindu*, July 2, 2014, at http://www.thehindu.com/news/international/world/india-among-jihad-targets-of-isis/article6167595.ece.
5. "'Negligible' support from Indian youth for Islamic State: Rajnath Singh", *Financial Express*, December 16, 2014, at http://www.financialexpress.com/article/miscellaneous/negligible-support-from-indian-youth-for-islamic-state-rajnath-singh/19780/.
6. Speech by Pranab Mukherjee, Minister of External Affairs, at the Emirates Centre for Strategic Studies and Research (ECSSR), Abu Dhabi, on the "India's Foreign Policy and

India-Gulf Relations: Meeting the Challenges of the 21st Century", May 12, 2008, at Ministry of External Affairs, New Delhi http://www.mea.gov.in/Speeches-Statements.htm?dtl/1533/Speech+by+Shri+Pranab+Mukherjee+Minister+of+External+Affairs+at+the+Emirates+Centre+for+Strategic+Studies+and+ResearchECSSR+Abu+Dhabi+ on+ the+Indias+Foreign+Policy+and+IndiaGulf+Relations+Meeting+the+Challenges+ of+the+21st+Century.

7. "IM suspect Fasih Mohammed deported from Saudi, arrested in Delhi", *Business Standard*, October 23, 2012, at http://www.business-standard.com/article/economy-policy/im-suspect-fasih-mohammed-deported-from-saudi-arrested-in-delhi-112102302011_1.html.
8. "Key IM logistics man deported from UAE", *The Indian Express*, May 3, 2014, at http://indianexpress.com/article/india/india-others/key-im-logistics-man-deported-from-uae/.
9. Prasanta Kumar Pradhan, "Arab Spring: Redefining Regional Security in West Asia", in S.D. Muni and Vivek Chadha (eds.), *Asian Strategic Review*, New Delhi, Pentagon Press, 2013, p. 185.
10. India's Permanent Mission to the UN, "India's Explanation of Vote after the vote on Libyan Resolution in the UN Security Council delivered by Ambassador Manjeev Singh Puri, Deputy Permanent Representative", March 17, 2011 at https://www.pminewyork.org/pages.php?id=1013&page=3.
11. See the "Six-Point Proposal of the Joint Special Envoy of the United Nations and the League of Arab States", as annexed to Security Council resolution 2042 of April 14, 2012 at http://www.un.org/en/peacekeeping/documents/six_point_proposal.pdf.
12. India's Permanent Mission to the UN, "Explanation of Vote on the Resolution concerning Syria by Ambassador Hardeep Singh Puri, Permanent Representative of India at the UN Security Council", April 14, 2012, at https://www.pminewyork.org/adminpart/uploadpdf/92334ind2011.pdf.
13. P.M. Mathew, "What Nitaqat means for Kerala", *The New Indian Express*, April 13, 2013, at http://newindianexpress.com/opinion/What-Nitaqat-means-for-Kerala/2013/04/13/article1542322.ece.
14. Ibid.
15. "Workforce nationalisation in the GCC", *The Peninsula*, May 18, 2012, at http://thepeninsulaqatar.com/qatar/194886-workforce-nationalisation-in-the-gcc.html, accessed on July 12, 2013.
16. Kasim Randeree, "Strategy, Policy and Practice in the Nationalisation of Human Capital: 'Project Emiratisation'", *Research and Practice in Human Resource Management*, Vol. 17, No. 1, 2009, at http://rphrm.curtin.edu.au/2009/issue1/emiratisation.html.
17. "Workforce nationalisation in the GCC", *The Peninsula*, May 18, 2012, at http://thepeninsulaqatar.com/qatar/194886-workforce-nationalisation-in-the-gcc.html.
18. "Swaraj pushes for India-GCC Free Trade Agreement", *The Hindu*, October 1, 2015, at http://www.thehindu.com/news/national/swaraj-pushes-for-indiagulf-cooperation-council-free-trade-agreement/article7710985.ece.
19. Embassy of India, Doha, Qatar, "India-Qatar Bilateral Relations", at http://www.indianembassyqatar.gov.in/.
20. "Export-Import Data Bank", Ministry of Commerce, Government of India.
21. Fact Sheet on Foreign Direct Investment (FDI) April 2000 to June 2015, Department of Industrial Policy & Promotion (DIPP), Government of India, at http://dipp.nic.in/English/Publications/FDI_Statistics/2015/india_FDI_June2015.pdf.
22. Ministry of External Affairs, Government of India, Press Release, "Official Visit of the Secretary General of the League of Arab States to India, 16-18 December 2013", December 17, 2013, at http://www.mea.gov.in/press-releases.htm?dtl/22656/Official+Visit+of+the+Secretary+General+of+the+League+of+Arab+States+to+India+1618+December+2013.

23. Ibid.
24. "Export-Import Data Bank", Ministry of Commerce, Government of India.
25. "Annual Economic and Commercial Report: 2012", Embassy of India, Cairo, at http://www.indembcairo.com/Portals/0/com.pdf
26. "Export-Import Data Bank", Ministry of Commerce, Government of India.
27. Trade Promotion Organisation of Iran, at http://en.tpo.ir/documents/document/12236/12247/portal.aspx.
28. "Rouhani Calls for Iran-India Cooperation in Fighting Terrorism, Radicalism", *Fars News*, May 6, 2015, at http://en.farsnews.com/newstext.aspx?nn=13940216001370.
29. "President Rouhani: Iranian, Indian Economies Complete Each Other", *Tasnim News Agency*, May 6, 2015, at http://www.tasnimnews.com/en/news/2015/05/06/732133/president-rouhani-iranian-indian-economies-complete-each-other.
30. Speech by Foreign Secretary Nirupama Rao at IDSA-IPIS Strategic Dialogue, Institute for Defence Studies and Analyses, New Delhi, on "India and Iran: An enduring relationship" on July 5, 2010, at http://idsa.in/KeynoteAddressIndiaandIrananenduringrelationship_nirupamaroy.

# Index